FIFTH ARMY IN
ITALY
1943–1945

FIFTH ARMY IN ITALY 1943–1945

A Coalition at War

Ian Blackwell

Pen & Sword
MILITARY

First published in Great Britain in 2012
By Pen and Sword Military
an imprint of
Pen and Sword Books Ltd
47 Church Street
Barnsley
South Yorkshire S70 2AS

ISBN 978 1 84884 487 2

Printed and bound in England by
CPI Group (UK) Ltd, Croydon, CR0 4YY

Typeset in Times New Roman by
L S Menzies-Earl

Pen & Sword Books Ltd incorporates the imprints of
Pen & Sword Aviation, Pen & Sword Family History, Pen & Sword Maritime,
Pen & Sword Military, Pen & Sword Discovery, Wharncliffe Local History,
Wharncliffe True Crime, Wharncliffe Transport, Pen & Sword Select,
Pen & Sword Military Classics, Leo Cooper, Remember When,
The Praetorian Press, Seaforth Publishing and Frontline Publishing

For a complete list of Pen and Sword titles please contact
Pen and Sword Books Limited
47 Church Street, Barnsley, South Yorkshire, S70 2AS, England
E-mail: enquiries@pen-and-sword.co.uk
Website: www.pen-and-sword.co.uk

Contents

List of Maps

Maps based on those in *The Fifth Army History*, the majority of which were reproduced by 517 Field Survey Company Royal Engineers.

Photographs used in the plate section are from the United States National Archives.

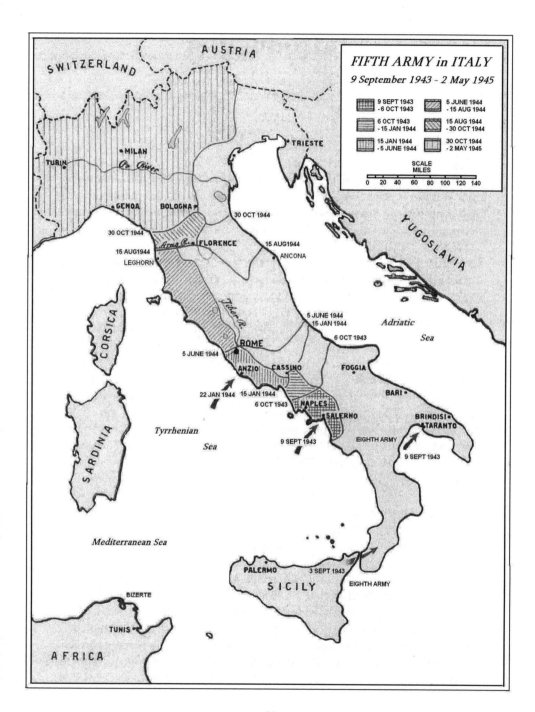

FIFTH ARMY in ITALY

9 September 1943 - 2 May 1945

9 SEPT 1943 - 6 OCT 1943
6 OCT 1943 - 15 JAN 1944
15 JAN 1944 - 5 JUNE 1944
5 JUNE 1944 - 15 AUG 1944
15 AUG 1944 - 30 OCT 1944
30 OCT 1944 - 2 MAY 1945

SCALE
MILES
0   20   40   60   80   100   120   140

Introduction

There is a widespread perception that the Second World War was fought between two groups of partners: on one side, the Germans, Italians and Japanese – the Axis; and opposing them the British, Americans and Russians – the Allies. This somewhat limited view is even more restricted by some of the school textbooks used in the United Kingdom, where coverage of what was essentially the most destructive war in history has been reduced to a comparatively few pages.[1]

Part of the reason for this brevity lies with the designers of the examination syllabus, of course, who have to be selective about what can be crammed into a limited amount of classroom time and the relative priority of competing historical topics, but the net result has been to leave the majority of today's school-leavers with a woefully inadequate understanding of events which have shaped the world in which they now live. A degree of parochialism is inevitable when students from a particular country are taught what their forefathers did over sixty years ago; still more so when history is being used for nationalistic and political purposes. By and large, spokesmen are inclined to portray their home states in the most positive and sometimes heroic light, and one way of doing this is to ensure that only the 'official' version of history is taught. Nonetheless, the net result can be a general ignorance of the extent to which the conflict was a 'world' war, covering not only great geographical areas but also involving people from a large number of nations.

Several years' experience of organizing battlefield studies for the British Army has driven home the fact that it is all too easy to make assumptions about the level of background knowledge of even the most senior officers, let alone that of youthful junior ranks fresh from school. I include myself in the former category – senior in age, if not in rank – for in preparing briefing packages for battlefield studies, the limitations of my own knowledge became ever clearer. The number of nationalities that fought in the Italian campaign grew with each book and official history I read, and the 'soundbite' approach to history served up by many accounts became ever more inadequate. Far from having two armies, the British Eighth and the American Fifth, composed of British and American soldiers respectively, slogging their way northwards up the leg of Italy, there were many contingents from other nationalities playing their part in the fighting. The armies were not 'British' or 'American' except in name and in the nationalities of the commanders. The exact number of different countries that contributed men and women to the Allied cause in this campaign is far from straightforward to determine. Since the war ended boundaries have been redefined; for example the India that existed in 1943–45 is now three countries: India, Pakistan and Bangladesh. Newfoundland was a dominion in its own right until it became part of Canada in 1949, and what were then colonies of the United Kingdom and France – with the variations in government that each power employed for their overseas possessions – are now largely independent and often with different names. Macmillan's 'Wind of Change' has swept through more than Africa since the end of the Second World War.

That there were many nationalities involved is of more than academic interest. Their presence brought all sorts of difficulties for leadership, administration, command, control and communication, and just about every other facet of war-fighting. The war in Italy has often attracted the comment that it was hard-fought, frustrating, and possibly irrelevant to final victory. To appreciate why this observation should have been made, it is necessary to understand the nature of coalition warfare – and in Italy during the last two years of the Second World War those who opposed the Germans were a coalition of an unprecedented number of nations. Their experiences have become increasingly relevant for today's armed forces during the past few years as reliance on allies has grown, and the topic has engendered many battlefield study discussions for today's officers.

The reason that coalition operations should be regarded as relevant today is straightforward: the end of the Cold War led NATO members to reduce the strength of their armed forces, using the diminished threat of a major conflict as the stated reason, which – particularly since the economic downturn after the turn of the twentieth century – was more accurately explained by financial constraints. It is extremely unlikely that the individual European members of NATO will again be capable of acting independently in anything other than the smallest of conflicts, but for several years after the process of contraction began they were able to look to the United States for leadership and the provision of the great bulk of manpower, matériel and capability resources. The post-Cold War heritage was to leave the Europeans with comparatively immobile armed forces that were located on or near the anticipated battlegrounds on which they would have faced the Warsaw Pact, while the Americans retained the ability to deploy significant troop numbers swiftly across the Atlantic to man and to reinforce pre-positioned equipment. Becoming involved in conflicts such as Iraq and Afghanistan highlighted the differences in the ability of NATO's European partners to project their power overseas.

Many of the European nations have been accused of relying upon the United States to provide their defences while they were able to reduce their expenditure in that area: in terms of the Alliance, they have not been pulling their weight. As long as Americans were relatively content to play the leading role and saw their own interests as being furthered this situation was broadly acceptable, but changing international and strategic circumstances since the invasion of Kuwait in 1990, and then the events of 11 September 2001, which turned American attention from Europe to the Middle East, combined with the rise of Chinese power, have led them to redefine their priorities. The commitment of great manpower and equipment resources to Western Europe has been questioned when America is fighting in Iraq and Afghanistan and having to look at a potential threat across the Pacific Ocean, and the other NATO members are being asked to play a greater part in the affairs that affect them directly. The 2011 Libyan situation is a prime example of this growing American reluctance to be drawn into events which they see as being increasingly the responsibility of the Europeans – or at least, that the Europeans should not be able to start a conflict and automatically rely upon their transatlantic partner for the means to carry it out. That Britain pushed for intervention in Libya within months of making heavy defence cuts under the Strategic Defence and Security Review, which was published on 19 October 2010 highlights the point; that Britain continued to announce defence cuts before the country's involvement in Afghanistan and Libya was resolved raises the highlight to a glare.

The combined effect of reduced national military capabilities and pressure for individual nations to play their full part in operations which affect their security leads almost inevitably to a greater cooperation between those states, a cooperation which encompasses training, equipment procurement, operational procedures, and so on. Reduced budgets lead to reduced capabilities, which in turn lead to a degree of reliance on partners to fill the gaps in the armoury. Some progress has been made in areas such as joint equipment development, but improvement has been sporadic. Against the imperative for co-ordination and cooperation other interests come into play, such as pressures to maintain national defence industries rather than purchase equipment from other countries. While pooling and sharing resources may appear commonsensical and beneficial, they are not always seen in those lights by powerful interest groups in the individual countries, and politicians seeking re-election are unlikely to sacrifice votes by closing defence industries in favour of overseas competition, however cost-effective it may be.

International cooperation often fails to deliver the requirements even when several years have been devoted to cementing alliances: for example, the combined Franco-German brigade was not deployed to Afghanistan because the two nations could not agree on its role there. Differences between national strategic cultures could not be resolved, and neither could those between Britain and the Netherlands with respect to the deployment of their joint amphibious force. The concept of Anglo-French naval forces sharing an aircraft carrier may sound a promising solution to economic difficulties, but the precedent of the Franco-German brigade does not augur well: would the French, for example, be willing to commit their forces to the South Atlantic to combat a threat to the Falkland Islands? National governments want to retain the authority to deploy their own forces, and unless the case for a particular course of action is overwhelming in terms of their own self-interest they will stand back. There is a conflict between making economic savings through alliances and retaining control of national forces, and governments will be reluctant to release control over what they consider to be operations which are not directly related to their own self-defence. In the NATO context there is the possibility of a conflict of interests between those who support the Anglo-French cooperation and those, in France, who look to greater Europeanization.

There is a popular analogy drawn between the game of chess and fighting battles – the chessboard is often used as a jacket design for books on strategy, and the parallel recurs time and again in books of military history: Graham and Bidwell entitle a chapter on Salerno 'The Board and the Pieces', for example.[2] It is useful shorthand, but it is misleading, especially in the context of coalition warfare. The pawns are not all the same, even if they wear the same uniform, are equipped with the same weapons, have passed through the same training and owe allegiance to the same flag. The chessboard comparison does not bring out factors such as morale, leadership, motivation, and a host of other variables. With armies formed of coalition partners this lack of uniformity is greatly exacerbated, and the individuals tasked with leading such bodies of men have to deal with these problems in addition to those of warfighting in the single-nation context. Not since the 1982 Falklands Conflict has a NATO member acted alone in a significant war outside a coalition of several states (although some of them have carried out smaller operations on their own, such as the French interventions in Côte d'Ivoire in 2002 and 2011, the British in Sierra Leone in 2000, and the Italians in Albania in 1997), and this pattern has become the norm.

Generals and their political masters who command coalition forces are compelled to pick and choose the tasks they assign to formations of different nationalities; in management terms they assign manpower to jobs by selecting competency matches that ensure, as far as possible, that the best match is made between employees and workplace roles. In the military field the match also takes into account equipment and other factors, and the political implications of having troops of particular nationalities fighting and possibly dying in battle. An alternative way of looking at this factor is to consider it as providing the opportunity for specialization, whereby troops from a particular nation assume dedicated roles (for example in the context of this volume, the French Expeditionary Corps, which was skilled in mountain warfare and was often given operational tasks which made good use of this expertise). In this scenario national contingents meet part, but not all, of the capabilities required by an army to fight a war. Providing that these constituent parts are prepared to act together, then – at least in theory – the overall commander has a multi-functional toolbox with which to carry out his task. The difficulties come when the parts fail to work wholeheartedly together. Even when, as during the Second World War, the threat that the coalition faced was sufficiently strong to bind its members tightly together, a degree of friction remained between them which, in some respects, rendered the Fifth Army less competent than its enemy.

To gain some understanding of the difficulties under which the men who fought in Italy laboured, I believe that it is essential to have a grasp of the wider strategic picture as seen by the decision-makers at the highest levels of government and military command, which imposed limitations on the manpower and equipment that were available to them. Without this background understanding it is hard to grasp the reasons for the shortages of these commodities that the Allies experienced in Italy, particularly in comparison to the relative largesse they had in North West Europe. The decisions of men far away from the Mediterranean, who were concerned with the global conflict rather than just the local war, would cause them to place their priorities elsewhere, just as today's politicians in different international and domestic environments have placed other concerns above defence expenditure. 'Guns or butter' has been a choice which national governments have had to make for generations, and in times of low threat butter tends to take priority, a priority which involves a degree of risk because of the time it now takes to raise, train and equip modern fighting forces.

A further difficulty in enabling today's soldiers or readers to understand what happened over sixty years ago may be summed up in that oft-repeated (but nevertheless still appropriate, hence its popularity) line from Leslie P. Hartley in *The Go-Between*: 'The past is a foreign country; they do things differently there.' The men and women who lived and fought in Italy in the Second World War were almost as different from us in their beliefs, outlooks, opinions and characters as are the inhabitants of some remote island. Discussing the events of 1943–45 with veterans opens fresh perspectives which today's soldiers sometimes find difficult to comprehend; the upbringing, training, equipment and skills of those who served all those years ago make it hard to relate to modern warfare. The comparatively sheltered – in terms of awareness of what goes on outside of one's immediate surroundings – lifestyle of many of the Second World War recruits who had no access to modern media meant that transporting them many miles from their homes to a foreign country was what is now termed a culture shock, and a considerable one at that. From the perspective of operating as part of such a diverse coalition, this shock was all the more pronounced and exacerbated the difficulty of welding everyone together into a cohesive whole. It was not just the matter that Clark raised during the interview he gave for the *World at War* television series, of differing religions, diets, and so on; simpler prejudices such as the attitudes of soldiers from North America who felt that the Italians were unhygienic and slovenly[3][4] played their part in hindering a seamless partnership between fighting men of different nations, allies though they might have been. What attempts the generals and their political masters made to understand the morass of cultural, ethnic, and religious differences between the coalition members, and what effect these might have had on their ability to work together, is a question to which the answer must remain – at best – patchy.

Woodrow Wilson once said that 'the ear of the leader must ring with the voices of the people' (speech at the University of Tennessee, 1890). The leaders who planned and fought the Italian campaign must have found their ears ringing with the sounds of the Tower of Babel. Some of them, those who had their roots in one of the colonial empires, may have had some small advantage in that they had been accustomed to leading native administrations or military forces, but even here their experience was generally limited to the particular colonies in which they served: for the British, their Empire and Commonwealth; for the French, mostly their North African and Middle

Eastern properties. The American experience was even more limited, a fact which was recognized with respect to the difficulties of working with at least one ally: a 217-page booklet which attempted to explain the differences between US and British military terminology was produced and circulated to officers.[5] On the positive side, the challenges facing the coalition members gave an impetus not only to working together, but to working through the difficulties engendered by sometimes conflicting practices. The opportunities for misunderstandings were immense, of course. These were not confined to problems of interpretation of language, but also of interpretation of motives and intent. Mark Clark's insistence that the Fifth Army be written up as 'Mark Clark's Fifth Army', for example, has been widely taken (especially by British authors) as evidence of his desire for self-aggrandisement. A more charitable interpretation might be that Clark, faced with commanding an army which was under-resourced and under-supported by his superiors in Washington, sought to give it a distinctive identity which would give at least its American members a sense of uniqueness and pride, and in this – as evidenced by remarks made by some (but by no means all) American veterans – he succeeded. The British Eighth Army had already achieved this status in the eyes of the wider world, although without personalizing the issue by calling itself after its commander. A similar motivation to give his troops a sense of pride and achievement may have been a factor in Clark's much criticized decision to prioritize the capture of Rome above carrying out the plan to cut the German line of retreat once the Gustav Line had been breached.

As will become apparent in the following chapters, the Fifth Army was American in name but not totally in composition. While Clark may have raised the morale of some of the American contingent in Fifth Army, he did not necessarily do the same for the other nationalities: British servicemen of both the Eighth and Fifth Armies were to adopt the 'D Day Dodgers' lament which reflected their feelings that they were generally forgotten by their countrymen and newspapers which became focused on the North West Europe campaign after the Normandy D Day. And among American soldiers, there were many who regarded Clark as failing as a military leader – especially those of 36th (Texas) Division which was badly mauled on the Rapido river, for no good reason that they could see.

Clark found himself, partly as the result of his own ambition to take command of the Fifth Army, consigned to fighting a campaign which his superiors in Washington had sought to avoid. He commanded an army that was repeatedly robbed of its American manpower as divisions were hived off, firstly for the invasion of Normandy and the following campaign in North West Europe, and then for Operation ANVIL, the invasion of the Mediterranean coast of France. Clark's command was regularly bolstered by the attachment of foreign formations, and was American in name only. He also had to deal with the difficulty of having a British general (Alexander) as commander of the 15th Army Group, of which Fifth Army was a part, and, from January 1944 a British general (Wilson) as Supreme Allied Commander of the Mediterranean theatre.

Both the American and British generals were well aware that America was in the ascendency as the more powerful of the two western allies, and this fact was to colour the relationships between Clark and Alexander in Italy. Although Clark may have felt that Washington had comparatively little interest in what he did, provided that he did not commit too many errors and waste too many lives, the fact that he commanded the American army in theatre meant that Alexander had to treat him with a degree of reserve that he would not have employed when dealing with subordinates from the British Army. This careful approach was to have consequences, some of which were unhelpful to the pursuit of coalition warfare.

As some compensation – in his own mind at least – for finding himself as being subordinate to the British, and having to rely on British, French and other nations' troops to make up the gaps in his order of battle, Clark felt himself able – to a certain degree – to question or ignore orders from Alexander. The counterpoint to Alexander's reluctance to 'grip' Clark was to give Clark a degree of independence not accorded to other generals.

In Italy the Allied forces were, in a sense, fighting not only the Germans and the Italians who remained loyal to Mussolini and his Italian Social Republic, but were also involved in a battle with the Joint Chiefs of Staff in Washington who had little faith in continuing the war in the Mediterranean theatre and who imposed strict limitations on the numbers of men and the amount of matériel that would be sent there. Indeed, the priority that was given to the cross-Channel strategy meant that many of these assets would be removed from Italy for OVERLORD and later ANVIL/DRAGOON. I have always maintained (probably because this approach works for me) that to understand any conflict it is necessary to consider the context in which it occurred, for it is only by looking at the wider picture that the objectives which the participants aimed to achieve, and the constraints under which they operated, can be appreciated. I have therefore taken a 'big hand, small map' starting point of 'Why Italy?' and considered the wider strategic question before digging down into the operational and tactical levels. For Italy, it is necessary to appreciate the agreement between the United States and Britain that OVERLORD was to be the priority, an agreement which was to rob the Allied forces in the Mediterranean of amphibious shipping, the more generous provision of which would have allowed them to make a better fist of Anzio, and to have outflanked the enemy defences at numerous points along the vulnerable Italian coastline. The OVERLORD agreement, in turn, came from debate in which American and British interests and strategic cultures played their part. The difficulty, as ever, is in deciding where such an analysis should stop, before the book reaches unmanageable length and begins to stray from its original theme. The inclination is always to attempt to reduce the complexity and confusion of the battlefield to clarify events and enhance understanding, while making it easier to draw out lessons, but this tendency does little service to portraying the 'fog of war' which pervaded much of what happened, especially at the 'sharp end'.

As if the foregoing does not present enough problems, the multinational composition of the Allied force throws up yet more difficulties for the researcher, on at least two levels. The first, perhaps more obvious one, is that much of the history of national formations and of personal memoires was written in the appropriate language. One is left relying on translations, where they exist, into English. The unthinkable alternative would be to attempt to learn, and at a sufficiently competent level, a whole series of foreign languages from Afrikaans passing through Portuguese to Urdu, and so on. The differences between American and British English are at times enough of a challenge.

The second problem, even assuming that translations are available (and these are only likely to have been made if there has been sufficient demand for them), is that national and personal histories are very much influenced by the political and personal interests of the writer, and of the individual or organization which commissioned the work. To take one example, that of France during the Second World War, the postwar history had been skewed to emphasize the importance of de Gaulle and his Free French, and of the Resistance. Until comparatively recently elements of French Second World War history such as collaboration (including the deportation of Jews) were swept under the carpet. France was not alone in seeking to portray the most favourable interpretation of its part in the war, for writers of other nations have been as guilty of presenting a sanitized version of events; after the war the majority of senior British officers played down or completely ignored the morale problems that afflicted their troops, although their shyness about telling the whole truth did not always stop them from being critical about their fellow generals. It is the job of the historian to disentangle the fact from the fiction – not always a straightforward task – and to identify when a writer has attempted to manipulate the memory for purposes other than a dispassionate recording of facts.

The focus of this book is not tactical although I have sometimes found it necessary to deal with events at that level to illustrate the pressures under which the coalition and its commanders operated; there are, in any event, numerous volumes covering both the Italian campaign and the Fifth Army's part in it which I have drawn upon in researching and writing this book. These are listed in the Bibliography, and the reader who wishes to delve deeper into the grittier end of the fighting is advised to look there. In examining the coalition's difficulties during the campaign I have chosen to take a chronological approach rather than to address concerns such as national or racial tensions (or cooperation and integration) under separate headings. These matters are considered as and when they arose, for I find that this approach aids understanding of the development of attitudes and frustrations, and indeed of finding compromises and solutions which enabled such a disparate group of nationalities to work together effectively. To what extent the campaign was executed poorly is a matter for debate, as is the part that individual statesmen and generals played, for positive or negative effect. While adopting a fairly broad-brush approach to the history of the campaign, I hope that I have included enough to maintain an understanding of the principal events while highlighting the coalition factors. I have resisted the temptation to fight a page-by-page, river-crossing-by-river-crossing and mountain-ridge-by-mountain-ridge interpretation of the campaign – much as the Joint Chiefs of Staff in Washington wanted to avoid becoming involved in such a sequence of events.

I have to thank, in order of their appearance in my life, the following people who generated an interest in the multicultural nature of the subject of this volume. Firstly, my late father, whose engineering career took him (and me) to far-flung corners of the world. In common with many Cornishmen during the last and previous centuries, he felt the urge to travel widely; indeed, we have relatives in many continents, drawn there by the dual pressures of the failure of the mining industry at home and the desire to look over the horizon for fresh opportunities and adventures. With him I lived – for various periods – in India, Southern Rhodesia, Aden and British Honduras (to give these countries the names they were known by at the time) and to appreciate and be sensitive to their different cultures. Secondly, my wife Bonnie: American by nationality (although born in Austria when her parents served there after the Second World War) and educated in the United States, Hong Kong, and the United Kingdom, she shares with me a love for the history and heritage of Europe, and has been the more-or-less willing visitor to many battlefields. Thirdly, Barry Cummings, a former Army colleague who has set up both home and a successful consultancy business in Dubai, and who invited me to work with him there on management development projects. The United Arab Emirates hosts a melting-pot of nationalities working together – with obvious similarities to this book's theme. A major consultancy was focused on producing core competency standards (i.e. those qualities common to all management positions, be they in advertising, accounts, or whatever; these include communication skills, leadership, ability to analyze information and to make informed decisions, and so on) to develop managers from a wide range of nationalities and cultures so that they might work more effectively together. And finally, Chris Davis, sometime officer in the Royal Irish Regiment, whose commanding officer appointed him 'battlefield studies officer' with the responsibility for organizing half-a-dozen trips each year, the purpose of which was to further officer and senior NCO education and training while engendering a greater esprit de corps in a battalion of part-time soldiers. Chris took to this task like a duck to water and employed me as the historian on these visits, which have taken us across the battlefields of Europe. In particular, our studies of the Italian campaign have led directly to this volume. More anonymously, I have to thank those officers who have stood with me in Italy on Staff Rides and debated the decisions of their forefathers, with which they have often disagreed (although that may be a product of hindsight). In particular, those who brought with them the experience of working in the coalitions that operated in Iraq and Afghanistan, have had much of relevance to offer to my thought processes when compiling this book.

As ever, I have also to express my thanks to the staff of the Prince Consort's Library in Aldershot, without whose assistance much of the source material for this book would have been beyond my reach. The search for even the most unlikely titles has often ended, successfully, on their bookshelves – or if not there, then they have generally managed to track them down for me, and to be most kind when I have held on to them far past the return date.

Having thanked those who helped inspire this book and who assisted during the writing stage, I have now to express my appreciation to Richard Doherty for reading the manuscript and for adding his comments and suggestions. These have been most valuable, and have been incorporated with gratitude. As always, however, the buck stops with the author and any errors that have crept in despite Richard's thorough examination are down to me alone.

Notes

1. Foster, *The British Empire and Commonwealth in World War II: Selection and Omission in English History Textbooks*
2. Graham & Bidwell, *Tug of War: The Battle for Italy 1943–45*
3. Lewis, *Naples '44: An Intelligence Officer in the Italian Labyrinth*
4. Patton, *War as I knew it*
5. Military Intelligence Service Special Series, *No 13, 'British Military Terminology', dated 15 May 1943*

CHAPTER 1

Rome

On the morning of 5 June 1944 General Mark Clark entered Rome. In a jeep with Major Generals Gruenther and Hume, his driver made his way along Route 6 into the city, but then lost his way as he tried to find the Capitoline Hill, which Hume had suggested as a suitable location for the Fifth Army Commander to meet his four corps commanders. After a confused journey they arrived in St Peter's Square where they asked directions from a priest who, it transpired, came from Killarney (Clark claimed that it was Detroit). Once more on their way, they found the route blocked by enthusiastic crowds celebrating the arrival of the Americans, through which they were assisted by a young man on a bicycle who proclaimed to one and all the presence of General Clark himself, an announcement which served more to enhance the excitement rather than to clear the path.[1]

The previous evening Clark stood before a city sign bearing the word 'ROMA', posing for photographs while fighting for the city continued in the background. By Clark's account, the sign was punctured by a sniper's bullet as he posed.[2] Clark had sent Major General Keyes to ensure that the spot would be clear of the enemy before a deadline of four o'clock; this would allow sufficient time for the photographs to be wired to the world's newspapers for publication the next day, as indeed they were.[3] That same evening, over 800 miles away in Southwick House in Southern England, General Eisenhower deliberated whether or not to launch the invasion of Normandy, already postponed for a day because of poor weather. His decision to go ahead would limit the attention given to Clark's achievement in taking Rome.

In Washington, President Roosevelt broadcast to the American people: 'The first of the Axis capitals is now in our hands. One up and two to go!' He went on to say that Rome's importance was not merely as a military target, and that many of the main objectives of the campaign had long since been gained. The symbolism of Rome's fall extended to the city's place in Christianity, and the liberation of the Pope and of the Vatican City, which had been achieved by the American, British, Canadians, New Zealanders, French, Moroccans, South Africans, Poles and 'East Indians' (sic), and lastly the Italians, came at 'an excellent time, while our Allied forces are poised for another strike at Western Europe'. The President then went on to praise the Italian people, who had spread their talents throughout the world, and who should now go on to develop their arts, craft and sciences for the benefit of the world at large.

Roosevelt's closing remarks were as follows: 'And so I extend the congratulations and thanks tonight of the American people to General Alexander, who has been in command of the whole Italian operation; to our General Clark and General Leese of the Fifth and the Eighth Armies; to General Wilson, the Supreme Allied commander of the Mediterranean theater, (and) to General Devers his American Deputy; to (Lieutenant) General Eaker; to Admirals Cunningham and Hewitt; and to all their brave officers and men.

'May God bless them and watch over them and over all of our gallant, fighting men.'[4]

It was as if they had achieved what they had been tasked to do and were now being stood down.

In the House of Commons Winston Churchill's first reference to the fall of Rome came the next day, 6 June. His speech opened with a statement in which he referred to the event as the 'liberation of Rome', recognizing that the Italians were now a co-belligerent power fighting alongside the Allies. Unlike Roosevelt, he did not mention the fact that the Italians had been one of the Axis powers. He gave an overview of the situation in Italy since the Anzio landings on 22 January that year, in which he listed the principal Allied nationalities that had participated in the battles to break through the Gustav Line on the advance to Rome. The liberation of the city was not General Alexander's primary objective, he stressed, despite the 'moral, political and psychological advantages' that it brought. Rather, Alexander's aim was the destruction of the enemy's army. The 'relentless pursuit' of the enemy continued. He concluded his comments on the Italian campaign by expressing his gratitude to Alexander for the skill with which he had handled this 'Army of so many different States and nations', and recognized in General Clark a 'fighting leader of the highest order'. The qualities of all Allied troops had 'shone in noble and unjealous rivalry'.

Churchill then moved on to the burning issue of the day. To some in the House it must have appeared that the time he spent on the events of the Italian campaign had been deliberate teasing, for he only now came to the landings

2

in Normandy which had taken place during the night, and which were still being fiercely contested. Again he stressed the brotherhood in arms between Great Britain and the United States and the complete unity that existed between the Allied Armies.[5]

Try as he might, Clark could not put Italy on the front page of the newspapers for more than a day. Events had overtaken both him and his Fifth Army; to some, the purpose of the Italian campaign had served its purpose and those who continued to fight there had done their bit towards final victory; theirs was to become a sideshow, a feeling summed up by some British soldiers who came to look upon themselves as the 'D Day Dodgers', and to put their own sardonic words to the haunting melody of 'Lili Marlene', the tune that was beloved of the Eighth Army and their German opponents alike.

In the speeches of Roosevelt and Churchill it is possible to decipher the underlying differences of opinion between their two governments about the worth of the Italian campaign. For the President, the fall of Rome appeared to be a tick in the box which completed the conquest of the first of the Axis nations before moving on to other things; to Churchill, it was more important – sufficiently important for him to have made it the central point of his address to the Commons, outweighing OVERLORD.

The German perspective – at least as presented to the wider world – was, understandably, to place as positive an interpretation on the fall of Rome as possible. According to the version of events from Berlin, Hitler had declared that the Eternal City should be demilitarized the previous March, a noble German gesture designed to preserve Rome as a monument to the history of Christian civilization and western culture. Rather than turn the city's buildings into rubble, as happened in Madrid during the Spanish Civil War, or into defensive fortresses, as in Stalingrad, the temptation to fight for it was resisted in favour of preserving it and emphasizing the strength of the bond between National Socialism and Fascism. While the defence of Rome might have stalled the Allied advance for weeks or even months, the awareness of the historical links between Rome and the Holy Roman Empire, which had been based in Germany for almost a millennium, led Hitler to allow it to fall into Allied hands without a battle which would have destroyed much of its glories. Besides, Rome's occupation would be as temporary as had happened before, when it had been captured by the Bourbons and by Napoleon. Or so the propaganda went; Rome's fall, to be closely followed by the Normandy landings, must have left a hollow feeling in German stomachs, regardless of Goebbels' best efforts.[6]

The propaganda that the various participants and observers placed upon the fall of Rome reflected their differing views on the importance of the Italian campaign and the worth of Rome as a military objective. For the Washington-based Americans, such as Roosevelt and his Chiefs of Staff, Italy was little more than a diversion from the main task of getting to grips with the Germans through North West Europe. The purpose of the campaign was scarcely more than to show the world, and Stalin in particular, that America was committed to fighting the enemy while preparations for the cross-Channel invasion progressed. For the Italian-based Americans – or at least one in particular – capturing Rome was a prize worth practising a degree of deceit and disobedience to acquire.

For the British, both in London and in Italy, the campaign had more significance and had more to offer as a strategy for winning the war and securing a more favourable world once Germany had been defeated. While some in London, such as Churchill, felt that Rome was a desirable target in itself, others were prepared to see it in the context of crippling the enemy forces in Italy, in which context it became a by-product of a much more important goal, that of crushing the German Army in Italy as a precursor to positioning the Western Allies to counter the spread of communism.

From the German perspective the object of the campaign was to keep the Allies as far away as possible from their homeland. There had been some debate between Rommel, who had argued that most of Italy could not be defended and that the line should be drawn in the north, and Kesselring who took an opposing view and maintained that not only was it possible to fight for every mile but that it was necessary to do so to deny the Allies ground which was within easy bomber flight of the Reich. His argument prevailed with Hitler; his reward was to be given the job of putting his thoughts into practice, a job in which he had managed to hold the Allies out of Rome for nearly nine months.[7]

Notes

1. Clark, Mark W., *Calculated Risk*
2. Ibid
3. Ellis, John, *Cassino: The Hollow Victory*
4. Radio Broadcast 8.30 pm Eastern War Time, 5 June 1944
5. Hansard *HC Deb 06 June 1944 vol 400 cc1323-4*
6. "Rom," *Berlin Rom Tokio. Monatschrift für die Vertiefung der kulturellen Beziehungen der Völker des weltpolitischen Dreiecks,* VI (June, 1944), pp. 2-3
[7] Mavrogordato, Ralph S., *Hitler's decision on the defence of Italy*

PART I – BUILDING A COALITION

There is only one thing worse than fighting with allies –
and that is fighting without them.
Winston S. Churchill (1874–1965)

CHAPTER 2

Coalition Warfare

The Allied armies that fought in the Italian campaign of 1943–45 included perhaps a larger number of national delegations than any other force in history. In his *Memoirs* Field Marshal Earl Alexander listed no fewer than twenty-six: British, American, Canadian, New Zealand, South African, Newfoundland, Indian, Singhalese, Basuto, Swazi, Bechuana, Seychellois, Mauritian, Rodriguez Islanders, Caribbean, Cypriot, French, Polish, Nepalese, Belgian, Greek, Brazilian, Syro-Lebanese, Jewish, Yugoslav, and Italian.[1] He underestimated, for the foregoing list does not include the Algerian, Moroccan, Tunisian and Senegalese who served with the French, or the Rhodesians who fought with the South Africans. There were also nationalities that served in the Mediterranean under their own flags in the Allied navies (the Dutch) or air forces (such as the Australians), but not the armies. And one should include those nationalities which have gained separate identities since the war, the Pakistanis and Bangladeshis. The foregoing includes only formed units or sub-units such as battalions or companies that had a recognized national identity, but there were individuals from a greater variety of countries who served under others' flags, such as Irish citizens who enlisted in British units and those of many others who served with the French Foreign Legion. There are even two soldiers from the Red Army buried in the Commonwealth War Graves Commission Cemetery in Cassino. It was truly a World War.

Not all of these nationalities served with the Fifth Army. Its commander for most of the Italian campaign, General Mark Clark, counted sixteen nationalities but did not list them by name.[2] An army is a fluid organization through which flow formations and units as circumstances dictate; it does not remain still, and Fifth Army was subject to a great number of changes during its twenty months of fighting in Italy. Although it was the 'United States' Fifth Army, at no time during the campaign were its troops entirely American. Indeed, on occasions, for example when it landed at Salerno and for a period during the winter of 1944–45, Americans were outnumbered by soldiers of other nationalities. Commanding such a disparate group of nationalities, races, religions, cultures, languages and aspirations was not simple. Even were it to be accepted that some units (for example from the British Commonwealth) might have a shared organizational structure and a common training, for example for staff officers, there were still major differences between the constituent parts of the Fifth Army that made interchangeability impossible. A brigade or battalion from one country could not simply be withdrawn from the line and replaced by another from a different nation. Even troops of one American division were not necessarily able to fill the shoes of another. Differences of training, specialization, experience, manning levels, equipment states and a host of other factors had to be taken into consideration; the range of nationalities compounded the problem. As Clark said during the television programme *World at War*, whereas the Germans were homogenous, being of one nationality (he was not entirely correct, for the Fifth would face, for example, the *162nd Turkomen Division* which was manned by former Russian prisoners although with German officers and senior NCOs; there were also Poles and other Eastern Europeans who had been conscripted into *Wehrmacht* units [some of whom were recruited into the Polish Corps after being taken prisoner by the Allies[3]], and there were Italians from Mussolini's Italian Social Republic who continued to fight on the German side), the Fifth Army included soldiers of many races and creeds, many of whom were equipped with weapons that were incompatible with those that the Americans used.

The Anglo-American Alliance

All of the governments that contributed troops to the war, on both sides, had their own reasons for doing so. This may appear painfully obvious, but it is sometimes necessary to dig beneath the surface to understand that their ultimate reason was one of national self-interest – they were not in it for reasons of altruism, despite public protestations at the time which may have indicated otherwise. The apparent unity of purpose presented by the Allies does not survive a thorough investigation.

In 1946 Winston Churchill used the phrase 'Special Relationship' to describe the close political and cultural links between Britain and the United States of America. A rapport between the two nations had been recognized since the middle of the nineteenth century, although it had passed through peaks and troughs in the intervening years. At times relationships had been positively frosty, for example during the American Civil War when it appeared on more than one occasion that war between Lincoln's government and Palmerston's was a real possibility. The superficial similarities between the nations' interests (which George Bernard Shaw characterized by stating that England and America were two countries separated by a common language), especially during the years of the Second World War when they were presented to friend and foe alike as being hand-in-glove, should not blind us to the fact that each country had its own agenda to follow, and was using the alliance to further its own ends. Differences were inevitable, although carefully kept behind closed doors which concealed debates that at times became heated. It should be borne in mind that Churchill made his 'Special Relationship' speech at a time when he was seeking to bind the United States into a clear post-war alliance to face the growing power of the Soviet Union in Europe. Likewise, his six-volume history *The Second World War,* which began appearing in 1948, was published under the same international conditions. The titles of two of the volumes, *The Grand Alliance* and *Closing the Ring* emphasize the relationships between the Allied powers and Churchill's own preferred strategy for winning the war by closing around the Axis from a number of directions, including from the Mediterranean – which was not the American view of the way to achieve this aim.

Histories are rarely written without some form of bias or interpretation creeping in, and Churchill's are no exception. 'I will leave judgements on this matter to history – but I will be one of the historians', he has been quoted as saying on more than one occasion. His writings are best regarded as personal memoirs, not least because when he penned them he was restricted by considerations of national security: he was unable to make reference to Ultra secrets, for example. To this must be added the fact that he was, above all, a politician who sought to portray his own actions in the best light and to justify himself. He was not alone in this. General Mark Clark wrote his own memoirs under the title of *Calculated Risk*. This work reveals more about his character than about the campaigns in which he fought, and – like Churchill – he played up the importance of the Italian campaign. For Churchill the reason for doing so was because he was its architect; for Clark it was because he was the senior American officer engaged in a campaign which virtually all of the other high-ranking Americans regarded as an irrelevant sideshow to the battle for North West Europe in which they were engaged. Ironically, Churchill's statement that history would be the judge of his actions proved more favourable to both him and Clark than appeared during the war years, for had the Italian campaign been given more weight and progressed as they had hoped, post-war Europe would have been a different place.

Both Britain and the United States had reduced their armed forces after the First World War. A combination of a belief that they had just passed through the 'war to end all wars' and the years of the Depression distracted them from preparation for any future large-scale conflict. Despite relatively isolated voices warning of the need to re-arm, such as Churchill's, little was done until it became apparent that the resurgence of Germany and Japanese expansionist policies were presenting an increasing threat to peace. Britain and America began to give serious consideration to the state of their armed forces and their readiness for war. Whereas Britain had the Commonwealth as an automatic basis for forming partnerships for mutual support, America was in a different position.

During the inter-war period between 1918 and 1939 United States' national policy was strongly guided by the belief that she should not become involved with military alliances, or indeed maintain forces which were able to carry out offensive operations. The pervading ethos was one of seeking to avoid war through a network of international agreements which outlawed it – although the United States never joined the League of Nations – an aim which was supported by limiting naval construction and by introducing legislation which kept the United States out of European and Asian wars. Although small groups of officers were engaged in producing war plans for both the Navy and Army, which were intended to prepare them for a variety of situations which might emerge unexpectedly, attention was largely focused on a doctrine of isolationism.

As the international situation became more tense towards the end of the 1930s, President Roosevelt became increasingly concerned about the limitations and weaknesses of the country's stance, and in the summer of 1939 work commenced on drawing up plans for the possibility that America would become drawn into a conflict in the Pacific in which she would form a coalition with the European colonial powers to resist Japanese expansionism. The Japanese had expanded their influence in that region during the early stages of the First World War, a process which continued in the 1930s when she took control of Manchuria, an act which the League of Nations refused to recognize; the Japanese promptly withdrew from the League, and announced their intention to disregard the agreements on limiting naval construction. The reaction of American military planners was to conclude that a war with Japan would be both long and expensive, and that the Philippines would be lost to the enemy at an early stage. The view that the United States should not become engaged in a war in the Western Pacific gained momentum, and the weakness of its position became more evident as the threat increased. American reluctance to address the problem extended beyond the Pacific. Throughout the world the financial crisis of the 1930s had caused social and political upheavals. In Germany the Nazi Party emerged and re-armament commenced; in the United Kingdom and France, faced with economic and domestic problems, the threat remained unchallenged except for initial agreements between Britain and the Dominions to facilitate command arrangements for Commonwealth forces which might have to operate together at some time in the future.

German aims for control of the Danzig Corridor in 1938 caused American war planners to turn their attention to Europe. The realities of Hitler's ambitions, his reintroduction of conscription and the remilitarization of the Rhineland, together with his alliance with Italy, *Anschluss* (the annexation of Austria) and the involvement of German forces in the Spanish Civil War, could not be ignored; the possibility of America being drawn into a European war had to be considered. The Munich Agreement, in which Britain and France refrained from opposing Hitler's move to annex Czechoslovakia's Sudetenland, may have eased the situation temporarily, but Roosevelt recognized the danger and warned the world at large that the United States would act to meet it, particularly in the Western Hemisphere. Nevertheless, his words failed to carry weight: Americans at large generally maintained their belief that they would not become involved in another European war. The military planners in the United States did not have this luxury – the possibility of conflict with Germany, Italy and perhaps also Japan had to be addressed. Plans were therefore drawn up in which the assumption was made that an alliance of the United States, Britain and France would oppose Germany, Italy and Japan.

The American contingency plans for European operations were thrown into disarray by the success of the German offensive in Western Europe in 1940. With France knocked out of the war, and with the possibility of Great Britain also being defeated, the United States faced the situation that there might well be no allies strong enough to contain Germany, Italy and Japan. A real possibility emerged that the Axis powers, having disposed of their enemies in Europe and having come to an understanding with the Soviet Union, would then move on to seize the worldwide overseas possessions of the European colonial powers, perhaps aided by the use of the British and French navies should they fall into Axis hands.

Faced with this scenario, US Army planners warned that their forces were insufficient to do more than protect American interests in the Western Hemisphere. Any attempt to spread the Army to other areas, such as the Far

East, South America or Europe, would be dangerous and would squander what resources existed. Manpower considerations apart, the Americans had been selling large quantities of naval and military munitions to the British and French nations, and their own stocks were being seriously depleted. There seemed little scope for other than a limited defensive posture. President Roosevelt rejected this worst-case scenario and ordered a reconsideration based on other hypotheses, including the premise that Great Britain would continue to be 'an active combatant'. The underlying situation remained, however: with the forces then available and for the immediate future, America could not become engaged in a war with the totalitarian powers which were equipped with navies, armies and air forces in such superior numbers.

The nation's resources, of course, could and would be mobilized. The National Guard would be called into Federal service and the Regular Army expanded, and the production of munitions increased. Consideration was given to seizing British and French possessions in the Western Hemisphere to prevent their use by the enemy in the event that the two nations had surrendered to the Germans, and – having based his policy on the continuing ability of Great Britain to fight on – Roosevelt gained the authority of Congress for Lend-Lease.

In the autumn of 1940 it became clear to United States' planners that Britain was able to continue its resistance to the Germans, despite having to rely on American support. They were able to address the longer-term problems of providing that assistance, which might eventually mean becoming involved in British operations worldwide; in other words, Britain would be taking the lead on grand strategy, with America following in a supportive role. This perception sat uneasily upon American shoulders.

In September 1940 two senior US Army officers, Major General Emmons and Brigadier General Strong, returned to Washington from a lengthy visit to London. With Rear Admiral Robert Ghormley, USN, who had been appointed as a 'special naval observer', they had discussed future plans with the British. Although the respective nations' navies had been working together for some time, this was the first opportunity the armies had been given to do the same thing. The British had made it clear to them that they were very much relying on the continuance of aid; moreover, the possibility of more active co-operation by the Americans was also hoped for. Although the Americans could not become directly involved in the European conflict it was felt that they could possibly assist by greater presence in the Pacific, where the Japanese threat to British interests was increasing as they continued their expansion into south-eastern Asia. Malaya lay in their path, but Britain could not send a fleet to the Far East to protect it – at that time it was fully occupied facing the Germans. The presence of the US Navy in the Pacific provided a deterrent to Japanese ambitions in the Dutch East Indies and Malaya. To the Army planners a show of strength in the Pacific, together with the President's policy of providing the British with munitions at the expense of their own resources, was disturbing. The former action could be interpreted by the Japanese as no more than a bluff that could be called; the latter was placing the nation's military security at risk on the assumption that America would not have to fight. It was calculated that the Army's requirement for munitions for a year's operations was almost as much again as was currently held, and that it would take two years to make up that deficit. Sending supplies to Britain was the last thing they wanted to do when preparing to fight their own war. In the words of General Marshall, then Chief of Staff, 'We have scraped the bottom of the barrel so far as the Army is concerned.'[4] A request to the President that no further munitions be sent to Britain fell on deaf ears: he preferred to continue with his policy of encouraging the British while threatening the Japanese, a policy which ran very close to the one that Churchill had proposed to him soon after he assumed the position of Prime Minister. While Britain continued to receive strategic materials, exports to Japan stopped.

The British standpoint was that the United Kingdom's security was paramount. While Churchill expressed confidence that any attacks on Britain could be withstood, there were concerns about British interests abroad, and at that time the most pressing was for the Middle East. Here an Italian attack on Egypt was seen as being imminent, and troops were being moved there from India, South Africa, and the United Kingdom in anticipation. The elimination of Italy from the war was a strategic aim of the first importance, for it would remove the threat to the Middle East and allow the Royal Navy to improve the blockade against Germany – defeat of which was the ultimate purpose – and to meet the Japanese threat in the Far East.

As for the defeat of Germany, the British agreed that a land campaign would be necessary, although by the time that became practicable the enemy would have had to have been weakened by naval blockade and by overstretching their forces. For the coup de grace to be possible, certain factors were necessary: the British Isles must remain secure, to provide the base from which the land offensive would be launched; and because British manpower alone would be insufficient, troops from other countries – including the United States – would be required. For American planning purposes, therefore, the way forward was to be strongly supportive of offensive action in the Atlantic as an ally of Britain, while remaining on the defensive in the Pacific. While not expressing total agreement with these points, Roosevelt authorized 'conversations' between American and British staffs to consider them. British officers travelled to Washington under the cover story that they were members of the British Purchasing Commission, and on 29 January 1941 the first discussions began, continuing until 29 March. They became known as the 'ABC' meetings (American-British Conversations).

Held under conditions of great secrecy, because public knowledge of them might have threatened the Lend-Lease Bill then before Congress, the initial discussions dealt with the two nations' military positions, consideration of joint strategy in the Atlantic and Pacific and the operations necessary to implement the strategy, agreement on the division of areas of responsibility, force levels to be committed, outline operating plans, and arrangements for command. At the suggestion of the British, strategy in the Mediterranean and the Middle East was added to the agenda.

The British presented three points of strategic policy:[5]

Firstly, Europe was the vital theatre, and it was here that a decision must be sought.

Secondly, Germany and Italy should be defeated before Japan was dealt with.

Thirdly, the security of the Far East, including Australia and New Zealand, was essential to the cohesion of the British Commonwealth and to the maintenance of its war effort. As the key to the defence of these interests, Singapore had to be retained. From Britain's perspective, the island's defence was symbolic of its determination to protect its Dominions and colonies. It would also be vitally important once Germany and Italy had been defeated and the time came to deal with Japan. The defence of Singapore was based as much on economic, political, and sentimental considerations as on military ones.

The first two points were in agreement with the American position; the third was not. To commit United States naval forces to Singapore would be to protect the prestige of the British Empire, which was not a consideration paramount in American minds. Deploying their limited resources to a 'non-decisive' theatre implied that the United States was accepting responsibility for the safety of a large part of the Empire. There was no way that America, especially when considering its history, would support colonialism. The American planners' response was to assert that their most effective contributions to achieving the objective of defeating Germany would be by concentrating on the Atlantic and by using their naval strength in the Mediterranean region. Tactfully, they recognized that Singapore was valuable, but providing forces to protect it would dilute their ability to affect matters in the primary theatre. Japan would have to wait.

Already national interests and differences were affecting the way in which the war, in which of course the United States was not yet directly involved, would be fought by the Allies. The British, as supplicants, could hardly press their preferences other than by attempting to convince the Americans of the strength of their argument – as indeed they continued to try to do throughout the war years. American power grew as the nation moved to a war footing, while Britain was steadily finding that her abilities were limited. On manpower issues alone, Britain's strength was to prove a growing problem. Although the United States needed Britain, not least as a base from which to launch a land campaign against Germany, the balance of power shifted: as the war progressed the position of the Americans became steadily more dominant and their ability to influence strategy increased accordingly.

As the debates over strategy illustrated, the two nations had differing objectives, particularly for the longer term. Nevertheless, they had much in common. Above all, they both feared Germany. It was easy for them to agree that US Army forces should be concentrated in areas of mutual interest, in other words the North Atlantic. With their presence there, the British could feel confident about sending additional forces to the Middle and Far East theatres. For the Americans, the positioning of their strength in the northern Atlantic simplified Anglo-American command relationships. They wanted to take responsibility for specified areas and for their units to remain under national command rather than to be divided into groups under the British.

Should the United States become involved in the war, the planners considered that Greenland and the bases leased from Britain should be garrisoned and US Naval and Army bases established in the United Kingdom. American air power would be used to take the offensive against Germany, again from Britain, which would also make it easier for Churchill to deploy more forces to the Middle and Far East.

This necessarily brief overview of the initial Anglo-American agreements concludes with the exchange of military missions. In London a flag officer from the US Navy and a US Army general, with supporting staff, would be established; in Washington the British equivalent, but with the addition of an officer from the Royal Air Force, would provide the same function. If America went to war the existence of these missions would be announced as being the representatives of their respective Chiefs of Staff. Although not all dealings between the two nations would be smooth sailing during the forthcoming years, a firm basis for the coalition was set in place.

Following the entry of the United States into the war after the attack on Pearl Harbor on 7 December 1941 the Anglo-American alliance emerged from the shadows. Churchill arrived in Washington on 22 December for the ARCADIA Conference, which was to lay down the basis for future cooperation between the two nations. These arrangements included the establishment of the Combined Chiefs of Staff, which comprised the United States' Joint Chiefs of Staff (the heads of the Army, Navy and Air Forces – at that time still part of the Army) and the British Chiefs of Staff.

The United Nations
Among the decisions taken during the conference was the Declaration by the United Nations – the 'Big Four' (USA, the United Kingdom, the Soviet Union and China); the four British Dominions (Australia, Canada, New Zealand and South Africa) and British India; nine American allies in Central America and the Caribbean (Costa Rica, Cuba, the Dominican Republic, El Salvador, Guatemala, Haiti, Honduras, Nicaragua and Panama); and eight Allied Governments-in-Exile (Belgium, Czechoslovakia, Greece, Luxembourg, the Netherlands, Norway, Poland and Yugoslavia) – a total of twenty-six. The term 'United Nations' was coined by Roosevelt to denote those who were allied in their resolution to ensure a complete victory over the Axis powers; membership grew to include a further twenty-one states by the end of the Second World War. It was to become the foundation of the modern UN.

Although the newly-formed United Nations was lauded amongst the member states, with much flag-flying and parades, in reality it was more of a political achievement than a military one. To the world at large it appeared that twenty-six countries were moving as one in the fight against Hitler, Mussolini and the Japanese warlords. The term 'United Nations' was used in communiqués to emphasise the solidarity and unity of purpose, but in reality – for the promulgation of the war – the UN boiled down to the Anglo-American alliance. The other two 'Big' nations, the Soviet Union and China, played a comparatively small part in the strategic planning that followed the

UN's establishment; indeed, Stalin's participation in the major conferences was limited (Churchill attended fourteen conferences, Roosevelt twelve, and Stalin only five). The British Commonwealth signatories were not individually represented, and the remaining members were either governments-in-exile (for example Poland and the Netherlands both worked under British direction, reliant on her for support and equipment) or of no great military significance anyway. The United Nations was a coalition with great ambitions for a co-ordinated approach to resolving global problems in the context of which it offered its members a say in the formation of the postwar world through reconstruction, thereby – hopefully – avoiding the shortcomings of the League of Nations. But it was not an effective mechanism for planning and fighting a war; with so many members it could not be, lest it turn into a debating society which spent its time arguing rather than acting.

The British and Americans brought differing strategies for winning the war against Germany to the conference. From the British perspective the way forward was to emphasize speed and manoeuvre, to engage the enemy's weak points, and to wear him down through attrition. Weakening the Germans through Norway (one of Churchill's particular thoughts throughout the war) or via the Mediterranean, by clearing Axis forces from North Africa and then moving through Italy and either Greece or the Balkans to Germany itself, suited Britain's limited economy and manpower reserves. It also reflected their 1940 experience of facing the blitzkrieg which led to Dunkirk, and the respect that they held for the enemy's fighting prowess. Rather than large campaigns which would meet the full strength of the *Wehrmacht*, which would require massed armies, the task could be achieved through gnawing away at the enemy in smaller actions where the enemy was attacked where he was at his weakest.

The Americans saw things quite differently. From their standpoint the Germans must be faced and defeated on the ground, sooner or later. It was a theory of mass and concentration – which the planners saw as requiring a United States Army of some 215 divisions – which would achieve a decisive victory. Behind this thinking was the confidence inherent in the nation's industrial potential and in the ability to raise and train the enormous army required. The plans which they developed from this line of argument called for a build-up of US forces in Great Britain (codenamed BOLERO) in preparation for an early cross-Channel attack (ROUNDUP). One factor would militate against the success of this plan: the dispersal of troops and matériel to meet crises in other parts of the world – the Pacific, the Far East,

North Africa and the Middle East – or to assist the Soviets and Chinese who were desperate for aid. To meet these demands would, the planners believed, erode the United States' ability to play a decisive part in shaping coalition strategy.[6]

On 14 January 1942 the conference ended; on the next day the first American troops, 4,500 men of 34th Division, sailed for Northern Ireland. A month later, on 16 February, Eisenhower was appointed Chief of the War Plans Division in the War Department General Staff, and then – on 2 April - Assistant Chief of Staff in charge of the Operations Division, Office of the Chief of Staff. In this role, he was to produce a series of studies on wartime strategy, which were guided by his belief that Germany should be attacked *'through England'* (my italics). Indeed, asserted Eisenhower, 'The United Kingdom is not only our principal partner in this war; it offers the only point from which effective land and air operations against Germany may be attempted.'[7]

The Anglo-American relationship, all public appearances to the contrary, was far from being a smooth one; there were too many conflicting pressures on the two nations, some of which could be put down to differing national interests, others because of the need to pay heed to other nations' concerns and interests, for example those of the Soviet Union and China, both heavily engaged against Axis forces, and who were competing for support in strategy and matériel. The United States was faced with the enormous problems of raising and deploying sufficient armed forces and weapons to fight a war which had spread across the world and which had already consumed many of the assets possessed by her allies. Of the initial signatories of the United Nations Declaration, America was the only one which had the potential to produce the necessary manpower and industrial output to swing the balance and win the war. The others had either already fully committed or expended all of their resources, or – like the Central American and Caribbean states – had little to offer in terms of taking the fight to the enemy anyway.

When balancing the requirements of supporting the various allies and ensuring that they remained in the war, it became necessary to make promises and to arrive at compromises which were not always seen as the optimum way forward. For example, in his discussions with Soviet Foreign Minister Molotov at the end of May 1942, Roosevelt found that, in order to reassure the Soviets, he had to express his hope and expectation that the Western Allies would open a second front against Germany that same year. His words were more encouraging than the Soviets had received from the British, who had hedged their intentions about a second front with a caution about the dangers of failure, which might result in a repeat of the evacuations from Dunkirk, Norway and Greece; they would not commit themselves until the situation was seen to be sufficiently favourable as to ensure success. British reservations would prevail, and no cross-Channel invasion was mounted that year. Indeed, their arguments against such an operation being mounted without thorough preparation were to cast doubt on ROUNDUP, the plan to invade in 1943.

Cross-Channel or Mediterranean? The Anglo-American Debate

The possibility that United States ground forces would not become involved against Germany and Italy until 1943 or even 1944 could not be accepted by Roosevelt, who directed that the feasibility be studied of diverting American divisions to the Middle East or for operations in French North Africa, instead of to England to await the cross-Channel landings. Churchill had already briefed Roosevelt on GYMNAST, a proposed landing in Morocco and Algeria, but further planning on this had been halted during the ARCADIA Conference. Nevertheless, Churchill had urged Roosevelt to keep this option in mind, and the President now turned to it as a way to bring American troops into the war comparatively quickly. The British and the Anglo-American forces were not yet ready for cross-Channel, but there were enough to undertake GYMNAST. Although General Marshall and Secretary of War Henry Stimson were both against diverting the effort from the build-up for North West Europe, Churchill's warning about 'standing idle' led Roosevelt towards considering committing American forces to the Mediterranean. The option of sending them to Egypt to support the then hard-pressed British who were fighting against Rommel's *Panzerarmee Afrika* was rejected partly because of the length of the lines of communication and the difficulty of integrating American forces with the British, but mainly because such a move could be politically and tactically embarrassing – politically in that such a move would be interpreted domestically as giving support to British colonialism, and tactically because there was no more guarantee of success against the enemy here than there was should the cross-Channel venture be attempted prematurely. GYMNAST, however, was more promising. The lines of communication were shorter, establishing American bases in North West Africa would give air cover to Atlantic routes, and the use of US forces rather than British for the landings would be more acceptable to the French and would hopefully lead to fewer casualties.

In coming around to the proposal to deploy to North and North West Africa the Americans in no way saw GYMNAST as being a substitute for the cross-Channel strategy; it was a stop-gap operation which would send the message to the Soviets, in particular, that the United States was ready to apply pressure on the Axis. A second understanding that the Americans had was that any subsequent operations actually inside the Mediterranean, would be carried out by the British.[8] As far as they were concerned, GYMNAST – to be re-named TORCH by the Combined Chiefs of Staff on 25 July 1942 – had strictly limited aims.

As planning for the operation proceeded, the Americans began to accept that it had wider implications than they had first assumed. The GYMNAST concept had been for American forces to land on the Atlantic coast of Morocco at Casablanca, which would give them a port through which to mount further operations. SUPER-GYMNAST, its development, introduced additional landings at Oran and Algiers – inside the Mediterranean – and the involvement of British troops. The strategic objectives became more ambitious, and included the establishment of bases for offensive operations against Libya and Italy. In more modern terms, mission creep was rearing its head. After much debate between the American and British planners, the objective was defined as:

> A Combined land, sea, and air Assault against the Mediterranean Coast of ALGERIA, with a view to the earliest possible occupation of TUNISIA, and the establishment in FRENCH MOROCCO of a striking force which can insure control of the STRAITS of GIBRALTAR, by moving rapidly, if necessary, into SPANISH MOROCCO.[9]

The objective may have been spelt out, but not everyone was committed to it, nor convinced of its wisdom. General Marshall and his staff were fearful that TORCH would lead the Allies to adopt the British aim of gaining control of the Mediterranean – a major change in the previously agreed grand strategy of taking Germany out of the war by the most direct means of an invasion of North West Europe. To Marshall, the strategy agreed during the ARCADIA Conference, of 'tightening and closing the ring around Germany' would not, in itself, defeat Germany. For the Americans operations in the Mediterranean were not operations against the Germans but a misdirected irrelevance. Some of their planners went so far as to consider that the possibility of the British being driven from Egypt might well be a blessing in disguise, for such an event would compel them to concentrate their efforts on cross-Channel, in line with the American preference.[10] Apart from other considerations, TORCH would relegate BOLERO (the build-up of forces in

20

England in preparation for Normandy) well down the priority list; shipping would be devoted to the North African operation, taking precedence over other commitments in the Middle East, the Pacific, and in ferrying supplies to Russia. The transfer of convoy escorts to TORCH meant that only the *Queen Mary* and the *Queen Elizabeth* were available for transporting troops to Great Britain – they were the only vessels fast enough to make the North Atlantic journey unprotected. Ships, aircraft, men – all were to be diverted to an operation that was hedged about with doubt, at least in the minds of many American planners, who saw the hoped-for 1943 cross-Channel invasion being postponed to some indefinite time. Apart from the disappointment and frustration that this brought to some in the Western Hemisphere, there were the Russians to consider – Stalin would have to wait for the opening of the Second Front, and it fell to Churchill to explain this to him. He brought the news during a critical moment in the battle for Stalingrad, and although the Russians had little option but to accept the case, they were nevertheless – and understandably – disappointed. The news of TORCH gave them some encouragement, as did Churchill's airing of a thought to send limited Anglo-American air force units to support the Soviet Union in the Caucasus. As may be imagined, the proposal was not welcomed by General Marshall, although Roosevelt showed interest. The idea died off when the Soviets argued that, instead of an air force, the Western Allies should send additional aircraft to the Soviet Union for use by the Red Air Force, over and above those already being sent under Lend-Lease. The concept of Allied servicemen fighting alongside the Soviets in Soviet territory was unacceptable to Stalin. After failure to reach a compromise, the idea was dropped, another example of the difficulties of trying to get nations to work together.

The decision to go ahead with TORCH had considerable ramifications, and was not taken lightly or without opposition. Understanding the unwillingness among influential Americans to exploit the gains of TORCH eastwards into the Mediterranean explains much about the way in which the campaigns in Sicily and then Italy itself were prosecuted: those tasked with fighting in these areas had to do so without the unstinting support – moral or matériel – that was to be given to those who would later land in Normandy. Having gained Roosevelt's support for TORCH, Churchill had now to persuade him on the way forward once North Africa had been secured. He introduced the 'soft underbelly' concept, striking at the Axis through Sardinia or Sicily, through moving against Italy, Greece and other Balkan areas, and optimistically bringing Turkey into the war on the Allied side, which would facilitate an attack through the Black Sea against Germany's flank. Again, Marshall demurred. There were logistic problems with regard to Mediterranean operations, any involvement there was 'dabbling', and moving away from the main question of dealing with Germany; the spectre of the Dardanelles expedition of the last war hung over Churchill's proposals.

On 10 December 1942 President Roosevelt and the Joint Chiefs of Staff took up the question of what would follow the North African campaign. Marshall argued against any further Mediterranean operations, in favour of returning to a swift build-up of forces in the British Isles. He wanted to be ready to take advantage of any German weaknesses by launching an operation in the west of France; the President's ruling was to continue the build-up in both the United Kingdom and in North Africa, so as to be able of taking advantage of whatever opportunity might present itself. He went so far as to say that the Turkey options should be given consideration, but did not commit himself to any particular course of action at this stage. Planning for the Mediterranean had to continue.

The Mediterranean was not the only course open. The US Army Air Forces were as enthusiastic as ever to push the concept of reducing Germany through strategic bombing from bases in Great Britain and North Africa; six months of sustained effort should, General Arnold believed, open the way for a land offensive. Army planners were less impressed, pointing out that weather would play its part, in addition to British reservations about not invading until the enemy was on the verge of collapse.[11] To them, the Air Forces' claims for strategic bombing were overstated. There were three possible courses of action for 1943, as the Army saw things:

Firstly, the strategic bombing option. This they rejected on the grounds that only a concerted air and land assault would defeat Germany.

Secondly, the cross-Channel invasion, which meant returning to the original strategy once North Africa had seen the last of the enemy. The difficulty here was deciding how this could be achieved in 1943. The logistics for such a venture would not be ready until mid-1944, and to turn away from the Mediterranean would be to sacrifice the advantages obtained by TORCH, both psychological and geographical. It would also ignore the fact that it would still be necessary to retain large force levels in the region to ensure its future security. There was the additional consideration of the Dieppe experience in August 1942, where heavy casualties incurred during the raid did not augur well for a contested landing in France. The postponement of this option had to be accepted.

And thirdly, to maintain pressure in the Mediterranean. With the other two options discarded for the forthcoming year, the possibility of knocking Italy out of the war and continuing a limited offensive in the Mediterranean which would serve to take some of the pressure off the Soviet Union, while continuing the bombing of Germany and the assembly of forces for cross-Channel, seemed the best way forward.

Reluctant though many of the planners were to adopt this strategy, the fact that the United States was already engaged in the Mediterranean provided them with a workable course of action for the next year. In early January 1943 the Joint Chiefs and their planning teams were on their way to Casablanca to thrash out an agreement with the British. On Boxing Day 1942 they circulated a summary of their views on operations in 1943 to the British Chiefs of Staff, which would provide an agenda for the conference. In this summary they reiterated their position that the principal offensive effort should be directly against Germany – in Western Europe rather than peripherally. No mention was made of post-TORCH exploitation, except in that the position in North Africa should be consolidated and that preparations for air operations against Italy should be put in place. Surplus forces in North Africa should be transferred to the United Kingdom.

On 2 January 1943 the British Chiefs of Staff replied that they were in agreement on most points, but that the main difference was with regard to the Mediterranean where they saw the requirement for a follow-up to TORCH, which would take Italy out of the war, giving the enemy no time for recovery.

Five days later Roosevelt and Marshall met in the White House to discuss their preparations for the forthcoming conference – the only such meeting they held on the subject, despite the President's warning that the British would be well-prepared with their plans.[12] In Marshall's view the different strategic approaches of the two nations had boiled down to a choice between cross-Channel versus Mediterranean operations; Roosevelt recommended a compromise wherein plans be assembled for both options, while the actual decision be postponed until circumstances developed sufficiently to indicate which way to go.

A further issue emerged during the meeting. Roosevelt declared his intention to seek the 'unconditional surrender' of the Axis powers as the basic aim of the war. This policy had been given no study by the Army planners, and its consequences had not been considered. The reason for Roosevelt's decision has been partly explained by a number of earlier events, which date back to his December 1940 speech in which he stated that the United States was 'The Arsenal of Democracy', the provider of military supplies to Great Britain and the Soviet Union in their fight against Nazi Germany and Fascist Italy, without actually becoming involved in the fighting itself. In this he had clearly placed his country on the side of freedom – which he underlined only a week later in his State of the Union Address in which he laid out the goals of 'The Four Freedoms': Freedom of Speech and Expression, Freedom of Worship, Freedom from Want, and Freedom from Fear. Together with the Atlantic Charter, which he agreed with Churchill during their pre-war meeting on the USS *Augusta* off Newfoundland in August 1941, these statements laid down the American aims for the war and for the postwar world. Amongst these was the right of all peoples to self-determination, an aspiration which neither the British, with their Empire, nor the Soviets, who controlled the Baltic States, could accept without caveat. Nor, for that matter, did all of the stated goals sit easily with Roosevelt's intention of spreading United States' influence and of establishing bases outside North America – let alone the question of segregation at home. Nevertheless, the three statements had given the Allies a framework within which to plan for the future, both during and after the war, and were unwavering in their rejection of fascism.

Like all such well-intentioned statements, putting them into practice was less straightforward than putting them on paper. During the planning for TORCH it had been decided to try and broker an agreement with the Vichy French forces in North Africa as a way of stopping them resisting the landings. Unfortunately for the high ideals of the Atlantic Charter and the United Nations, the deal was struck with Admiral François Darlan, who was widely seen as being a German collaborator and a supporter of fascism. General Eisenhower agreed to Darlan's self-nomination as the French High Commissioner for North and West Africa, a move which outraged many Allied leaders, including the head of the Free French, Charles de Gaulle. Fortunately for Allied relations, Darlan was assassinated shortly afterwards, but the episode exposed the disarray in the Allied camp and left many questioning the morality of a leadership that was prepared to come to agreements with men such as Darlan. Roosevelt's decision to opt for unconditional surrender went some way to restoring their confidence by clearly stating that no deals would be made with the Axis powers.[13]

On 14 January 1943 Roosevelt, Churchill and their political and military advisers met in Casablanca for the SYMBOL Conference. Here the two leaders discussed the strategy of unconditional surrender, but Churchill was taken aback when Roosevelt announced it at a press conference, thereby ensuring that the news was spread throughout the world in the shortest possible time. Churchill's fear was that the policy would only make the enemy fight all the harder in the final stages of the war, and the decision still remains controversial. Unconditional surrender, as important a policy as it undoubtedly was, was not of course the only item on the agenda. The discussions included the war in the Pacific and – of particular relevance to this volume – the decision to invade Sicily once the North African campaign was won.

With strong American feelings against becoming involved in the Mediterranean rather than making an all-out effort for the cross-Channel invasion as soon as possible, the Sicily decision was not taken easily. Initial planning for the operation had been undertaken, but it remained to be approved. There were several matters to be resolved, including the knock-on effect on the cross-Channel landing, particularly with respect to naval plans. Opening the Mediterranean and the route to the Suez Canal by clearing it of enemy shipping meant that fewer escort vessels would be required for the convoys; but undertaking landings on Sicily would tie down considerable numbers of warships, transports, landing ships and assault craft, all of which were needed in England. Keeping them in the Mediterranean meant that any opportunity to mount a swift invasion on the French coast would be jeopardized. A further consideration with regard to naval planning, particularly for the Americans, was the war in the Pacific, for which shipping was a vital requirement.

The question boiled down to whether or not to exploit the successes of TORCH and the ensuing North African gains. The Americans were wedded to the intention of invading North West Europe and regarded the British as being far too conservative in not agreeing to an early date for this operation. Closing down further operations in the Mediterranean would allow the Allies to revert to the earlier priority of cross-Channel and to devote all of their energies to that purpose. The British felt that the Americans were too inexperienced and were underestimating the difficulties of landing on a heavily-defended French coastline. To support their argument, they had the experience of the Dieppe raid; and they were also suspicious of American capabilities – their performance in North Africa, particularly in the Kasserine Pass, did not fill the British with confidence. What they did not make allowances for, however, was the American ability to learn from their mistakes and to improve matters.

Consideration of the need to draw German forces away from the Eastern Front and to take some of the pressure off the Red Army was an important issue. On current planning, there would be thirteen British and nine American divisions available in Great Britain by August 1943; if these were to be landed in France, they would not be sufficient to ensure that significant German forces would be withdrawn from the east. There were already forty-four enemy divisions in France, and these would be more than enough to hold the Allies. The best that could be hoped for was to take a foothold in an area that could be used as a base from which to expand as more divisions became available – the Cherbourg or Brest peninsulas, for example. But such a move would not improve the situation in the east, and the forces landed in either of the two alternatives would be placed out on a limb, without adequate air cover: Cherbourg was within limited fighter range from England, Brest was beyond it. Overwhelming *Luftwaffe* forces could play havoc with the ground troops. Cross-Channel was looking very unlikely for 1943, but the Western Allies could not sit on their hands until the following year. Some activity was necessary to show the Soviets, the enemy, and the public at home in the United States and Great Britain, that the Western Allies were prosecuting the war to their full ability, and the Mediterranean was the most promising place for this. The Italian campaign was becoming not just a possibility; it was becoming inevitable, whether the Americans wanted it or not.

The wheels may have been inexorably turning towards Italy, but the United States Joint Chiefs of Staff were determined to make sure that it did not hinder their preparations for France unduly. In agreeing to the Sicilian landings, they were keen to emphasize that they were not writing a blank cheque for further Mediterranean operations. Preparations for cross-Channel (BOLERO) would continue; and the answer to the final American question – was the Sicilian operation the means to an end, or was it an end in itself? – remained in the air.

With the British and American delegations in Casablanca unable to produce a definite plan for defeating Germany by resolving the cross-Channel-Mediterranean question, the SYMBOL Conference came to a close. Planning would proceed for both eventualities but with the understanding that cross-Channel would come about, either as Marshall favoured with a ROUNDUP-style main thrust through France against Germany, or as a coup de grace delivered once the enemy had been worn down through 'peripheral' operations, as Churchill wanted.[14] Short-term objectives would include Sicily (Operation HUSKY). A further gain was the agreement of a series of guiding principles on a command system which would control combined Anglo-

American operations: they would take place under a supreme commander. If the coalition was not yet able to see eye-to-eye on strategy – apart from Unconditional Surrender – at least they were able to find a way of actually working together once operations commenced.

One other difference between British and United States approaches to decision making became apparent during the aforementioned conferences. The British Chiefs of Staff arrived in Casablanca well-supported by a team of staff officers and pre-prepared plans on which to base the discussions. The Americans had made comparatively fewer preparations, and went away from the meeting feeling that they had been out-manoeuvred. They also felt that the long experience that the British had in international negotiations had played a decisive part in the decisions that were taken.

A recognition that US Army planning was characteristically opportunistic, and therefore comparatively poorly prepared to counter British arguments, led General Wedermeyer (the Army planner) to stress the need for a long-range vision on how Germany and Italy were to be defeated. With such a concept agreed, long-term logistical planning could proceed; but before this could be undertaken two fundamental topics had to be addressed: the role of airpower and the limits that should be placed on future Mediterranean operations.

Views on what airpower might achieve were split along service lines. The Air Forces held to the belief that overwhelming bombing would render Germany defenceless, allowing the ground forces little more than a mopping-up operation as a finale. The Army's opinion was that, while airpower could inflict damage on the enemy, the ground part of the strategy would be far larger than the airmen understood. No Allied victory had thus far been won by sustained mass bombing, but rather through co-ordination between air and ground. With Wedermeyer now estimating that the cross-Channel invasion would not be possible until late 1944, the proposal for a combined bomber offensive against Germany – outlined at Casablanca – would go ahead. The offensive was solidly linked to cross-Channel, and for the Air Forces their role in the defeat of the enemy had been clarified – and the focus was on building up their strength in the United Kingdom.

The Mediterranean question was less straightforward. HUSKY had been agreed, but both Marshall and Wedermeyer felt that if it could be advanced – brought forward rather than wait for Axis forces to be defeated in Tunisia – then the commitment to this theatre might be wound up at an earlier date, and attention could then focus, again, on BOLERO-ROUNDUP. Practical difficulties led Eisenhower's staff to rule this option out, which Marshall found unduly cautious. HUSKY could not go ahead until July 1943. This ruling meant that planning for limited Mediterranean operations had now to be put in place for post-HUSKY. Various alternatives were considered, with Italy, Southern France, Sardinia, Corsica, Crete, the Dodecanese Islands, and even the Iberian Peninsula being looked at as possible objectives. US Army planners were not of one mind on whether or not the Mediterranean operations could be brought to a close once Sicily had fallen. Political considerations – continuing to bring pressure on the Axis to satisfy Soviet requirements, as well as those of home country populations – and British preferences, had to be recognized. However, at Casablanca Wedermeyer had advocated that that any post-TORCH operation be carried out only by those forces already in the Mediterranean and that the Western Mediterranean was the most suitable area for whatever commitment might be undertaken. In general, Southern Italy was the most promising target, offering the opportunity to divert German forces from the Eastern Front, of knocking Italy out of the war, and of providing bases from which to bomb targets in the Balkans. The planners also drew up the advantages of limiting Mediterranean operations post-HUSKY to the minimum, and of transferring all surplus forces to Great Britain: if enough veteran divisions could be brought back before the end of 1943 then ROUNDUP might be launched in the spring of 1944. On 27 April Marshall asked Eisenhower to have plans drawn up for various post-HUSKY alternatives, including Sardinia and/or Corsica, and the heel of Italy, but he emphasized that any thought of an all-out invasion of Italy could not be taken without very serious consideration. The fear of forces being drawn into the Mediterranean and away from ROUNDUP was foremost in his mind.

In early May the Joint War Plans Committee recommended to the Joint Chiefs that consideration be given to moving troops back to the United Kingdom, and that future Mediterranean operations be limited to those that could be carried out by existing forces in the region – and that they should be confined to the Western Mediterranean. These proposals were approved on 8 May 1943, a few days before the TRIDENT Conference opened in Washington.

For TRIDENT, the United States' negotiators had determined not to repeat their weaknesses during SYMBOL, where they had felt themselves to be out-prepared and out-manoeuvred by their British counterparts. Now Wedermeyer proposed that the Americans prepare papers for British consideration before the conference. This would go some way towards ensuring that it was not only British suggestions that were discussed. The number of US representatives was also increased, and several committees established which would specialize in matters such as logistics. To these changes was added the establishment of a working group, known as the Joint War Plans Committee, which would deal with the production of detailed studies on future joint deployment and operations. Hitherto the American and British approach to future operations had been different, the former not undertaking detailed planning until a course of action had been authorized, the latter spending some time and effort in studying the possibilities before agreeing on what action to take. While the United States' procedure meant that time was not wasted on operations that might never come to fruition, it also meant that their feasibility was not fully explored at an early enough stage to affect decisions; the British approach produced the information, but at the cost of many man-hours which might not have been needed. In recognition of the close relationship between the political and military worlds, attempts were made to improve liaison between the Joint Chiefs of Staff and the White House and State Department. Marshall's perception of the British approach was that, when they arrived for a conference, their ideas were fully developed in detail and had been agreed by everyone from Churchill downwards. For TRIDENT things would be different, and the US planners undertook studies on all 'reasonable courses of action' for post-HUSKY follow-up. They were ordered to give special emphasis to planning for cross-Channel operations.

While the planners maintained that, because of logistics and terrain, ROUNDUP held more promise than the Mediterranean, they were prepared to cede the point that limited operations in the latter theatre could tie down strong Axis ground and air forces and possibly even force the enemy to move divisions from the Eastern Front. The conflict between maintaining the primacy of ROUNDUP while taking short-term opportunities against the 'soft underbelly' was still unresolved, and the American planners were split in their support for the alternative courses of action. Eventually a set of proposals was produced for the President's approval, which emphasized the build-up of Army Air Forces' strength in the United Kingdom in preparation for the cross-Channel operation in 1944. This basic strategy should not be hazarded by other operations – but there were certain merits in implementing post-HUSKY exploitation, to keep the momentum going, to make best use of the resources already in the area, and to threaten Italy and the south of France. These were contingent upon a reduction, rather than an increase, in forces in the Mediterranean. The United States must not get involved in operations east of Sicily. Far from clarifying the issue, the planners appeared to have advanced matters not a jot.

For two weeks, 12 to 25 May 1943, the Anglo-American delegations debated the strategy of the war. Yet again, the problem of cross-Channel and Mediterranean operations dominated the discussions. While Roosevelt pushed for the former, to take place in the spring of 1944, he stated that he had strong reservations about committing large armies into Italy. Churchill's response was that the first objective for operations after HUSKY was to eliminate Italy from the war. This was the only large-scale way to take the pressure off the Soviets in 1943, for the Germans would have to replace Italian forces in the Balkans and in Germany itself. To achieve this aim, he felt, it would not be necessary to occupy Italy itself – but the opportunity to take control of Italian airfields and ports to facilitate operations against the Balkans or Southern France should not be missed. The real problem, he stressed, was what to do between the anticipated end of the Sicilian campaign (late August) and the launch of ROUNDUP (spring 1944). The two leaders agreed that their forces should not remain idle for this period.

How to employ them was then debated by the Combined Chiefs of Staff. The British and Americans held to their arguments for and against the amount of effort that should be put into the Mediterranean. In essence, it boiled down to how much could be done without jeopardizing a spring 1944 date for ROUNDUP – a question of what strength of men and resources could be allocated. Trained US troops had to be safeguarded for ROUNDUP, and there was the number of available landing craft to be considered. Not only did the planners have to estimate those required to land the required number of divisions on the coast of France, but they had to balance the needs of the Pacific War and the rates of production of these vessels; adding further landing operations to the shopping list was an unwelcome complication. The Americans maintained that any post-HUSKY amphibious operation in the Mediterranean would rule out the possibility of providing enough for ROUNDUP. Landing craft availability became the defining concern of the conference. Using 1943 landing-craft production rates, the planners calculated that Mediterranean operations could continue after HUSKY, but ROUNDUP could only rely on sufficient vessels to land five divisions simultaneously (two airborne divisions would also be employed). The Americans were now arguing not against Mediterranean operations as such, but only about whether or not they might delay ROUNDUP.

In the ensuing compromise the British accepted the cross-Channel operation, with a defined date and size, and preceded by a combined bomber offensive which would destroy and disrupt the German military and economic infrastructure. Planning would proceed for an emergency cross-

Channel landing should circumstances demand it. For the Americans the concessions were made on Mediterranean operations. Agreement was reached that planning should continue to take Italy out of the war, but without specifying how this might be achieved. The planning was to be undertaken by General Eisenhower, Commander-in-Chief in North Africa, but the Combined Chiefs retained the right of taking the final decision. In making his plans, Eisenhower was restricted in the forces he could use, for the Americans had extracted an agreement from the British that four United States and three British divisions would be transferred from the Mediterranean to Great Britain, starting from November 1943. Eisenhower was to plan on the basis of having twenty-seven divisions available for operations and garrisons in the Mediterranean, post-HUSKY.[15]

As the North African campaign extended into the early months of 1943 an increasing number of United States troops were deployed: from 180,000 in December 1942 to some 388,000 by the first week of May 1943 when the campaign entered its mop-up stage. Much of the strength intended for the United Kingdom under BOLERO was diverted to the Mediterranean (in the United Kingdom American numbers fell from approximately 168,000 in November 1942 to about 59,000 at the end of March 1943).[16] ROUNDUP was being pushed further into the future. Not only were troop numbers being diverted to the Mediterranean, but the United States took on the task of rearming the French. The ability to employ French formations was of undoubted benefit, but equipping them was not straightforward – such a procedure would have its effect on American and British production, training and equipment programmes. A re-armament committee, which included US, British and French representatives, was established and a French liaison officer was sent to Washington. It soon emerged that he and the American officials had a differing view of what had been agreed at Casablanca; his expectations were in excess of what Roosevelt had intended when he agreed 'in principle' to the rearmament. In fact, the phrase 'in principle' was interpreted differently by British, Americans, French and Russians, and was the source of much misunderstanding within the coalition. It was a salutary lesson in semantics which continues to cause problems today; in 1943 it led to a degree of friction between the Americans and French, and by the end of the North African campaign one armoured and two-and-a-half infantry divisions, and some smaller units, had been – or were being – equipped. The French had hoped for three armoured divisions, eight motorized divisions, and a host of other matériel – including an air force of some 500 fighters, 300 bombers and 200 transport aircraft, all to be delivered by the summer.

They were to be disappointed, not least because their requirements had to take their place in the queue for shipping.[17]

Equipping the French to fight a modern war was not the only issue that the British and Americans had to deal with. The political question of the future French government had to be addressed. At Casablanca a strained cooperation between the two claimants to the French leadership – Generals Giraud (who had succeeded Admiral Darlan as head of the French in North Africa) and de Gaulle (head of the Free French) – had been achieved by Churchill and Roosevelt, and the two became joint heads of the French Committee of National Liberation until de Gaulle manoeuvred Giraud out later in the year. The Americans, however, suspected de Gaulle of being in Churchill's pocket and he was distrusted by Roosevelt, and neither he nor Churchill saw the Committee as being other than a wartime administrative organization which did not have the potential to become France's postwar government.

Agreement on Italy

And still the question remained unresolved: what the Western Allies were to do once HUSKY was completed? The Sicilian landings went ahead as planned, and their initial success brought the matter to a head. Within a week of the landings the British urged that General Eisenhower be permitted to retain a number of vessels that had not yet been allocated to BOLERO or to the Pacific theatre; this was resisted by the US Army planners, backed by Marshall. However, he now came up with a proposal which was at odds with his previous stance: a bold amphibious assault on Naples as a post-HUSKY option. An intelligence report dated 15 July, only five days after the landings on Sicily, outlined the deterioration in Italian military capabilities, and an attack in the Naples area would exploit this weakness and offer an opportunity to move onto Rome. Marshall felt that taking such a risk was justifiable under the circumstances, a decision that was received with delight in London, where US Secretary of War Stimson was conferring with Churchill. To Stimson's dismay the Prime Minister interpreted Marshall's proposal as an endorsement of Churchill's Mediterranean policy, an interpretation which Stimson was at pains to clarify by emphasizing that Marshall's intent was to maintain pressure on the enemy while preparations for cross-Channel continued, rather than to launch an extended large-scale operation on the Italian mainland. Nevertheless, and while professing their support for ROUNDUP, the British were highly satisfied with the prospect of their plans for the Mediterranean being given a boost.

Plans for taking the war into Italy now proceeded in earnest. On 18 July Eisenhower requested approval from the Combined Chiefs of Staff to move onto the mainland as soon as Sicily was in Allied hands; this would give him the opportunity to take the best advantage of failing Italian morale and to force that country out of the war, while tying down the maximum numbers of German forces, so assisting both the preparations for ROUNDUP and the Soviet Front. Two days later approval was received, and AVALANCHE – the codename for an Allied landing south of Naples, to take place in late August – was given the blessing of the Combined Chiefs of Staff (CCS). But the American planners still resisted calls for any more shipping to be made available; nothing should be permitted to threaten BOLERO or operations in the Pacific and Far East.

On 25 July Mussolini fell. The news was considered by both the Joint and the Combined Chiefs of Staff, and Marshall again moved his stance on future operations against Italy. The state of Italian morale and military capabilities now signalled to him that AVALANCHE should take place at the very earliest opportunity. Moreover, Allied casualties in Sicily were relatively light, and there would be some 60,000 men over and above the numbers agreed during TRIDENT that were available for post-HUSKY operations. Add these factors to the opportunity to assist the new Italian government in freeing itself from the Germans, and the opening was too good to miss. For all that the Americans had held out against the British policy of peripheral operations, they had now been drawn towards them – but they were not ready to do so unreservedly, and they would not commit forces to the Mediterranean that might better be used – in their eyes, at least – in attacking Germany directly. Whatever the planners felt, the prospect of an Italian campaign was now firmly on the cards. A later generation would have used the expression 'mission creep' to explain what had happened as events overtook earlier intentions and fresh opportunities appeared which became too attractive to ignore. An Italian campaign which did not endanger BOLERO-ROUNDUP, which tied down German divisions, which gave airbases from which to bomb Germany, and which was short-term and had limited objectives, did not seem too unattractive, especially when compared to a slow 'flog' up the leg of the country which would suck in more and more forces, which was what some had anticipated from the British proposals.

Churchill's preferred option was to push on at least as far as Rome, to open up opportunities in both the Mediterranean and southern Europe. This, he held, would considerably enhance the odds for the success of ROUNDUP. The Americans felt differently. They feared that such a campaign would draw the Allies into the Balkans, Greece, and possibly Southern France. This fear was not groundless, for they learned that the British Foreign Secretary Anthony Eden supported the idea of landings in the first two localities. Italy might even supplant ROUNDUP. More than this, there was American concern that Portugal might be drawn into the war on the Allied side. This would have proved to be a mixed blessing, for it was felt that were this to happen then Allied forces might have to be sent to the Iberian peninsula to support them – and away from the cross-Channel build-up. The planners urgently needed decisions to be taken in order to assemble their manpower and matériel in the right locations.

Eisenhower's staff produced two alternative plans for Italy: BUTTRESS envisaged invading Calabria (the 'toe') in the area of Goija, the operation being mounted from North Africa; and AVALANCHE. They also made a plan for a swiftly-mounted version of AVALANCHE in which a division-sized force would land to exploit a sudden Italian collapse. Eisenhower maintained that a landing on the Italian toe was necessary before AVALANCHE went ahead. This should ensure that the Germans would be prevented from moving their reserves directly to the AVALANCHE site, but at this time (2 August) he was undecided where the preliminary landing would be. The choice lay between BUTTRESS and BAYTOWN (crossing the Straits of Messina).

The next Anglo-American conference, codenamed QUADRANT, took place in Quebec from 14 to 24 August. In his pre-conference meeting with President Roosevelt, General Marshall pressed the argument that the two limited operations currently underway against the Axis – in the Pacific and the Mediterranean – would take so much of the Allied resources that OVERLORD would be threatened. Marshall felt that the time had come for a final decision on European strategy, which in his mind was to clearly prioritize OVERLORD, and he therefore sought Roosevelt's support in bringing the British around to committing themselves unreservedly to this course of action. The President's response was to point out that seven battle-experienced divisions were scheduled to leave the Mediterranean for the United Kingdom – but could they not be replaced in the Mediterranean by an equal number of freshly-trained formations so that more might be achieved there? Not to be used, of course, in the Balkans, but they could help secure an area north of Rome, take Sardinia and Corsica, and threaten Southern France.

Marshall replied that moving the three US and four British divisions from the Mediterranean for OVERLORD was about all that could be achieved without threatening preparations for that operation. Any use of shipping to bring divisions from the United States to replace those taken from the

Mediterranean would be a price which OVERLORD would pay for. The planners maintained that the forces already there, minus the seven divisions identified for withdrawal, would be sufficient to meet Roosevelt's requirement. In this they were supported by Eisenhower, who stated that after achieving the proposed objectives of capturing Rome, Sardinia and Corsica, he would have fourteen divisions available for an invasion of Southern France in co-ordination with OVERLORD. Thus reassured, Roosevelt expressed himself satisfied with preparations for the Mediterranean. The Joint Chiefs of Staff now had the President behind them in their stand on the primacy of OVERLORD.

Early in the conference news came of the fall of Sicily. Although Eisenhower had been directed to draw up plans for operations on the Italian mainland, the American and British delegates had yet to formalize their views on the cross-Channel-Mediterranean debate. The British argument was that operations in Italy would assist OVERLORD for the reasons outlined above; further, the retention of the seven divisions in the Mediterranean would open up more opportunities – to choose between an OVERLORD or Mediterranean strategy, General Brooke maintained, would be 'too binding'. The American counter-argument was that if operations in the Mediterranean were to be extended and the seven divisions retained there, then the conditions for OVERLORD might not be met. Unless OVERLORD were given the overriding priority Marshall wanted, it would become a 'subsidiary operation'; the entire Anglo-American strategic concept for winning the war would have to be revised – and this could result in the United States taking a different view on the secondary role of the war in the Pacific.[18]

Compromise was reached and OVERLORD was given the priority that Marshall wanted, but the question of how far to take the Italian campaign remained. Churchill assured the conference that he was not committed to an advance further than a line drawn between Ancona and Pisa. Both parties agreed that it would be advantageous to capture airfields as far north as possible from which to extend the range of Allied bombers in their offensive against Germany. But there was disagreement about the suggestion that the south of France should be invaded by Anglo-American forces as a diversion or support for OVERLORD. While the Americans wanted to place limits on Mediterranean operations, they also saw a need to open up another front in Southern France, which the British felt might as easily be achieved by striking westwards from Italy, should the Allies get far enough north.

Keeping the Italian war limited, while ensuring that it contributed to OVERLORD, was the problem throughout the QUADRANT discussions. There were differences in the two nations' strategies for winning the war which came down to the importance each accorded to peripheral operations and the timing of the main blow against Germany – to a programme of attrition compared to a policy of concentration in a particular area. Yet again compromises were arrived at: OVERLORD was to be the main effort, with a target date of 1 May 1944. But the Americans had to forfeit their wish that it be given overriding priority, instead accepting that it was the 'main object', which would be recognized as such in the event that decisions had to be taken regarding the allocation of scarce resources. As for forces available for Mediterranean operations, they would be those previously agreed 'except insofar as these may be varied by decision of the Combined Chiefs of Staff'.[19] The limiting statement 'with available Mediterranean forces' was omitted.

Mediterranean operations would be continued in three phases, the first of which was to eliminate Italy from the war and to establish air bases at least as far north as Rome. The second phase would be to seize Sardinia and Corsica, and the third would be to maintain pressure on German forces in northern Italy while creating conditions for the entry of Allied forces (including most of the French formations) into southern France.

One other decision was to affect the future of the war in the Mediterranean. Hitherto the understanding had been that since the Americans, in the person of Eisenhower, commanded in that theatre, then the British would take command of the cross-Channel operation. Churchill had gone so far as to nominate General Sir Alan Brooke for the appointment, and had informed Brooke of this in early 1943. Now, however, Churchill felt that an American should have the job because of the numbers of United States forces that would be involved. He proposed this to Roosevelt, who had already been thinking the same thing, and who had Marshall in mind. In the event neither Brooke nor Marshall got the job, not least because they were irreplaceable in their current appointments.

QUADRANT achieved a degree of agreement. OVERLORD was to be the principal means by which Germany would be defeated; operations in the Mediterranean would tie in with this decision to help create the conditions for its success; and compromises had been reached on the extent of Mediterranean operations – for example ground offensives would not extend to the Balkans or the eastern Mediterranean. And an agreement to allocate twenty-nine divisions to OVERLORD and its follow-up, by 1 May 1944, effectively set limits on future Mediterranean involvement. Nevertheless, the United States planners, in particular, kept a wary eye on events in case they threw up attractions that might draw resources away from OVERLORD.

It was becoming apparent that commanders in the field were taking a bigger part in the planning process than hitherto; until American forces became engaged on the ground, all planning had been done in remote headquarters well away from the operational theatres. Now Eisenhower and his staff were busy planning the invasion of the Italian mainland. On 16 August he informed the Joint Chiefs of Staff that he intended to launch Operation BAYTOWN across the Straits of Messina between 1 and 4 September, and AVALANCHE on 9 September. The delay between the two operations would allow his limited number of landing craft to be used for both operations. BAYTOWN was to be mounted by Montgomery's Eighth Army, employing two divisions in the assault. They were to move up the toe of Italy and to link up with the AVALANCHE landing, and also towards the east to link up with a landing near Taranto, which had been given the unhappy codename of SLAPSTICK.

On 3 September the Eighth Army began crossing the Straits of Messina, supported by a bombardment of 29,000 rounds of ammunition fired from 630 artillery pieces. More shells came from the guns of three cruisers, five destroyers, three monitors and four gunboats, and some 100 bomber and fighter-bomber sorties were flown in direct support of the landings.[20] There was no resistance – the Germans had withdrawn the comparatively few troops of the *15th Panzer Grenadier Regiment* that had been in the area to prepared positions twenty-five miles deeper into Italy. On the same day, and a few miles to the south of Syracuse in the town of Cassibile, General Giuseppe Castellano signed the Italian surrender on behalf of Marshal Badoglio.

The invasion of mainland Italy had – at last – begun. After months of argument between the British and the Americans, watched suspiciously by the Soviets, the die was finally cast. But the drawn-out debates had meant that preparations were not properly in place to support the probability of months of fighting that lay ahead. Not only were the commanders on the ground constrained by the limited resources that their superiors had allowed them to use in this venture, they were to lose seven of their most experienced divisions with no guarantee that they would be replaced by similar numbers of men. The campaign was to be fought with limited amphibious capabilities, for the great bulk of the shipping was to be redirected to OVERLORD, which meant that the opportunities to outflank the enemy by making further landings behind their defences would be few. And the logistic support for the operations was not in place: the delays in making the decision to invade meant that many essential facilities – such as base workshops for the repair of both armoured and soft-skinned vehicles – were still located in North Africa, and with the limitations placed on shipping capacity the problems of back-loading vehicles, let alone bringing fuel, ammunition and all other supplies forward, became serious. To all of the foregoing difficulties had to be added that of morale and motivation, at least at the senior levels of command, for the commanding generals were well aware that theirs was to be a sideshow designed to do little more than to keep the enemy occupied until the main effort could be made across the English Channel. As the campaign progressed, this malaise also began to affect those further down the chain of command, to the extent that British Army desertion rates in Italy rose dramatically after the fall of Rome – and after D Day in Normandy.[21] The United States forces were in little better state: Marshall was compelled to address the problem of their morale in a letter dated Christmas Day 1944, in which he proposed that American press reports which placed the importance of the Italian campaign well below that of the fighting in North West Europe, and which made it a 'forgotten theatre', be countered by a statement from the President which restored the balance.[22] The confusion that had surrounded the determination of the Mediterranean strategy did not augur well for the future of the campaign. It was symptomatic of coalition warfare, at least as fought by this group of allies.

Notes

1. Alexander, Field Marshal Earl, of Tunis, *The Alexander Memoirs 1940–1945*
2. Clark, Mark W., Interview in *Tough Old Gut, World at War*
3. Alexander, op cit.
4. Quoted in Matloff, Maurice & Snell, Edwin M., *Strategic Planning for Coalition Warfare 1941–1942*
5. Ibid
6. Matloff, Maurice, *Strategic Planning for Coalition Warfare 1943-1944*
7. Note in his personal files 22 Feb 42, quoted in Matloff & Snell, op cit.
8. Matloff & Snell, op cit.
9. Outline Plan Operation TORCH, HQ ETOUSA, 21 Aug 42, quoted in Matloff & Snell, op cit.
10. Matloff & Snell, op cit.
11. Ibid
12. Ibid

13. Plesch, Dan, *America, Hitler and the UN*
14. Matloff & Snell, op cit.
15. Ibid
16. Ibid
17. Ibid
18. Ibid
19. CCS 319/5, 24 Aug 43, title: Final Report to the President and Prime Minister quoted in Matloff & Snell, op cit.
20. Malony, Brigadier C. J.C., et al, *The Mediterranean and the Middle East* Vol V
21. Peaty, Dr John, *The Desertion Crisis in Italy*
22. Letter from Marshall to MacLeish (Assistant Secretary of State for Public and Cultural Relations) The Marshall Papers #4-622

CHAPTER 3

The British Commonwealth

The British Commonwealth contributed many formations to the Fifth Army during the Italian campaign. Their presence was the almost inevitable consequence of American insistence that cross-Channel was to take precedence over the Mediterranean, and their decision to withdraw large numbers of United States forces to England in preparation for OVERLORD. At the same time, however, America had to be seen to be playing its part in a campaign which kept the pressure on Germany until the Normandy plans came to fruition; an American army could not be absent from the line of battle until the summer of 1944. One Commonwealth nation after another – Britain, Canada, New Zealand, South Africa, India, and several smaller members – had troops under American command in the Fifth Army at some time. While their presence bolstered its strength and enabled it to take its place alongside the Eighth Army, these countries brought with them the heritage of British pre-war military planning and preparations (or lack of them) for a major conflict against a European power. By 1943 the Commonwealth armies had suffered a series of setbacks which undermined the confidence of generals and private soldiers alike, a lack of confidence which was only recently being countered by success in North Africa. For those who had to build and command an effective coalition, these factors had to be considered and appropriate steps taken to ensure that the capabilities and morale of British forces continued to grow, steps that would not always be easy to make.

In the histories of the Second World War the relationships between the three great Allied powers and their leaders dominate discussions about political and military cohesiveness. The difficulties of cooperation between the Western Allies and their Soviet counterpart loom large, outstripping the problems encountered between the Anglo-Americans. While the predominance given to these issues is both unavoidable and correct, sight should not be lost of the less visible – and certainly less dramatic – differences between the smaller partners in the Alliance.

For the Italian campaign the Anglo-American alliance was the most important, in that the two nations were the most powerful in terms of resources dedicated to fighting the Germans there. It was inevitable that countries which contributed the strongest forces to the fight should have the loudest voices in the decision-making process, a situation which was to become more evident as the war progressed and American strength increased as Britain's began to wane. The coalition comprised a great number of other states which, as previously noted, had individual and independent reasons for contributing forces to the conflict. These will be considered in the following chapters as and when the various national contingents appear on the scene in Italy, but one group's reasons for participating might well be addressed at this stage, because they became combatants within a week of the war's outset and continued to fight without break against the Axis: the British Commonwealth. To follow the usual practice of lumping all of its countries together under one heading is a convenience, but is misleading.

The British Army After The Great War – The Wasted Years
Britain itself had come relatively late to the realization that another major European conflict might follow the 'war to end all wars', the Great War. Since 1918 successive governments beset by other concerns, economic and social, had reduced the nation's armed forces and done away with the conscription of the First World War. There was little indication of any threat to national security until the late 1930s, and neither the government nor the population at large, from whence the recruits would come, saw the need for large armed forces. In many respects the British Army returned to what it had been before 1914 – an Imperial police force with limited capability for fighting a modern, industrialized war. What attempts had been made to ready it for the future were often misguided: the pre-Great War ethos of selecting officers on the basis of their social status had crept back, and trying to turn cavalry regiments into armoured units was often an unhappy experience, for example. More critically, officers of all ranks (with some notable exceptions) failed to appreciate the effects of changing technology on the practice of warfare. As in the Victorian Army, intellect and ambition were not attributes looked for in the British officer – 'character' was. To these, and other, limitations must be added the comparatively low priority which the Army had been given by the inter-war politicians who had favoured the navy and air force when the question of allocating resources had been addressed.[1]

In the 1920s the General Staff had come to the conclusion that a comparatively small, highly professional army with the most up-to-date weapons offered the best prospect of avoiding the casualty lists and stalemate of the Great War; a swift victory achieved by professionals with the assistance of such weapons was the objective, an aim which was not to be realized. The Staff were also determined to restore mobility to the battlefield and to avoid the stagnation of 1914–18 trench warfare. Their intentions were not to come to fruition, firstly because of unwillingness by the government to make the necessary financial investment in the Army, but also because of a different opinion on the way forward. When the British government saw Hitler's Germany as posing a threat during the following decade, the reaction (in March 1939) was to double the size of the Territorial Army as a deterrent. This was not the option that the Army itself would have preferred – it increased numbers, but not professionalism nor quality of equipment; and the move threatened a re-run of 1914–18 with a large British army deployed to the Continent.

In its development of doctrine after the Great War the British General Staff sought to analyze events on the battlefield, to condense them down to separate phases in which the combatants manoeuvred, seized critical geographical features, fought and won, and then pursued the defeated enemy. This approach reduced a battle to a series of events which could be understood and controlled, in much the same way as psychologists of the time had applied a scientific approach to the industrial process, breaking it down into manageable phases which could be examined and massaged to improve productivity; what the Staff did not do was to give sufficient recognition to the reality that chaos is an inherent feature of battle and to take account of that fact – or indeed, to take advantage of it, as the Germans did in their development of *blitzkrieg*. The desire to impose order on the field of battle had another unwelcome effect – British Army doctrine reduced initiative among subordinate commanders. Senior officers needed to be kept informed of events on the battlefield, but the technology of the time did not allow intelligence to be communicated swiftly: in the British Expeditionary Force in France in 1939–40 great reliance was placed on the French telephone system (there were only seventy-five radio sets in a division at that time, compared to nearly 1,000 in 1944). The alternatives, of laying cable – not conducive to high mobility – or using despatch riders, were not time-saving measures. Taken together with the expectation that those on the frontline should not exercise more than very limited initiative, the tempo of operations was not increased – which it had to be, if *blitzkrieg* was to be countered effectively.

British Army doctrine was radically different from that of the Germans.

While the difficulties of contemporary communications equipment led the British to believe that delays in the passage of information and orders were inevitable, the Germans found an alternative solution which not only avoided the delay but took advantage of their opponents' tardiness to allow a rapid development of the battlefield on their terms. *Wehrmacht* policy was to encourage – indeed, demand – that all ranks be proactive and to exercise as much initiative as possible to achieve their commanders' intent. The fact that a plan rarely survives the first encounter with an enemy was both accepted and catered for, by ensuring that troops were thoroughly familiarized with all-arms tactics and by ensuring that commanders made their intentions understood. The British saw this type of training as imposing a series of drills on the troops, which they believed diminished, rather than increased, their imaginations and their ability to improvise and innovate. It was a complete misreading of the situation: the German thoroughness in instructing soldiers was intended to give them an understanding of the tactical doctrine so that they could carry on despite a change in circumstances. Their doctrine emphasized shattering their enemy's moral and physical cohesion; it relied on subordinates using their initiative to take the immediate opportunity of hitting hard to achieve this purpose, and schooling them by means of drills gave all ranks a common understanding of what should happen – there was little need to wait for orders if everyone knew the commander's overarching aim.

This basic misunderstanding of German military ethos came from the British Army inclination to believe that every foreign army worked in the same way as did the British; the notion that there might be an alternative, workable and war-winning, doctrine did not appear to occur to those who wrote the British manuals. At one level this mindset might be explained by a form of social Darwinism, in which senior British ranks found it impossible to accept that anyone but themselves could have come up with the best solution to dealing with the problems of the battlefield. To believe that there was only one way to fight a war was to commit the most elementary of military errors: when facing an enemy that had another methodology, such as the German Army, this error could be fatal because they might well be (and were) outmanoeuvred; when operating alongside allies who had their own doctrines, the error could at best be a source of confusion and misunderstanding which resulted in a less than harmonious working relationship. For a coalition such as the one that fought in Italy, the implications were enormous.

There had been very real attempts to learn from the lessons of 1914–18, not all of them successful. One legacy of the previous war was the emphasis placed on avoiding unnecessary casualties, which led British commanders to consolidate gains on the battlefield before exploiting success – in practical terms, 'going firm' on the objective rather than pushing on beyond it while the enemy was disorganized. The emphasis was very much on avoiding risks which might repeat the casualty figures of the First World War, an attitude which was to play its part again in Italy, but which meant missed opportunities to make the best of enemy confusion as they withdrew after a failed defence. A contributory factor to this thinking was that soldiers of the 1940s would not accept the casualty figures of their fathers' war; they would be better educated and less inclined to blindly follow their generals uncritically, and senior officers' concepts of leadership had, of necessity, to be reconsidered – they would have to lead by a process of give and take rather than by unthinking authority. While some senior officers were prepared to reflect on the changing relationship between ranks, an overwhelming number still considered that soldiers were not intelligent enough to exercise sufficient resourcefulness to act independently; indeed, there were those who felt that even allowing platoon commanders to use radio sets was a step too far.

New technology brought its own difficulties to the development of British doctrine, as a couple of examples will illustrate. Although it was the British who had introduced tanks to the battlefield, the lessons they drew from the experience were not always the correct ones. During the inter-war years a distinction was drawn between two tank types – the 'infantry' and the 'cruiser' tank. The job of the former was to support the infantry, operating almost as mobile pill-boxes which would advance at the pace of the foot soldier to effect the 'break-in' to enemy defensive lines and open a gap through which the cruiser and light tanks could 'break-out', striking at the enemy's flanks and deep towards his headquarters positions. This distinction was to introduce a complication into tank design and into combined arms co-operation which was to endure for much of the war. A second example of confusion and missed opportunity was with regard to the use of aircraft on the battlefield. Although they had been successfully used to support ground troops in 1918, the wrong lessons were drawn from the experience because of the casualties suffered by aircrew, and little attention was given to the co-ordination of air power other than to state that local air superiority was necessary for ground operations. Close air support was played down and the concept undeveloped both by the Army and the Royal Air Force because of the likelihood of heavy aircraft losses. The RAF was also reluctant to become involved in close air support because, as a separate service, they did not want to be seen as an ancillary to the ground forces at a tactical level. To the RAF their role was to achieve air superiority and to carry out long-range interdiction bombing operations against the enemy's lines of communication. This contrasted strongly with the *Luftwaffe*'s concept of operations, which included close air support with specialist dive-bomber units and a command system which worked with the ground troops to put it into action. The close air support debate was to continue through until the last years of the war, although there were times – for example in North Africa – when co-operation between the ground and air services was good.

The examples of tanks and aircraft illustrate an underlying problem in the British Army's thinking. Although in the four years leading up to the declaration of war in 1939 the horse was replaced by mechanical technology and new weapons were introduced, the Army failed to recognize that new equipment opened up new possibilities; these changes were not reflected in a change of doctrine, which did not address whether or not the system of command and control needed re-examining, but were incorporated into the existing policies. While new technology increased the pace of warfare, little was done to prepare commanders to react appropriately, to speed up the planning system and the communication of orders. Doctrine and technology had drifted apart.

There was also a difference between the professionalism of the British and German armies, a difference which reflected recruiting and training practices and policies rather than any inherent differences in the two populations from which the men were drawn. The British attitude towards officer selection, as previously noted, was to favour character over ambition and intellect; this extended to the feeling that the British aptitude for improvisation (if, indeed, such an aptitude existed) would enable officers to muddle through and to come up with a way to achieve success – again, there was resistance to an over- formalized educational and training regime. German army training was designed to produce junior officers who fulfilled the doctrinal requirements: all cadets were fully-trained soldiers before they went to cadet school, where they were taught everything up to and including what a battalion commander needed to know. Theoretically, any newly-commissioned officer was prepared to command a battalion in combat, which established a system that could readily absorb casualties because trained replacements were immediately available to step into their shoes. Moreover, they understood the operational procedures that their superiors went through in planning and executing missions. British subalterns, on the other hand, learned the bare essentials of platoon command before being commissioned and sent off to special-to-arm schools to learn the skills of their cap-badges – artillery, signals, and so on. For the infantry and cavalry no such school existed, the required training being carried out – for good or bad – in the regimental depots, where the quality of their professional development depended upon the skills and enthusiasm (or lack of them) of the commanding officer. It was not until March 1939 that the system changed when a tactical school was established, too late to have an impact on the officers who went to France later in the year. Officers of the Territorial Army were even less well catered for, as their training was done in their units, often under the auspices of the adjutant. In some cases the trainee officers did not have sufficient numbers of soldiers with whom to carry out training exercises and on whom to hone their professional skills.

For the other ranks the systems were again different. In Great Britain service as a soldier, especially in the infantry, was generally not regarded as a desirable career and the Army had problems recruiting men of intellectual quality or technical ability. Such individuals were more likely to be attracted to the Navy or RAF. In contrast, the Germans increased army pay, relaxed the discipline, and improved living standards to attract better educated men able to meet the requirements of the doctrine: they had to be capable of acting on their own initiative and to understand their officers' concept of operations, whereas much British Army training emphasized blind obedience to orders.

The Outbreak of War

In September 1939 the British Army numbered 53,287 officers and 839,410 other ranks. The Regular Army mustered 224,000 all ranks, supported by the Regular Army Reserve (ex-Regulars with a call-up commitment) of 131,100 men – of whom only 3,700 were fully trained. These were men who had left the Army within the previous year, the others having been civilians for up to thirteen years, who needed re-training on new equipment and procedures. The bulk of the reserves were the Territorial Army (18,900 officers and 419,200 other ranks) with its own reserve of over 20,000 all ranks. These figures may have appeared impressive, but the Territorials – although generally of higher intelligence than the regulars – needed between eighteen months and two years to train. Conscription was introduced in April 1939; by September the first intakes had just completed their basic training.[2] In the period from September 1939 to June 1941 the size of the British Army nearly tripled. It was to peak at 2.9 million men in June 1945, but demographic factors dictated that it would become increasingly difficult to maintain recruiting rates.

The falling numbers of men available to the Army caused increasing difficulties as the war went on. The quality of the educational backgrounds of conscripts during the later years fell, although this may have been the result of the disrupted schooling they had received during the early years of the war, before they reached the age when they were liable for military service. Army policy had been to send the least academically qualified recruits to the infantry, reserving the more technical arms – or at least those that worked with mechanical equipment or heavier weapons – for those men who it believed were best prepared to cope with machinery. At the outbreak of war about forty per cent of recruits went to the infantry, a proportion that was to decline as the needs of modern warfare emerged. Two years after the war started the Army identified over 500 trades or highly skilled jobs, and over a quarter of the Army's strength was recognized as tradesmen. The initial system for identifying men with appropriate skills for particular jobs was haphazard, with the consequential problem that they had later to be reassigned, and it was not until mid-1942 that personnel selection became systematic and a closer match was made between an individual's capabilities and the job he was sent to in the Army.

After 1941 the manpower shortage became increasingly acute, with the infantry being particularly affected. By mid-1943 virtually all but the best conscripts were destined for the infantry: the Navy and RAF took the most highly educated men, a fact which led to some grumbling amongst army officers. As the shortage became more acute towards the end of the war personnel from the other two services were transferred to the army, and as the threat from the *Luftwaffe* decreased anti-aircraft units were disbanded and also transferred to the infantry – as happened in the United Kingdom, North West Europe and Italy in 1944.

The fact that the best educated men were posted to almost any service or arm but the infantry underlines the approach that commanders were to take on the battlefield. The emphasis was on fighting a mechanical war with artillery, tanks and bombs, not by taking unnecessary and avoidable casualties. This was done not only for reasons of preserving life, but also in recognition of the demographic reality that British manpower was finite, and could not easily be replaced.

The post-Dunkirk period presented the Army with a problem not solely about the loss of men and equipment in France. While the Army was going through a time of rapid expansion it was necessary to identify officers with sufficient talent for command appointments in the field, and to weed out those who were unsuited. Most of the Army, and virtually all units that had been formed with the new influx of recruits, was stationed in the United Kingdom; this factor meant that the best indicator of an officer's abilities – his performance in battle – was not readily available. The solution, for good or bad, was to favour regular officers as appointees to command positions. This preference was not without some justification for, as has been previously noted, the pre-war training of Territorial Army officers was suspect; during the first two years of the war a quarter of all TA lieutenant colonels in command appointments had to be removed from their jobs. The inheritance from the pre-war years had also left the Army with a large percentage of commanding officers who, in the light of modern battle conditions, were considered to be too old for the job. Consequently the decision was taken that no officer over the age of forty-five would be appointed to command a field force unit; by September 1943 that age limit would be reduced to forty-three. Furthermore, unless there were particular reasons otherwise, command appointments could not be held over the age of fifty. The Army was beginning to find that the available pool of officers qualified for command was becoming increasingly restricted, a problem that was to be compounded when casualties took their toll.

The lateness of the re-armament programme and the Dunkirk episode had stripped the Army of much of its weapons. The urgency to find new equipment meant that some mass-produced items were of dubious design or quality, but there was no alternative but to accept anything that was serviceable. Weapons such as the Sten gun, a crude attempt to imitate the much better German MP38 sub-machine gun, not only filled the gap but continued in use throughout the war. Other inadequate weapons, particularly the anti-tank Boys rifle and later the PIAT (which the Army took to Italy), were issued. It was quicker to produce weapons that were known to be obsolete than to wait for new designs to be developed and tested. Six hundred 2-pounder anti-tank guns, despite being known to be outdated, were manufactured and distributed in 1941 rather than turning the production lines over to make one hundred 6-pounders, which were the most up-to-date model then available.[3] The next weapon in this category, the 17-pounder, was to appear in small numbers in Tunisia in early 1943. Infantry weapons – small arms, light and medium machineguns, and mortars – could not match the firepower of those used by the Germans, who in any case had more light machine guns in a platoon than did the British, which was another reason the British made frequent use of their artillery to support their own attacks and to repel those of the enemy. Only in one arm, the artillery, did the British Army impress the Germans. The 25-pounder gun-howitzer, with a range of

13,400 yards, was a reliable weapon; but when the Royal Artillery went to war in 1939 all of its heavier guns were of Great War vintage. More modern guns, the 4.5-inch and the 5.5-inch medium guns, did not appear in service until 1941 and 1942 respectively. The pre-war Army's intention to bring mobility back to the battlefield had caused it to neglect the development of weapons which it believed to be too cumbersome for the battlefield that they envisaged for the future; when such a battlefield did not emerge, they were – at least for a while – without the guns that they now needed. Until they arrived, the British Army could not lay down the concentrations of fire it wanted.

The pre-war deliberations about tank design produced three versions by the beginning of the war: cruisers, such as the Cruiser (which saw service in France and North Africa) and Crusader (a Cruiser designed by Nuffield as a 'private venture' which saw service in North Africa); infantry tanks, such as the Matilda (again, France and North Africa); and light tanks used for reconnaissance. In general they were mechanically unreliable and under-armed, although the models produced later in the war, such as the Churchill infantry tank, proved more successful. The Churchill was used in Italy by the Tank Brigades in support of the infantry.

From mid-1942 American tanks began to replace many British models: the M3 Lee (known by the British Army in its modified form as the Grant) medium tank had an outdated gun-mounting design, with the main armament set in a sponson on the tank's side, in the fashion of British Great War tanks. With a high profile that made it a prominent target, it was replaced by the M4 Sherman as soon as production numbers allowed. The Sherman was armed with a 75mm gun, as was the Lee, but on this tank it was set in a turret, which allowed the tank commander to adopt a lower hull-down position. It was relatively cheap to produce and was to become the mainstay of British and United States armoured units. Initially successful against the German *Mk III* and *IV* tanks, they were more evenly opposed by the later *Panzerkampfwagen IV,* which was up-gunned; against the *Panther* and *Tiger* the Sherman was generally outmatched. A particular weakness was the Sherman's tendency to burst into flames once hit, a failing which was to lead to the tank being nicknamed the 'Tommy Cooker' by the Germans and 'Ronson' by the British – like the cigarette lighter, it lit first time. In an attempt to enhance the Sherman's performance some models were fitted with the successful 17-pounder gun, which enabled the tank to level the ground against the *Panther* and *Tiger*. This variant, the Firefly, was introduced to British and Commonwealth units in Italy late in 1944. Other American armoured vehicles were used in Italy by the British – the M3/M5 Stuart light tank, sometimes with the turret removed and used in the reconnaissance role; and the M10 tank destroyer was used by the Royal Artillery.

Blitzkrieg was intended to destroy the enemy's moral and physical cohesion, and it certainly achieved that aim against the British and French in 1940. It was also to leave a legacy for the British, not just in depriving them of significant quantities of matériel but in eroding the confidence of senior officers about the ability of the British Army to defeat the *Wehrmacht* without the assistance of overwhelming numbers of troops and modern equipment. Neither asset was ready to hand for the foreseeable future after Dunkirk. In mid-1940 the Army assumed a secondary role to the Royal Navy and the RAF in the defence of the British Isles, and it was believed that any attempt to return to the Continent to engage the German Army would have to await the outcome of a naval blockade and air bombardment. The anticipated drastic weakening of the enemy's will to resist depended on warship and aircraft production to deliver the blockade and bombardment, and the Army had to take its place in line for industry to manufacture its requirements. For the time being the Army's role was to prepare to resist invasion, and home defence was its preoccupation until the end of 1942. Despite the objections of the Adjutant General, who recognized that the training system could not cope with the numbers, the government ordered some 324,000 men to be enlisted in the two months after Dunkirk. Initially they formed 122 new infantry battalions – not because there was a need for this particular number of infantry units, but because sufficient rifles were available to equip them. With the equivalent of eight to ten divisions' worth of equipment abandoned at Dunkirk, there was now enough left for only one fully-operational division. There were only fifty modern tanks available in the United Kingdom.[4]

In March 1941 the War Cabinet resolved that the British Army should have fifty-nine divisions, an increase on earlier figures – a field force of thirty-two divisions was planned in the spring of 1939, to which was added fourteen Dominion and four Indian divisions in September of that year. The 1941 figure comprised twelve armoured and forty-seven infantry divisions, and eight independent tank brigades. Britain was to produce ten armoured and twenty-seven infantry divisions and eight tank brigades; the remainder was to be found from the Dominions, India and allies in exile. The lack of equipment and of training facilities was to push the date for achieving such numbers further into the future, and the foregoing force was planned to be in place a year later. Manpower constraints placed the ceiling on this planning – men could either be employed in uniform or in war production, not both.

Raising an army by too great a number meant that they could not be equipped because industry would be stripped of their services. Understandably, the Army in 1941–42 experienced a real crisis of morale.

The intent to increase the number of divisions was hindered both by manpower and equipment shortages. Mechanical transport and artillery shortfalls compelled the War Office to reduce the establishments of divisions, for example by assigning them two, rather than three, field artillery regiments, and by doing away with machine-gun battalions. The numbers of Engineer and Service Corps units were cut, and it was only by cannibalizing independent brigades and other formations that divisions destined for overseas could get the required numbers of lines of communication troops. By 1943 this possibility had been exhausted, and field force units began to be disbanded: two armoured and three infantry divisions went during the year, with the limited compensation of having one airborne and a single weak infantry division formed in their stead. In 1944 a further three armoured and four infantry divisions were disbanded, and only one infantry division formed. By the end of 1944 the British Army comprised five armoured and twenty-one infantry divisions and seven independent tank brigades. Emphasizing mechanical, rather than human, warfare apart, attrition was biting and would continue to be a major cause of concern until the end of the war.

In June 1942 Tobruk fell to the *Panzerarmee Afrika*. The defeat highlighted many deficiencies in the British Army's way of warfighting, including weaknesses in combined arms operations and in the speed (or lack of it) with which communications and command worked. The British had performed well against the Italians at the end of 1940/beginning of 1941 when General Richard O'Connor's Western Desert Force had trounced Graziani's army, which far outnumbered it. O'Connor's better tanks and the mobility afforded by his mechanized transport gave him the necessary speed and manoeuvrability to win. In armour, communications, training and morale, the British had the upper hand, and they were able to do what the Germans had done to them in 1940 – increase the tempo of the battlefield so that their opponent could not react quickly enough to avoid defeat. The success, however, was to cause Hitler to deploy the *Afrika Korps* to Libya to support his Italian ally. Rommel was swiftly to turn the tables on the British, who lost continuity by having no fewer than six commanders in a period of sixteen months. The British also had some twenty divisions pass through the Western Desert Force (or Eighth Army, as it eventually became in September 1941), only four of which took part in more than two battles. Neither generals nor divisions were profiting by their experience, for the opportunity to do so was not given.

Nor were the British swift to learn from their experiences in fighting the Germans in France and North Africa. The *Afrika Korps'* divisional commanders worked from command vehicles stripped of armament and fitted with radios which were tuned to those of units in the front line, which allowed them to listen to the progress of the battle without waiting for information to trickle up the chain of command. Their all-arms battlegroups moved and operated together, with tanks, motorized infantry, artillery and anti-tank weapons able to provide immediate mutual support. Acting on brief verbal orders which gave the commander's intent while relying on subordinates to use their initiative to achieve it, the system was swifter than that of their opponents. However, the British appeared unable to analyze the German procedures and to find a way of countering them – let alone emulating them, although commanders such as Auchinleck recognized that the British system was too slow for mobile warfare. The *Afrika Korps'* Chief of Staff, Colonel Fritz Bayerlein, was contemptuous of the Eighth Army's command, control and communications, regarding them as rigidly methodological and concerned with issuing over-detailed orders too far down the chain of command, which left no room for initiative.[5] Against this criticism it has to be recognized that the underlying strength of German doctrine lay with its use of what today would be termed 'mission command', and to train soldiers of all ranks to use their initiative took time – time the British did not have, even if they could convince the generals that this was a better way forward than the practices they had been wedded to for many years. They were left to play catch-up, but meanwhile they were inclined to search for reasons for their failures: incompetent or inexperienced commanders, poor training, poor equipment, poor air support, all of which may have had their part to play, but which were as nothing when compared with the underlying weakness that the British and the Germans had fundamentally different approaches to the place the military played in society as a whole, and the extent to which the nation should devote its efforts to preparing for war.

Until Montgomery arrived in North Africa in August 1942, the majority of British generals (with exceptions such as O'Connor – but he had been captured by the enemy when too close to the fighting) lacked the ability to fill the troops with confidence. Interestingly, Montgomery's technique for doing so, which was not universally appreciated by either his fellow officers or some of the other ranks, was to brief all men on his intentions. This was hardly comparable to the German doctrine of giving the commander's aim so that subordinates could use their initiative to achieve it, for his briefings were general statements along the lines of 'knocking the enemy for six', but they went much further than the remoteness of some of his predecessors who remained almost anonymously in the background, at least as far as most soldiers were concerned. His talks did, however, go some way to bolstering the morale of his troops, which many officers considered to be dangerously fragile after the procession of defeats which stretched back to 1940. It had sunk so low that Auchinleck had asked the War Cabinet to reintroduce the death penalty for deserters.

The presence of Montgomery was not, in itself, the answer to the Eighth Army's problems, but his generalship was part of the solution. By mid-1942 the equipment, some of which, like the Sherman tank, had come from America, gave the army superiority in numbers if not always in quality when compared to the enemy's. Monty brought not only an approach designed to raise confidence, but his operational planning was thorough and sought to minimize casualties. Partly this was because, as stated previously, Britain's manpower reserves were diminishing, but also because of the morale issue. Montgomery's operations were limited by sensible assessments of what he believed his forces could achieve, using maximum firepower and minimum manpower. With American industry behind them British generals were able to be extravagant with equipment and ammunition, but not with men. Manpower shortages were to limit commanders' options severely; they could not rely on early reinforcements, and the fear of taking unsustainable casualty numbers made them cautious.

Montgomery was able to impose his methodology on the Eighth Army; in the phrase of the time, he 'gripped' the Army and introduced elements which came closer to the German style of operations. Written orders were simplified and minimized, and were often put aside in favour of verbal, face-to-face instructions, or – when these were not possible – with the aid of radio. By introducing de Guingand as his Chief of Staff, with the task of coordinating all staff functions and with the authority to make decisions in his absence, Montgomery freed himself to concentrate on fighting the battle, which he did from a small tactical headquarters. While he could not re-educate the whole army into thinking along the German lines, even if he had wanted to, he could impose factors which speeded things up to cope with the tempo with which they had dominated events until now. There were differences between Montgomery's style and that of the enemy: he did not encourage too much initiative, and took steps to ensure that his subordinates kept to his carefully worked-out preparations by planning two levels down and by monitoring what commanders down to divisional level actually did. In order to impose his will on the enemy, his first step was to impose it on his own subordinates to ensure that – in his eyes, at least – misguided attempts at exercising initiative did not interfere with his plans. He also insisted that battlefield drills and rehearsals be carried out, and that his formation commanders were schooled in his thought processes by distributing a series of pamphlets and by giving lectures and holding study periods. In this fashion he was going some way towards ensuring that his commanders were able to understand his intentions. Monty also 'gripped' the training issue. Although the army had a doctrine, its promulgation was largely dependant upon individual formation commanders, whose interest in training was varied and who were inclined to place their own interpretations on the *Field Service Manuals* which were supposed to bring matters of tactics to a common standard across the army. Not only were units not thoroughly schooled in the thought processes of their superiors, but all-arms operations were an area of military instruction that was only addressed in a haphazard fashion. Little opportunity occurred to exercise infantry, armour, artillery and the support services together, and the skills needed to carry out such operations were seriously under-rehearsed until well into the war years.

In communications the army was again beginning to see an improvement over the first experiences of France in 1940. After El Alamein Montgomery's headquarters systematically monitored the activities of subordinate formations through listening in on their radio traffic, thereby ensuring that events were proceeding as intended. In all of this the army was helped, at last, by having more radios. Having waited in line behind the pressing needs of the Navy and the RAF, by 1942 supplies of this commodity began to arrive in greater numbers. By the end of the war over 550,000 radio sets were issued to the army and scarcity was much less of a problem, although the quality of signals sometimes did, for reasons of terrain or other factors.

Alamein also marked a change in the employment of artillery. With the emphasis on matériel-heavy (as compared to manpower-heavy) operations, overwhelming firepower had always been a desired objective. In 1942 increased numbers of 6-pounder anti-tank guns enabled commanders to release other artillery pieces from this role and to use them as originally intended. Improved procedures in both communications and organization steadily led to the time when artillery barrages could be called down by forward observation officers in concentrations from several batteries, and gunner officers took to the air as pilots in Air Observation Posts to direct fire, not only from Divisional Artillery regiments, but also from the newly-formed

55

Army Groups Royal Artillery (AGRA), comprising a number of heavy, medium and field regiments which could be employed to support operations in concentrations as required. With improved communications, artillery support could be summoned in short time: in Sicily it would be reduced to two minutes.[6]

Before leaving the subject of the state of the British Army that joined the coalition forces in Italy, it would be remiss not to take a brief look at the logistic 'tail', without which no army can hope to prosper. The support services are all too often undervalued in accounts of campaigns (and, indeed, by those who see battles as being fought solely by the teeth arms). Historically the British had a long tradition of waging campaigns over long distances, and they were used to putting in place supply and support services to feed, fuel, equip and arm their fighting men. Unlike the German Army, which – at least in 1939 – saw its anticipated wars in Poland and France as being waged over relatively short distances from its home bases, from which it could be supplied for much of the distance by rail, the British were more attuned to campaigning across the Empire; it can be argued that German over-stretch and insufficient logistic preparation contributed to their downfall in Russia, and in North Africa Rommel's fuel shortages played a part in his defeat at Alamein.

To maintain an army in the field, especially during offensive operations when the front line was – hopefully – moving away from its bases as swiftly as possible, presented very real difficulties. An armoured division swallowed up a thousand gallons of fuel to move only one mile, and an infantry division consumed 1,300 tons of food every month. Add to these requirements the re-supply of ammunition and weapon and vehicle spares (and the workshops to carry out repairs and servicing), and it becomes more apparent why, in an infantry division that mustered 15,500 men, only 6,750 of them were in the front line. The failure to understand that this balance was unavoidable is not confined to the armchair generals, for old soldiers such as Churchill found it frustrating that so many men could not be directly engaged in combat – although of course the type of army in which he had served ran along different lines. Churchill was not the only one to lack this understanding, as will become apparent later in this book: the French did not appreciate the importance of establishing a strong support service, and commentators remarking upon the length of time it took Montgomery's Eighth Army to get close to the beleaguered Salerno beachhead did not seem to understand that the delay was largely inevitable because there had not been time to put the required logistical service in place. Once again, it was the thorough planning that Montgomery insisted upon – frustratingly slow that it might have been – that brought success.

The British Army that first fought alongside its American ally in Tunisia had progressed a long way since the outbreak of war in 1939. Under-resourced because it did not feature as highly in the eyes of the government as did the other two services during the inter-war period, the belated recognition that it would probably have to fight another major European war came too late to equip it to do so. Through no real fault of its own, it had suffered the agonies of Dunkirk and of losing much of what matériel it had possessed in France, and until Alamein it had experienced one defeat after another, in Greece, Crete and North Africa, in Hong Kong and Singapore. Just as new weapons began to appear in earnest, manpower resources became even more of a concern.

The morale situation had improved with the victory at Alamein, but it was never going to be of sufficient strength that commanders could take it for granted; indeed, there were periods in both Italy and North West Europe when it would cause them serious concern. Despite such worries, there was an increased confidence in their ability to defeat the enemy, which unfortunately sometimes verged on the patronizing when they dealt with their newly-arrived American allies in North West Africa. The British Army entered a new phase in which, instead of being the senior partner in a coalition army of mostly Commonwealth countries and governments in exile, it steadily became the junior partner to the United States.

The Commonwealth

When Britain declared war on Germany on 3 September 1939 the act automatically committed India and the Crown Colonies to the conflict because they were governed from London. However, Australia, Canada, New Zealand and South Africa had independence of decision as Dominions: they were fully sovereign states theoretically equal to Britain despite having King George VI as their Head of State.

The four countries had raised large contingents to fight in the First World War. As 'self-governing colonies' their status was not that of dependencies, a factor which was to become increasingly apparent to both the political and military hierarchies in Great Britain. The contingents from these countries regarded themselves more as allies who fought as equals alongside the British forces rather than as part of them, and the contributions that they made during the Great War played an important part in achieving their move to Dominion status. That war also engendered a sense of national identity in which

Australians and Canadians, in particular, began to feel more a part of their countries of abode than of Great Britain; the experiences of Gallipoli and of Vimy Ridge gave soldiers a national pride in their nascent countries. This heritage of having a degree of autonomy together with their standing as middle-ranking powers placed the Dominions in the awkward position of making human and financial sacrifices during the Second World War without being able to influence matters overmuch. From the military perspective it was desirable to have the smallest number of decision-makers as possible, which meant that the smaller nations had to make sacrifices of sovereignty. Yet this arrangement did not always sit easily at home, where each Dominion's population at large – whose sons were being placed in the line of fire – had the reasonable expectation that their lives were not hazarded without good reason. The idea that they might be used as pawns to further the aims of one or more of the larger powers was not to be encouraged, and both the politicians and the generals had to operate with one eye cocked to watch for domestic reactions.

With Great Britain and the newly established Dominions no longer able to rely on automatic support from each other, in 1932–33 the United Kingdom, Canada and South Africa all passed Visiting Forces Acts which set a legal framework whereby one country's armed forces might be placed under the command of another's, should the need arise. Australia and New Zealand followed suit in 1939. There was at least an understanding that they might have to act together, and that some *modus operandi* ought to be established for this possibility. When war broke out in September 1939 this became a reality.

The Dominions quickly followed the lead of the 'Home Country' in declaring war on Germany. Australia and New Zealand did so immediately on hearing of Britain's action and Canada followed seven days later, once Parliament had met to consider the matter. In South Africa a major political crisis occurred when Prime Minister Barry Hertzog (leader of the anti-British National Party) and five government ministers determined to keep the country neutral. The Minister of Justice, General Smuts, and six more ministers favoured an immediate declaration of war against Germany, an impasse that was resolved when the House of Assembly formally voted for war in a division of eighty to sixty-seven. Herzog was overthrown and replaced by Jan Smuts and war was declared on 6 September, the motion stating that the Union would take the necessary steps to defend South African territory and interests, but should not send forces overseas as had happened in the Great War. South Africa was therefore prepared to support the

58

Commonwealth, but only on the African continent. The definition of where the line should be drawn crept northwards as the war progressed: in July 1940 South Africans were sent to Kenya to support the British in East Africa; they were later to participate in the North African and Italian campaigns, but it was a gradual progression, requiring a series of concessions and legal steps by the South African Government.

The Afrikaner community in South Africa was generally critical of Smuts' stance on the war, and placed obstacles against his intentions to support Britain – indeed, some extremists were actively engaged in sabotage against the war effort. They were hostile to the notion that South Africa should become involved in a conflict which did not directly threaten their country, and anti-war riots and attacks on off-duty soldiers broke out – some 140 were seriously injured in Johannesburg on 1 February 1941.[7] Low volunteer numbers hindered Smuts' plans to bring the under-strength army up to a useful force. The air force was also below strength, and the navy had the magnificent total manpower of three officers and three ratings when war broke out. Although a recruiting campaign was launched, Afrikaner resistance made conscription impossible and limited the numbers that could be raised for the armed forces. Prevailing racial attitudes in the Dominion ruled against enlisting the coloured and black populations into combat arms: public opinion dictated that Africans were not to bear arms, a factor which automatically relegated them to service in the newly-formed Native Labour Corps. Even this limited employment was attacked by the Afrikaners, the fear being that any form of military training would at some stage pose a threat to white supremacy. Opposition to using Africans outside the continent was initially supported by the British War Office, which saw them as being employed only in local defence duties, until manpower difficulties brought about a change of mind and Smuts was urged to make concessions.

South African policy inevitably affected the High Commission Territories in the south of the continent. Bechuanaland and Basutoland initially contributed manpower reinforcements to the South African Native Police Force, and it was soon realized that many whites were protecting essential services, a task which natives could carry out, thus freeing the whites for more active duties. Armed with knobkerries and assegais, the natives received the same basic training as whites – but not in firearms.

The status of the Dominions set them apart for as sovereign states they had to be treated separately, a further complication for those involved in fighting the war on the political and military fronts. By the time of the Italian campaign the Australian government had withdrawn its naval and ground forces from the Mediterranean theatre to face the Japanese threat closer to home, leaving only two Royal Australian Air Force squadrons to maintain a national presence in the region. The other three Dominions' armies continued to serve in the Mediterranean, but their units could not necessarily be employed willy-nilly. General Freyberg, commander of the New Zealand forces, was responsible firstly to his own government rather than to his military superiors in Italy for the use of the New Zealand Expeditionary Force, a situation which was formally approved between the governments of the United Kingdom and New Zealand, and Freyberg. This gave him the right to pick and choose which fights he committed his men to, based on whether or not the operation in question served the New Zealand national interest (not that this prevented their full participation in practice). Although the NZEF was little more than one division strong, its commander had direct access to his own government, a factor which effectively gave him the status of a subordinate commander-in-chief, who could by-pass his corps, army and theatre commanders. This was not an irrelevant issue: during the North African campaign before the arrival of Alexander and Montgomery, Freyberg's lack of confidence in the British commanders led him to demand that his troops be transferred to Syria for training and rest, to safeguard them from the blunders of his military superiors. This threat was not actually put into practice, but it did signal to the British chain of command that the New Zealanders had to be treated somewhat differently to other forces.

The Canadians relied upon the Visiting Forces Act for the legal position of their formations, and did not find it necessary to produce a separate directive. Unlike the New Zealanders, there was no occasion where they seriously began to lose confidence in the British higher command, and the relationship between the two was generally harmonious. There was no occasion on which Canadian commanders exercised their right to appeal to their own government. Nonetheless, they were in an analogous position to the other Dominions: the effect on home opinion had to be constantly borne in mind when planning and executing operations. It was this same consideration that caused General Smuts to divert his flight back to South Africa from a Chiefs of Staff meeting in England to Italy to consider the circumstances under which a South African infantry company had been taken prisoner by the enemy, the political and military consequences of which could have been serious at home.[8] The relationships between the British government and Smuts were extremely strong, so strong in fact that there was a plan for him to take Churchill's place in the event that the latter became incapacitated as Prime Minister. This plan had been formulated by John Colville, Churchill's private secretary, and put before the King in 1940.[9]

Although by the time of the Italian campaign the Australians had recalled the major part of their armed forces, for completeness it is worth remarking that they had been prepared to exercise an independence of command during the early years of the war. In 1941 they had insisted that their division in Tobruk be relieved, despite the difficulties that this caused to plans being put in place for a new desert offensive; and the following year they had refused to allow a division which was returning home to Australia from the Middle East to be diverted to Rangoon.

The Prime Ministers of the Dominions were not members of the British War Cabinet. Their participation in matters of grand strategy was carried out through long-distance communications or personal discussions as and when the need arose. The possibility of setting up an Imperial War Cabinet had been considered but rejected; the Canadian Prime Minister, Mr Mackenzie King, had opposed it on the constitutional grounds that Canada would be committed to decisions taken by her representative in London. Churchill himself was more than content to make such decisions himself, without the need to involve consultation with a War Cabinet that had been expanded to unwieldy size to accommodate the Dominion delegates. He also placed a major hurdle in the way by insisting that only the respective prime ministers could be members, a hurdle which made the whole idea impracticable. Australia was the only supporter of forming an Imperial Cabinet, but as a lone voice failed to achieve more than to ensure that its 'Special Representative' was in attendance in the War Cabinet when Australian interests needed addressing. Consequently, the role of spokesman for the Commonwealth at the 'top table' fell to Churchill. His communications to the Dominion prime ministers of decisions taken in consultation with Roosevelt and Stalin were sometimes haphazard; for example, the July 1942 decision that operations in the Mediterranean would continue was not conveyed to the Canadian Government despite its importance to the Canadians, whose troops were concentrating in the United Kingdom in preparation for the cross-Channel invasion. It was several weeks before they were informed.

Part of the reason for information not being communicated to the Dominions was Churchill's belief that too much was being passed on through the normal channels. He preferred to deliver important facts at a personal, prime-ministerial level, but the opportunities for doing this were limited. Consequently, the part that the Dominions played in matters of great import was very much under Churchill's control. All the Canadians could do, for example, was – like the New Zealanders – demand that decisions on the deployment of their troops be referred to them before being finally decided. When they discovered that operations were to be continued in the Mediterranean, it was the Canadian government that pressured Churchill into committing firstly a Canadian division and then a corps to that theatre. They felt that their forces had been out of the fighting for too long.

The underlying problem for the Dominions (and indeed for any nation participating in coalition warfare) was the conflict between their sovereignty and the efficiency of standardization and simplification in matters of command, operational doctrine, logistics, and the host of other factors which have to be considered when fighting a war. By and large, because of the scale of the threat they were facing and because they were able to fall back on shared traditions and military heritage, the Commonwealth countries worked together well. A degree of common sense, combined with a will to make things work, made them more united than otherwise.

> In seasons of great peril
> 'Tis good that one bear sway;
> Then choose we a Dictator
> Whom all men shall obey
>
> (Macaulay: 'Lays of Ancient Rome;
> The Battle of Lake Regillus')

In considering the nations from the British Commonwealth which participated in the Italian campaign, we now have to turn to India and the Crown Colonies. Unlike the Dominions they did not have the right to self-government but were ruled from the United Kingdom, in India's case through the person of the Viceroy, who in 1939 was the Marquess of Linlithgow. The Viceroy's commitment of India to the war without consulting the country's government was regarded as high-handed by Indian politicians and led to a split – the Congress Party had hoped for independence for India in return for passing a resolution conditionally supporting the fight against fascism, but was to be disappointed; it withdrew its representatives from the legislature in response. The Muslim League gave the Viceroy its unconditional support, largely for anti-Congress Party reasons. When the Japanese joined the war one group under Subhas Chandra Bose saw British weakness in the face of Axis offensives as offering the opportunity to force the independence question, and Bose travelled to Berlin and Tokyo before raising the Indian National Army in 1942 with the intention of overthrowing the British Raj.

Despite these divisions, the majority of the Indian population remained supportive of the British, and some two million Indians were to serve in the Army, the largest all-volunteer force in the world. Nevertheless, it would be a simplification to think that this support was universal, and the British authorities in India could not become complacent about it. Nationalist politicians continued to manoeuvre towards independence throughout the war, an issue which the authorities would have preferred to defer until after its completion.

India and the Crown Colonies were not given the choice of declaring war – Britain did that on their behalf. To all intents and purposes they were part of the 'Home Country', and in like fashion for command purposes their units were treated as part of the British Army, although they were often formed into their own divisions and brigades. Three Indian Army Divisions – the 4th, 8th and 10th – and 43 Independent Gurkha Brigade fought in Italy. Trained and commanded by British officers, these divisions were organized along British lines. Each division comprised three brigades of three battalions, one of which was usually British, the other two being Indian or Gurkha.

Indian Army battalions were commanded and mostly officered by British officers, who were all ranked higher than the comparatively few Viceroy Commissioned Officers, Indians who had been awarded commissions on their record of valuable service. Their status was that of junior commissioned officers, who served as a link between the British officers and the Indian other ranks. There was a third category of officers, the King's Commissioned Indian Officers, who were theoretically equivalent in status to the British, but who were much fewer in number. In 1918 ten places were reserved annually at Sandhurst for the training of these officers, the first of whom were commissioned in 1920 (the number of vacancies was later increased to twenty-five, but they were never filled and results were disappointing: during the years 1918–29 only seventy-seven Indians were commissioned from the 134 who actually commenced training). A further thirty-two Indians were trained at the cadet college in Indore in India, the intention being that eventually eight units would be completely 'Indianized', with all ranks coming from the sub-continent. With the slow rate of promotion, this was not anticipated to be possible until 1946 at the earliest.[10] Amongst these King's Commissioned Officers was Lieutenant Colonel D. S. Brar, commanding officer of the 5th (Royal) Battalion of the 5th Mahratta Light Infantry during the Italian campaign. He was the first Indian to lead one of his country's battalions in battle. The British who served with the Indian

Army had to become proficient in the language of their soldiers; during the war years Indian Army newspapers were produced in no fewer than eleven tongues,[11] but as recruiting was generally done by geographical area most battalions only used one of these. The practical implications of this were that whereas the officers were able to communicate across unit and formation boundaries, the soldiers might not have been capable of doing so. Nor were officers from the British battalions in a brigade fully able to communicate with soldiers from Indian battalions.

A similar situation pertained in the units formed in the Crown Colonies. As an example, British Colonial Pioneer units were drawn from India, Africa, Palestine, Cyprus, Mauritius, Syria and Lebanon, spoke a myriad of languages and were members of countless tribes and clans. The task of transforming recruits from these backgrounds into soldiers was immense, and had to be achieved in the shortest time possible; the Pioneer Corps Base Depot at Qassasin in Egypt managed to process 10,000 men a month, turning out a fully-equipped 350-man strong company six days a week. Every man had received weapons and gas training – no small task when one considers that few if any of the recruits had ever heard of poison gas or respirators. Not only had the native recruits to be trained, their British officers and NCOs had to learn the appropriate dialects and to gain a working knowledge of tribal customs, prejudices and diets. Unlike the battalions of the Indian Army, where there were years of regimental tradition and family ties to fall back upon, for the pioneers, Briton and native alike, this was all new. And yet, it worked. Not only did these men serve as pioneers, carrying out the usual tasks of labouring, moving supplies, constructing roads and airfields, and so on, but many of the companies were re-roled as 'Dilution' Companies, taking on different functions in the Mideast Fire Service, in anti-aircraft batteries, Royal Electrical and Mechanical Engineers' workshops, Signals units, and mechanical transport units.[12] The coalition was more diverse than might at first be imagined.

The question of segregation and racial discrimination also played its part in the armies of 1943. The numbers of King's Commissioned Indian Officers had not grown as quickly as some had wished, but at least there was an intent that a degree of 'Indianization' was to come about. For other nations' armies this was yet to happen. The South Africans, for example, did not even have coloured troops under arms, and apartheid – in practice, if not yet in name – held firm. Although Africans were employed by the South African forces in Italy, they were used for non-combatant administrative duties and were armed only with their traditional weapons, which did not include firearms except for self-defence and when on guard duties. The South Africans were not the only ones to segregate sections of their national communities – the Americans also practised discrimination, a subject which we will return to later in this book.

While the South Africans may not have armed their black population (although some white troops manning coastal guns were replaced by Zulus to free them for deployment elsewhere – presumably artillery in fixed emplacements pointing out to sea did not threaten white supremacy inland), their neighbouring British High Commission Territories did. Bechuanaland, Basutoland and Swaziland all produced recruits for the African Auxiliary Pioneer Corps (10,000, 10,000 and 500 men were called for, respectively). The British manpower crisis of 1941 presented the Army with an urgent requirement for both combat and labour units, which could not come from a South Africa which was experiencing difficulties in raising troops for the reasons explained above. Britain therefore turned to the High Commission Territories. In Bechuanaland the request fell upon willing ears – the tribal chiefs had already expressed their wish that the Protectorate play its full part in Britain's war effort, and although about 700 of its men enlisted in the South African Native Military Corps, their preference was to have units of their own. In the light of the British request the chiefs' proposal was re-examined, and within six months fifteen AAPC companies were on their way to the Middle East; in all, about twenty per cent of the country's manpower was to serve in the British Army.

The formation of AAPC companies presented difficulties with South Africa because of the country's stance on arming natives, and also because of the Great War experience when High Commission Territory men had served in the South African Native Labour Corps in South West Africa, East Africa and France. In Europe the SANLC had been officered by South Africans and accommodated in separate compounds; in the African campaigns they had been differentiated from units such as the King's African Rifles because they did not carry arms and participate in combat. The chiefs were adamant that their men would not serve under South African officers, a situation which caused white Territory officials who had enlisted in the South African forces to be released to command the AAPC units.[13] Furthermore, the British War Office brought them under the British Army Act, rather than the South African regulations, required an oath of allegiance to the Crown, and determined that service could be worldwide.

These measures notwithstanding, recruiting in Bechuanaland did not progress as successfully as the chiefs wished. British insistence that only volunteers would be accepted was unfamiliar to the chiefs, who had historically demanded that their subjects turned out for military service as ordered; this fact and the competing attractions of jobs in South African mines contributed to the limited numbers who enlisted. For many individual natives, service in the forces of the Crown was of little relevance – it was not their war. The solutions, at least as far as the chiefs were concerned, were to call up the age-group regiments of their tribal societies, and to forcibly enlist men with criminal records, solutions which were to cause a degree of friction with the colonial officials who did not want the chiefs to use methods of dubious legality. As in the United Kingdom, the conflicting demands for manpower – from the army and from industry (in this case the South African gold mines, which needed to maintain production for the war effort) – was the sticking point. Mine companies, while supporting the formation of the AAPC, did not want to see their workforce raided for recruits. Lowering medical standards did not produce the hoped-for increase in numbers, although by 1943 the strength was 9,194 men in twenty-four companies. For those that served, being part of the British Army and wearing a smart uniform was a source of pride, but not all was smooth sailing, for despite being legally equivalent to white British soldiers under the Army Act, there were instances of discrimination. These were commonest behind the front lines where an informal, but nonetheless very real, segregation was found, particularly for off-duty facilities. The closer to the battle, the more the races tended to ignore their differences, especially in those AAPC units which had converted to anti-aircraft duties. 1976 Bechuana Company was to land at Salerno as part of X (British) Corps, as did Basuto and Swazi pioneers. 1969 and 1977 Bechuana Companies were involved in bridging the Sangro River in November 1943, the latter company being specialized in smoke-laying; it was to perform the same duties at Cassino in March the following year, where 1983 Company suffered German shelling while working alongside the Royal Signals. Another eight Bechuana Companies also served in Italy.[14] Basutos also served as anti-aircraft gunners, including with 9th (Londonderry) HAA Regiment in North Africa and Italy.

Some 11,749 Greek and Turkish Cypriots enlisted in the Cyprus Regiment which had Motor, Mule and Inland Waterway Transport, and Pioneer Companies, some of which served in Italy to support operations (for example Cyprus Regiment Mule Companies were at Cassino). An interesting aspect of the regiment was that it was recruited from two ethnic groups whose motherlands were affected differently by the war: Greece had been invaded by Italy, and then by Germany, and fell fully into the Allied camp as a victim of Fascist aggression; Turkey remained neutral until February 1945, despite Churchill's ambitions to draw the country into the war earlier. Nevertheless the regiment, which also included a small number of Armenians and Cypriots of other origins, served with the percentages of Greeks to Turks (seventy-nine to twenty, respectively) being carefully monitored, although whether this was done merely out of statistical interest or in an attempt to regulate a particular balance is unclear. In the first instance the majority of officers and NCOs were British, preferably drawn from those who lived on the island and who were believed to understand the local population, but this restriction was later relaxed to allow Cypriots to apply for emergency commissions. The selection and vetting procedures that the Cypriots underwent before being commissioned appear to have been no stricter than those applied to British candidates in the United Kingdom, but nevertheless seem to have been interpreted as showing the authorities' reluctance to commission locals.[15]

The foregoing paragraphs illustrate the variations in practices only between members of the British Commonwealth, which might have been expected to have some degree of uniformity in military matters, if only because the majority of the armed forces of these nations came from a common background and sent their senior officers to Staff Colleges in England or Quetta, in India, where the same subjects were taught and studied. There was a shared approach to the composition of units, of procedures, and often of equipment which meant that inter-operability should have been straightforward – and indeed, to a degree, it was. This ignores other factors such as national sovereignty, which allowed the Australians to withdraw the majority of their forces from the Middle East when Japan threatened, gave the New Zealanders the right to be selective about operations, and the South Africans the option of not serving outside Africa, amongst other examples. The internal affairs of member countries had also to be considered – the independence movement in India, the refusal of the Bechuana chiefs to place their men under South African commanders. And there were also the issues of language, culture, religion, diet and so on, all of which meant that the Commonwealth armies were not a homogenous whole. Commanding such a grouping was not the same as commanding an expanded British Army, for the generals had to take account of numerous national sensitivities; at times they were treading on eggs.

If such variations were applicable to Commonwealth forces, then they were writ large when considering the jumble of national armies that fought in Italy in 1943–45.

Notes

1. French, *Raising Churchill's Army: The British Army and the War against Germany 1919–1945*

2. Ibid

3. Ibid

4. Ibid

5. *The Rommel Papers*, ed. Liddell Hart, quoted in French

6. French, op cit.

7. Schmitt, *The Bechuanaland Pioneers and Gunners*

8. Theunissen, *Major General W H Evered Poole, CB, CBE, DSO: 1902-1969, Personal Retrospects*

9. Colville, *The Fringes of Power*

10. Soherwordi, *'Punjabisation' in the British Indian Army 1857–1947 and the Advent of Military Rule in Pakistan*

11. Hingston, *The Tiger Triumphs. The Story of Three Great Divisions in Italy*

12. Rhodes-Wood, *A War History of the Royal Pioneer Corps 1939–1945*

13. Schmitt, op cit.

14. Bent, *Ten Thousand Men of Africa: The Story of the Bechuanaland Pioneers and Gunners 1941–1946*

15. Kazamias, *Military Recruitment and Selection in a British Colony: The Cyprus Regiment 1939–1944*

CHAPTER 4

The Americans

The American Army had passed through a series of changes and expansions before it, too, came to fight in Italy. As described earlier, the emerging threat to peace which came with German ambitions to control the Danzig Corridor in 1938 focused minds on preparation for war, which included plans to dramatically increase the size of the United States Army. On 16 September 1940 the Selective Service Act was approved, which established the first peacetime draft in American history.

The United States Army expanded from 134,024 officers and soldiers (of whom 824 were Army Nursing Corps) in 1932, to 174,079 in mid-1939, with a decision taken that September to expand it by another 17,000 and ultimately – in June 1940 – the Government declared its long-range intention to raise the numbers to four million men under arms by 1 April 1942 (although this was reduced to two million soon afterwards, to reflect the realities of American industrial capacity to produce weapons and equipment for such a force). In 1941 the United States Army comprised 1,460,998 officers and soldiers (of whom 5,433 were Army Nursing Corps). On 31 March 1945 the total Army strength was 5,848,573; the understrength twenty-seven divisions of the summer of 1940 became eighty-nine by the war's end.[1]

The rapid expansion of the army presented numerous problems, the most important of which was the shortage of experienced leadership at all rank levels. An understandable lack of confidence affected many junior officers and NCOs, and comparatively few senior officers had any background of working with large formations. Among the senior officers, both in the Regular Army and in the National Guard, several were overage or under-qualified for the appointments they held. The contradictory requirements of finding enough leaders for the new units while excluding those who were unfit to hold these jobs presented the planners and trainers with great problems. The solution, inadequate though it might have been in some circumstances, was to impose a standardized training regime which took many of the decision-making processes out of the hands of commanders of the smaller units. The problem of forming such an expanded army was compounded by a re-organization of the Army in a move to make it more effective; this involved the restructuring of infantry divisions from 'square' (i.e. with two brigades, each of two regiments) to 'triangular' (no brigade headquarters, but three regiments, and a reduction in divisional strength of twenty-five per cent of the riflemen). It was possibly not the best time to make such important changes, but America was in a hurry to bring its armed forces to readiness for war.

By late 1941 training was still incomplete and the divisions were not yet fully equipped, weaknesses that were highlighted during manoeuvres. An order to implement a training programme to correct the shortcomings was overtaken by events as the nation went to war following Pearl Harbor. Small-unit training took second place to the need for mobilization, and plans were made to activate three to four divisions each month. To speed up the process, centralized training was replaced by having draftees report directly to their divisions where they were trained under the principles of the Mobilization Training Program.[2]

The scheme for creating the new divisions was largely the creation of Mark Clark, at the time a brigadier general and G-3 to Lieutenant General Lesley McNair, the Commander of Army Ground Forces; if anyone should have been aware of any possible limitations of the training process, it was McNair – unless he was too close to the issue to recognize the problems. The selection of capable divisional commanders was key to the success of the sequence of turning recruits into an effective fighting force, and among Clark's responsibilities was the identification of candidates from whom General Marshall would make the appointments. Marshall was helped in this by the notes he habitually kept throughout his career on officers he considered to show outstanding ability, and consequently the list of those appointed closely mirrored the names of officers who had served under him, particularly when he had been assistant commandant of the Infantry School at Fort Benning. Such a procedure is only of value, however, if the criteria which Marshall employed proved to be relevant and accurate. As Martin Blumenson, the American military historian who produced many of the books on the Second World War, noted, when acting as divisional commanders few of these officers proved themselves to be brilliant, showing a tendency to play safe rather than to demonstrate imagination.[3] Performance between the years of 1927 and 1932, the period Marshall was at Fort Benning, was not necessarily an accurate predictor of performance between the years of 1942 and 1945. During the inter-war years preparation for higher command included attendance at the Command and General Staff School and the Army War College (although not all of the officers who later rose to high rank completed these courses), where – amongst other things – a common way of examining and resolving military problems was acquired, not necessarily for the better. The institutionalized approach produced capable, but not outstanding, senior officers and the more talented of them – as in all walks of life – went beyond their education and thought for themselves.

A further drawback of the system was that too many officers were unable, especially in their first exposure to the enemy in North Africa in 1942, to recognize that the lessons from their studies of the First World War were now outdated, if not downright dangerous, especially with respect to the new tempo that *blitzkrieg* tactics brought to the battlefield. The Americans were not alone in this, of course, but by the time they came into the war their allies had learned – usually the hard way – lessons which they were beginning to put into practice. Such criticism of American officers does not take into account, however, the ability of many of them to learn rapidly from their early experiences and to turn their new knowledge into practice quickly – an attribute that was not readily recognized by their allies nor their enemies, both of whom underestimated American abilities long after they had been improved.

The Mobilization Training Program should have prepared every division for its role when deployed overseas, but this objective was only partially realized because of the quality of the officers, from divisional commander downwards, who bore the responsibility for delivering the training. Experienced men were few and far between, and they were in high demand for the first divisions to go overseas. Consequently the training situation was sometimes that of the blind leading the blind. Provision of equipment (or lack of it, for sending it to Great Britain and the Soviet Union under Lend-Lease robbed the US Army of matériel which it needed for its own purposes, a situation which was not to improve until 1943), placing the emphasis on training senior leaders rather than individual basic and combat skills, and a number of other factors, meant that the training timetable was rarely met. One failing of the system was that junior officers' initiative was stifled by the centralized nature of the training, which emphasized regimental operations and procedures rather than battalion or company levels of command. While this might be understandable given the need to produce large numbers of deployable divisions in short order, the consequences would be felt later, on the battlefield where battalions, companies and platoons were the basic fighting units, often operating in comparative isolation. The failure to give adequate training to commanders at these levels was not easily remedied in the field.

Initiative was also smothered in many junior ranks by the system of sending partially-trained replacements to units in operational theatres. Such men could generally not be brought up to standard before they went into combat areas nor, needing close supervision, could they be trusted to operate independently. A consequence of these limitations was that American infantrymen tended to lack aggressiveness, especially when compared to some of their allies and certainly in comparison with the Germans. The lack of American divisions in Italy was to mean that soldiers were kept in the front line for longer periods than they should have been. Unable to withdraw for rest, re-training, and with little time to integrate replacements, the result was a high rate of casualties amongst reinforcements. Collective exhaustion was a feature displayed by many divisions, particularly the ones which fought through the Italian winters of 1943–44 and 1944–45. By mid-November 1943 the American divisions in the Fifth Army had taken significant casualties in their attacks on the German defences, leading to a replacement crisis which forced Army Ground Forces at home to strip units still undergoing training to make up the numbers overseas, and replacements which had been trained for other roles in other branches of the army were diverted to the infantry. The quality of the reinforcements was inevitably sub-standard: men were either not trained for the job they were sent to do, or arrived in Italy having spent almost as long on the voyage from the United States as they had spent undergoing initial training. Their skills had eroded with little or no time to renew them, particularly for those men sent to the 3rd, 34th, and 45th Infantry Divisions who had to join their formations directly at the front during the period between 9 September and 6 December 1943. The casualty rates for these replacements were as much as three times as high as veterans; and among the veterans junior leader casualties were particularly high.

Although there may have been a lack of aggressiveness in the junior ranks of the United States Army, the same criticism was not applicable to some of its commanders. The training and education of formation commanders sometimes led them into an assertiveness that was not matched by, for example, British commanders who felt themselves to be constrained by the overwhelming need to preserve manpower, an attitude which was to be scorned by Clark in particular, who on several occasions awarded the label of 'feather duster' to generals such as Alexander and McCreery.

THE AMERICANS

There were similarities between the British and American armies in that their respective nations had not prepared them for the war in which they found themselves. Neither army had the manpower nor modern matériel ready to hand in 1939, although both had a relatively few hurried months in which to attempt to bring themselves up to strength and up to date. Neither army had sufficiently well-qualified junior officers and NCOs to provide adequate training and leadership to the greatly swollen numbers of soldiers that were to be enlisted; and, most importantly, neither army had a doctrine that could match that of the Germans. All-rank initiative was not expected in the armies of the western allies.

The British did have the experience of facing the Germans from 1939 onwards, although this was not necessarily an advantage. While it brought lessons, they were not always the most welcome ones, for they had been learned the hard way and they damaged confidence. The British Army also had a generation of senior officers who had fought in the First World War; so, it might be argued, did the Americans, but they were fewer in number and their experience of that conflict was shorter. Again, this experience was a mixed blessing and the lessons were not always valuable under the changed conditions of warfare.

The American experience of combat before the invasion of Italy had been in North Africa and Sicily. Their participation in the TORCH landings, when United States troops had landed at Casablanca, Oran and Algiers (the last alongside British forces), had gone relatively smoothly despite some French resistance. Once consolidated, the Allies turned their attention towards Tunis with the intention of meeting Montgomery's Eighth Army, which was progressing from the east to squeeze the Axis out of North Africa. The Anglo-American advance from the west faltered against the terrain, the enemy, and the onset of bad weather. The way to Tunis and Bizerta lay inland, across rough countryside through which Axis forces were moving against them. After a period in which each side jockeyed for position, the enemy halted the Allied advance at the end of November 1942. Not pausing to give them the opportunity to gather their thoughts, the Axis forces launched their counterattack on 1 December, inflicting serious losses on manpower and equipment. A furious General Eisenhower sent a report to Marshall, in which he maintained that Allied operations had been a disaster – they had violated every accepted tactical principle of warfare, and would be used as examples of malpractice in military schools hereafter.[4] To cap the debacle the winter rains turned the ground into a morass. The Allies had lost the opportunity to swiftly cut off the Axis forces and the fighting bogged down. It was not an auspicious period for the Anglo-American partnership.

On 14 February 1943 the Axis force struck again, pushing through the mountains to attack Allied supply depots and airstrips. With American tanks spread too thinly to halt their attack, the Germans had little difficulty in penetrating deeply, fighting off an ineffective counterattack before taking some 1,400 American troops prisoner. Forced back to defensive positions on the Kasserine Pass during four days of disastrous battle, the Americans lost 2,500 men missing and the destruction of over 100 tanks. Only the perceived threat from an Eighth Army attack on his eastern front caused Rommel to halt his offensive against the Americans. Unimpressed with what they saw as the inexperience of American troops, the British sought to limit the participation of II (US) Corps for the remainder of the campaign.

An examination of what had gone wrong revealed the lack of an effective chain of command for the western forces. Eisenhower, the Commander-in-Chief, had been trying to fight the war while also dealing with political problems in North Africa. The problems of establishing relationships with the French (of which more later) occupied much of his time. Alan Brooke, the British CIGS, was left with the feeling that Eisenhower was preoccupied with politics; his military performance was less than inspirational[5].

Eisenhower did, however, take action to remedy the weaknesses which had contributed to the failures of November and December. Following manoeuvring by Brooke, 18 Army Group was formed under command of General Alexander to oversee the actions of the American, British and French forces, which would take some of the load off Eisenhower. The choice was not entirely judicious: Alexander, although outwardly urbane and diplomatic, did not have faith in the Americans; they were, he confided in Brooke, 'soft, green and quite untrained'. Nevertheless, Alexander was seen by many Americans as an officer with whom they could work. To remedy the shortcomings of American performance Eisenhower removed Major General Lloyd Fredendall – a man who held the British and French in poor regard, and who had attempted to command II (US) Corps from a bunker well behind the front line – from his appointment and replaced him with George S. Patton. Patton and his deputy, Omar Bradley, immediately began to turn II Corps around and to make it into a far more professional force.

Although these steps improved the situation, there would be more difficulties ahead for Allied working relationships during the campaign. Rommel may have savaged the Americans during the Kasserine Pass battles but the general flow of the campaign was against him and the Allies continued to squeeze his forces from both east and west. Alexander ordered an attack by 34th (US) Division to open the pass at Fondouk el Aouareb; this would allow his armoured units to push on and to cut off Axis units retreating northwards. The 34th's attack was forced to a halt short of the gap and failed to reach it. Under verbal instructions from Patton not to run risks the divisional commander, General Ryder, did not press his assault home and allowed it to bog down, which earned American soldiers a poor rating from the Germans. Recognizing that the attack had been made in insufficient strength Alexander brought in the British IX Corps and the French XIX Corps to join 34th Division in a second attempt. The combined force was placed under the command of Lieutenant General Sir John Crocker, an officer who had performed well in France in 1940 (and who was to be recommended, unsuccessfully, by Montgomery to replace him as CIGS in 1949), but who also regarded the Americans as 'green'. Ryder believed that Crocker's plan was flawed, as it would expose his division's northern flank when the attack commenced. His view was supported by General Koeltz, the French commander, but it was too late to change the plan and it went ahead without success – as the American and French officers had anticipated. The pass was not captured in time for the armour to advance through it to interfere with the Axis movements. The opportunity had passed, and by the time the British 6th Armoured Division had broken out only about 650 men of the enemy's rearguard were captured.

Inevitably, recriminations followed as British and Americans looked for the scapegoat. Crocker recommended the withdrawal of the 34th Division and the retraining of its junior officers under the guidance of the British Army; he saw the failure of the operation as being the American division's fault, an impression that was supported by the United States press which had led the public to expect an American drive through to the sea to split the German and Italian armies. American officers on the ground, however, put the blame on Crocker's plan, which had obliged General Ryder to attack with an exposed flank and which wasted American lives. Anglo-American relations became frosty, and Alexander and Eisenhower had to take steps to calm matters.

Inter-Allied tensions were felt at other occasions during the campaign, despite the damage-limitation efforts of senior officers. A dispute between Patton and Air Vice Marshal Sir Arthur Coningham, the Allied tactical air commander, grew into a near crisis when Patton criticized the 'total lack of air cover' for American forces. Coningham replied by sending a signal to all of the Mediterranean commanders, suggesting that Patton's comments should be likened to an April Fool's joke and that the real weakness was that II (US) Corps was not battleworthy. The matter was regarded so seriously in AFHQ that Eisenhower considered resigning, and it was only smoothed over when Air Chief Marshal Sir Arthur Tedder ordered Coningham to withdraw his statement and to offer a personal apology to Patton. Although the matter was dropped, it still left an atmosphere between officers of two nations which were supposed to be firm allies.

From North Africa the next step was Sicily, where Anglo-American relationships were again to come under strain. The earliest plans for the invasion had envisaged the Eighth Army landing on the south-eastern coast of the island before advancing northwards towards Messina. The United States forces (later to be named the Seventh Army) were to land on the northwest coast near the capital, Palermo, before progressing eastwards to Messina. The British and American landing areas were about as far apart as they could have been: about 140 miles as the crow flies, and separated by rugged countryside with second-class roads meandering across it. This plan was changed at the behest of Montgomery, who saw the intention of splitting the Allied formations into 'penny packets' spread around the coast as being dangerous and unlikely to succeed. His alternative proposal was for the Americans to land in the south, much closer to the British, and then to drive northwards across Sicily on the left of the British advance. Although this was militarily sound the Americans felt – rightly – that they were being relegated to a flank guard for Montgomery's army. Prompted by his subordinates to protest against this minor role, Patton's response was to refuse, saying that after thirty years in the army, his correct attitude was to accept orders and to carry them out to the best of his ability.

Patton's sense of duty in accepting orders without demur was soon to be tested in Sicily. Only two days after the landings, and after successfully defeating counterattacks by Axis forces, the Seventh Army's 45th Division was advancing northwards on a road within the American Army's boundary, but which Montgomery now decided that he needed, to give his Eighth Army more room to manoeuvre. Alexander agreed to the demand to shift the inter-army boundary westwards to bring the road under Montgomery's control, but his decision forced the Americans to pull the 45th back almost to the beach before it could be redeployed westwards. The decision rankled not only with Patton, but also with his staff, who saw it as confirming their opinion that Alexander's strategy was to have the British act as the sword arm while the American function was to do little more than to act as a shield which protected their left flank. Their view was not far off the situation, for on 14 July Alexander had sent a signal to Sir Alan Brooke in which he spelled out the way in which he saw the campaign progressing: the British would play the major part, with XIII Corps thrusting north from Catania to Messina and XXX Corps driving on to the north coast before turning eastwards to reach Messina from the western side of Mount Etna. Seventh Army would be sent to Trapani and Palermo once XXX Corps had split the island.[6]

Having been ordered to surrender the road to Montgomery and feeling the need to assert the status of the United States Army (in which he was supported by Eisenhower, who told him to stand up to Alexander or be removed from his command[7]), Patton decided to take matters into his own hands. On 17 July he arrived unannounced in Alexander's headquarters in North Africa to argue for a greater role for the Seventh Army. Montgomery's advance northwards had been halted on the Plain of Catania and both of the British corps were committed to the fighting; he had few options open to him to break the enemy's defences. Patton proposed that II (US) Corps, commanded by Bradley, be used to drive through the island and to cut Sicily in two, which would break the deadlock. The rest of Seventh Army would make a move westwards to deal with Axis forces there. Patton deliberately failed to make the point that Palermo lay in the west and that it would make an attractive prize. Having given Montgomery free rein over the inter-army boundary affair Alexander believed that he should now allow Patton his way.

Patton's movement on Palermo was swift. Alexander had already authorized a reconnaissance in force to the towns of Agrigento and Porto Empedocle, which would open the door to western Sicily as well as giving the Allies extra port facilities. Now Patton extended this manoeuvre and ordered an advance on Palermo. Belatedly, Alexander had second thoughts about the freedom he had given to Patton and attempted to limit his activities, an attempt which failed when the signal he sent to Seventh Army was 'garbled' and had to be repeated – a ploy by Patton's Chief of Staff to ensure that it was not received by Patton in time for him to call off his advance. The Americans were beginning to test the system and to find ways to achieve their own aims; while Palermo had little or no military value in the Sicilian campaign, the city was nevertheless a propaganda and political prize, the capture of which would do much to restore American confidence after their uncertain start in North Africa. Secondly, by placing II (US) Corps on the north coast Patton had a clear run eastwards to Messina on the route that Alexander had intended XXX Corps to take. Patton was determined to be the first to capture an Axis regional capital and to get to Messina before the British.

Contrary to the reservations held by some British officers about the competence of the American Army, it had been quick to learn and to put the lessons into practice. The performance of the 3rd (US) Infantry Division during the advance on Palermo was particularly notable; under Major General Lucian K. Truscott it had been trained to march swiftly and with the minimum of support. Truscott had spent some time as a liaison officer with the British forces and had been impressed with the training that commando units received. He proposed that similar units be formed in the US Army, a proposal which led to the establishment of the Ranger battalions. In April 1943 Truscott was appointed commander of the 3rd Division and instigated a strict training regime for all ranks which ensured that they could travel at a rapid pace, which became known as the 'Truscott Trot'. It was to prove its worth in Sicily when one of his battalions marched a distance of fifty-four miles cross-country in thirty-three hours, carrying all of its weapons, water and rations with it. This feat was performed in July, hardly the coolest month of the year, and was probably not bettered by any unit of any army during the war. As with all armies, there were formations that performed significantly better than others, and much of the reason for the disparity often lay at the door of the senior officers, whose qualities of leadership, attitude towards training and professionalism, and personal abilities could build or destroy his command. This factor was to re-appear in Italy.

Patton achieved his aim of capturing Palermo, which had little military significance but looked good in the American press as the first major Axis regional capital to fall to the Allies. Patton was learning to use the power of the media to further his own, and his army's, aims, lessons which Clark had already taken note of for his own career and which he was to build on for his Fifth Army in Italy. It was not only some of the British that believed that Patton's action was questionable – his II Corps commander, Lieutenant General Omar Bradley, saw no good reason to head westwards when the capture of Messina would cut off the enemy's withdrawal and inflict significant losses. To Bradley, Palermo was little more than a publicity stunt carried out to enhance Patton's reputation, which detracted from II Corps' drive up the centre of Sicily. Moreover, Bradley felt strongly that Patton should have resisted Alexander's earlier order to surrender the road from the landing beaches to Montgomery; had Bradley's Corps had use of it he would have been at the north coast before the Germans had time to establish their defences, and the deadlock now forming on the Catania Plain would have been avoided.

Moreover, Alexander let Patton get away with overplaying his hand.[8] Patton's action had unwittingly been encouraged by Montgomery who had advised him to ignore any orders from Alexander that he did not agree with. Monty had little respect for Alexander as a commander-in-chief, although he valued him as a friend – but his advice did little for coalition unity. His words reflected the reality that British practice was to discuss and if necessary debate orders rather than to carry them out without question, especially if they appeared questionable, a practice alien to the Americans, especially given the difficulties they were experiencing in training their greatly expanded army.

Alexander and Montgomery had, of course, exchanged thoughts on breaking the impasse facing the Eighth Army, discussions which did not include Patton. Alexander suggested placing one of the American divisions under Monty's command, which would extend the Eighth Army front to the west and allow him to swing around the Etna Line. The US Seventh Army was still being seen as playing a secondary role, having little more to do than to occupy the west of Sicily while the British made all the running to win the campaign. Montgomery's response was to suggest that an American division did, indeed, advance along the northern coast to stretch the enemy's defences, but the plans he had prepared for the Eighth Army would enable him to advance around the western slopes of Etna. Alexander informed Brooke that he saw the Americans being based in Palermo until such time as they were brought up to operate on the left of Montgomery's push to Messina.

Monty's ideas did not wholly match Alexander's. Failing to break the enemy on his right flank, he now proposed to reinforce XXX Corps, on his left, with 78th Division and push these forces to the west of Etna. He wanted more commitment from the Americans than the previously discussed one division: Seventh (US) Army should advance eastwards towards Messina on Highways 113 and 120. The first of these roads ran along the coast, in places carved into the mountain slopes above the sea; the second was parallel to it, but about twenty miles inland. Alexander agreed with Montgomery's proposal and directed Patton to transfer his supply lines from the south coast to Palermo and to use maximum strength in his move eastwards.

On 24 July, two weeks after the initial landings in Sicily, Alexander met Montgomery and the next day both generals held a conference with Patton. This was the first time that the three got together since D Day, and it is noteworthy that the meeting was convened at the instigation of Montgomery rather than Alexander. Throughout the preparation for the Sicilian campaign and its execution Alexander had held back and failed to coordinate the activities of the two armies, regarding Patton's as a flank guard for Montgomery's. Monty evidently felt that this situation could not continue and that an integrated approach should be taken. At his invitation Patton flew to meet him in Syracuse, where to Patton's surprise Monty proposed that the Seventh Army capture Messina, the prize objective of the campaign, even giving the Americans permission to cross the inter-army boundary in their manoeuvring to do so. Patton was profoundly suspicious of Montgomery's motives, suspecting him of some ulterior motive, but the latter general had recognized that if the campaign was to succeed without unnecessary casualties then this was the best way forward. As Carlo d'Este states[9] the view that there was a competition between the Americans and British to reach Messina first was a fiction promulgated in the minds of post-war American historians and film-makers – and in the mind of Patton. It was not Monty's view. Faced with the difficulties of breaking the enemy defences that lay before him, he proposed the most sensible strategy available. By the time Alexander arrived the deal had been agreed, a reflection on his personal style of leadership and the impatience which more dynamic men such as Montgomery experienced when serving under him.

Inter-allied relationships had still not been smoothed over to the satisfaction of Patton. At the Syracuse meeting he felt that he had been slighted by the lack of formal hospitality offered by the British: no lunch was forthcoming. Three days later Montgomery flew to Palermo for another meeting, where he was received by a guard of honour, a band and an impressive lunch, all of which were designed to bring home to him the failure of his hospitality to Patton, a lesson which was completely missed by the British general who noted in his diary that the Americans were delightful and a pleasure to work with. Moreover, he described their troops as being first-class.[10] The inter-Allied antagonism was one-way. Based on the perceived condescension of senior British officers ever since the first days of TORCH, many Americans now sought to prove their worth and to prove to the world that they were a match for anyone. To Patton this meant that he had to achieve an American triumph, and the way to do that was to get to Messina first. Which he did.

The press was a double-edged weapon as far as Patton was concerned. His career stumbled when the news broke that on two separate occasions during the campaign he had slapped soldiers hospitalized for what was then termed shell-shock. Emotional from visiting wounded men whom he believed to be heroes who had suffered for their country, Patton was unsympathetic when faced with men he considered to lack moral fibre. His actions were to rule him out of consideration for the command of all American forces engaged in North West Europe; it was not until August 1944 that he was again given command of an army. Desperate to become involved in the war, Patton even volunteered to command a corps under Clark, a request that was denied. It is interesting to ponder what might have been had his wish been granted.

Notes

1. Watson, *Chief of Staff: Prewar Plans and Operations*
2. Mansoor, *The GI Offensive in Europe*
3. Blumenson, *WW2 leaders in Europe: thoughts Parameters 19, no 4, Dec 1989* quoted in Mansoor
4. Center for Military History, *Tunisia*
5. Danchev & Todman (Eds), *War Diaries 1939–1945*, Field Marshal Lord Alanbrooke
6. Malony et al, *The Mediterranean and the Middle East* Vol V
7. D'Este, *Patton – A Genius for War*
8. Ibid
9. Ibid
10. Ibid

CHAPTER 5

The French

If each of the coalition forces engaged in the Italian campaign had its own agendas and problems to deal with, the French must stand apart as having a situation more complicated than most.

After the Germans had pushed deep into France in 1940 and the Franco-German Armistice had been signed on 22 June, the country had been separated between the northern and western areas which came under German occupation and the unoccupied region to the south, where the French government under Marshal Henri Pétain based itself in the town of Vichy. The government chose to abide by the terms of the Armistice, which included agreements on the size and composition of the French armed forces which were to operate under the overall direction of the Germans. They were reduced to some 100,000 men based in Metropolitan France, with a similar number for the overseas territories – essentially a police force for internal security purposes, for the Germans had no wish to deploy their own troops to French colonies. The French fleet was to remain in harbour.

Four days before the armistice was signed Brigadier General Charles de Gaulle, who had flown to London, made an appeal over the BBC for the French to continue the battle against the Germans. This broadcast was to earn him the support of Winston Churchill, who recognized him as the 'head of all free Frenchmen', but won him little applause in Vichy, where he was formally stripped of his military rank and tried and sentenced to death in absentia. Both de Gaulle and the Vichy Government regarded themselves as the true representatives of the French people, a dispute which was to have ramifications later in the war. When France was on the verge of defeat by the Germans, the government was divided between those (such as Prime Minister Paul Reynaud) who argued that the war should be continued by a government in exile from the North African colonies, and those who argued (including the Vice-Premier, Pétain) that the duty of the government was to remain in France to support the population. The Vichy regime was recognized as the official government of France by the United States, Australia, Canada and other countries, despite its legitimacy being challenged by the Free French, who maintained that it was run by traitors. The United Kingdom's relationships with Vichy were severed when the British attacked the French fleet in Mers el Kebir to prevent it falling into German hands. The Free French, on the other hand, were recognized by the British Government and their status formalized by the Charter of Free France. De Gaulle established a French National Committee in London under his presidency and his forces operated under the control of the British, who took on the responsibility for equipping them. In mid-November 1941 President Roosevelt announced that the Free French were eligible for lend-lease equipment, provided it was received via the British rather than directly. Until the end of the Tunisian campaign in May 1943 the Free French were almost entirely British trained and equipped.

British relationships with Vichy, already formally broken off after Mers el Kebir, worsened when Operation MENACE was launched in September 1940; this was an unsuccessful attempt to seize the port of Dakar in French West Africa and to place it under Free French control. Nine months later British forces invaded the Vichy territories of Syria and Lebanon, which German and Italian aircraft had been staging through; and from May until November 1942 the Battle of Madagascar was fought, when British and Commonwealth forces invaded the island to prevent its use by the Japanese. In the Syria-Lebanon campaign Vichy and Free French forces were pitted against each other, the former suffering some 6,000 casualties. The majority of the Free French troops involved were Senegalese, as were many of those serving in the Vichy ranks. Understandably some of them were reluctant to fire on their fellow countrymen, a factor which was to give the British a poor opinion of their abilities. The Vichy powers refused to surrender to the Free French, preferring to do so to the British, and when prisoners were offered the choice of being returned to Metropolitan France or joining de Gaulle, only 5,668 men took the latter option; 37,563 military and civilian personnel went back to France. Recruiting for the Free French did not progress as well as de Gaulle had anticipated, and it was not to pick up until the end of 1942; even following the TORCH landings Frenchmen rallied not to de Gaulle or the Free French as such, but to the wider Allied cause.

De Gaulle's forces had primarily been gathered from the French colonies in Africa and from members of the Foreign Legion who had been withdrawn from Norway. Of the 60,000 troops who had been evacuated from the continent during and after Dunkirk, only 3,000 chose to stay in England with the Free French. The remainder returned to France. De Gaulle received some support from the French colonies: Cameroon, Chad, Moyen-Congo, Oubangui-Chari and French Equatorial Africa declared for de Gaulle. These were later joined by the Pacific colonies of New Caledonia, French Polynesia and the New Hebrides, and Saint-Pierre and Miquelon (near Canada) joined the Free French after an 'invasion' on 24 December 1941, when supporters of the Free French overthrew the pro-Vichy administrator, despite United States opposition. The act contributed to Roosevelt's lasting distrust of de Gaulle.

By the spring of 1942 de Gaulle was confident that large numbers of Frenchmen would join his cause if landings were to be made in mainland France. He sought to tap into American sources for military equipment for both his current forces and for the anticipated increase in numbers following an invasion of his homeland, wanting it to be delivered directly to him rather than via the British. In this hope he was to be disappointed – the Americans had more pressing needs to meet, not only to their more significant allies who were already engaged in conflict with the Axis, but also for the rapidly-expanding US Army. Additionally, there was reluctance on the part of the American authorities to deal with the Free French military headquarters, which they considered to be very suspect on matters of security. Moreover, at the time that de Gaulle's request was made, preparations were underway for TORCH rather than a landing in France itself. De Gaulle and his staff were excluded from both the planning process and participation in the North African invasion; however, the planners were already negotiating with other French officers to gain their support. The Americans considered General Giraud to be the most promising Frenchman to bring French North and West Africa onto the Allied side. Giraud was highly esteemed in France: he had twice escaped from the Germans, once in each of the world wars, and had a record as a thoroughly professional soldier who had valiantly attempted to stem the 1940 German attack, albeit unsuccessfully. Now back in his homeland, Giraud was approached by the Americans with the request that he become the leader of the French forces. While agreeing to this proposal, he suggested that the North African landings would have more chance of success if there were also to be a landing on the Mediterranean coast of mainland France. He also suggested that the Americans bring some 150,000 tons of war matériel to southern France to equip the mainland French forces that would come across to the Allied side. With TORCH planning well advanced – indeed the assault convoys were already on their way – his proposals were out of the question. Accepting this, Giraud agreed to be transported to North Africa as soon as it was appropriate. In Africa his appointment was welcomed by those supporters of the Allied cause, including General Mast, their military leader. As soon as the United States had outlined its intention to re-arm the French, Mast produced a plan to re-equip eight infantry and two armoured divisions, as well as a number of tank, artillery, service and air units, all of which would be raised from the North African Army.

Whatever Mast may have wanted, and what the United States might have wished to provide, the facts at the time were that American resources were stretched in meeting the growing list of commitments worldwide. The Americans had launched a re-armament plan (the 'Victory' programme) in late 1941, which envisaged manning, training and equipping more than 200 United States divisions (let alone any Allied ones); this was an immense task, and even – at this stage – just equipping the divisions nominated for TORCH meant stripping equipment from other formations undergoing training in America. By September 1942 the negotiations between the United States and the pro-Allied French (excluding de Gaulle, of course) had made enough progress to indicate that the latter would join the Allies; the Mast Plan would have to be taken seriously. The relations between the French and Americans were at a delicate phase; although the French were supportive, they wanted assurances that their forces would be modernized, which would mean denuding twelve United States divisions of their equipment. In Washington the response was to offer only such matériel as was necessary to supplement what the French already had, and until the French reaction to TORCH was certain, nothing more would be committed.

As commander of the TORCH forces Eisenhower needed to know how and when equipment might be provided for the French forces which came across to the Allied camp, not that he could be certain of their strength. He therefore submitted a partial list of the Mast requirements to Washington, where the War Department agreed that the reduced schedule could be made ready for shipping by 20 December 1942, despite its affect on the twelve American divisions.

TORCH was launched on the night of 7/8 November 1942: some 83,000 United States and 26,000 British troops landed from shipping almost entirely supplied by the British. Although it had been hoped that the pre-invasion negotiations would result in little or no French resistance, at Oran and in and around Casablanca the French put up strong opposition. In the Algiers area things went more smoothly after the pro-Allied French brought the fighting to a swift end. On 9 November General Giraud arrived in North Africa, to find that Admiral François Darlan, the Vichy Commander-in-Chief, had assumed control of those forces which opposed the Allies. Darlan had agreed to the local ceasefire in Algiers, but was continuing to negotiate with the Allies while still maintaining communications with Pétain. It was not until 10 November that he ordered all resistance to cease; three days later he arranged a provisional French government based in Algiers which would renew hostilities against the Axis powers, and on 14 November General Giraud was appointed C-in-C of all North African army and air forces. Admiral Darlan and General Clark signed an agreement on 22 November, which set out the conditions under which French North Africa joined the Allies.

The Darlan-Clark agreement was not universally welcomed. Although the Allies had accepted Darlan's assumption of power as a temporary expedient to bring a halt to the resistance in North Africa, his close links to the Vichy Government made it impossible to merge his forces with de Gaulle's. The mutual distrust between the two camps was too great, and the recent history of bloodshed between them during the Syria-Lebanon campaign did nothing to heal the rift. The situation was – at least partially – resolved on 24 December, when Darlan was assassinated by a member of the French resistance, an act which went unmourned by the British as it removed an obstacle to de Gaulle's claim to French leadership. The newly-formed French Imperial Council appointed Giraud as High Commissioner for North and West Africa, while retaining his role as C-in-C. The events did not halt the difficulties for long, however. A series of crises was to affect French internal politics for the next sixteen months, although good relationships between the Anglo-American and French military authorities managed to ensure that these problems did not prove fatal to the alliance. For the moment, however, the French contribution to the Allied cause had considerably increased, although equipping this contribution to modern standards remained to be carried out.

The French African Army
On the outbreak of war the standing army in French North Africa comprised indigenous Arab and Berber volunteers in *Spahi* and *Tirailleur* regiments (cavalry and infantry, respectively), French settlers in *Chasseurs d'Afrique* and *Zouave* units (again, cavalry and infantry), and the Foreign Legion. There were also battalions of the *Infanterie Légère d'Afrique* (African Light Infantry), manned by convicted military criminals who still had time to serve on their military terms of engagement once they had finished their prison sentences. A brigade of Senegalese *Tirailleurs* was also stationed in Algeria. By May 1940 fourteen *Zouave* regiments, forty-two Algerian, Tunisian and

Moroccan Tirailleur regiments, twelve Foreign Legion regiments and demi-brigades, and thirteen African Light Infantry battalions were serving on all fronts.

Unlike the British policy of recruiting only sufficient African troops for immediate internal security purposes, the French had a tradition of maximizing the numbers and were content to use them outside Africa – colonial forces were seen as a valuable adjunct to those from mainland France. Many African troops had served on the Western Front during the First World War, and France had deployed colonial soldiers – an estimated 42,000 to 45,000 of them – as part of the occupation forces of the Rhineland after the war. This was seen not only by the Germans but also by many of the Allied nations as being unnecessarily humiliating to the Germans. At the root of this feeling was the fear of letting loose African soldiers on white women, a prevailing concern at the time.[1] The memory of this humiliation may have played its part in the German massacres of French colonial troops in France in 1940, although Nazi racial attitudes undoubtedly influenced matters. More than 75,000 black French soldiers served there before and during the German invasion, of whom about 10,000 were killed in the fighting. An estimated 1,500 to 3,000 *Tirailleurs Sénégalais* were randomly executed by German forces.[2]

In French North Africa (Tunisia, Algeria and French Morocco) and West Africa, the military authorities made the decision to preserve the unity of France under Marshal Pétain. Although the strength of the African Army had been reduced under the terms agreed with the Germans, there was still a useful force on the ground, which successively numbered 100,000, 120,000 and lastly 137,000 men, as progressively negotiated with the Germans.

In 1943 the French African Army numbered more than the officially recognized manpower laid down in the armistice agreement. Particularly in French Morocco, where the mountainous nature of the country encouraged clandestine training, extra manpower was raised. Short-term volunteers, civilian workers, auxiliary police and others formed units and trained with the 59,000 weapons and twenty-two million rounds of ammunition that local commanders had secreted immediately after the armistice. A total of 60,000 men was hidden, and a plan was formed to mobilize 109,000 men and to requisition supplies, transport vehicles and animals, in the event that hostilities were renewed. The preparations included improving the communications systems, both signals (radio) and physical (road and rail links).[3]

Among the French North African forces were the Moroccan Goumiers, Berber nomads originally recruited to police the mountain tribes from which they were drawn. Irregular troops, dressed in their native djellaba (a striped, hooded cloak), with French officers, they were often attached to the regular North African and Foreign Legion units as scouts. Their local knowledge of the tribes and the terrain made their presence invaluable when local tribes had to be brought to order during the process of colonization. These men were organized in groups numbering from seventy-five to 150, known as goums; when grouped together, several goums became a tabor; when North African forces were deployed to France following the outbreak of war with Germany, twelve goums were organised into tabors and sent to the Libyan border to defend it against the Italians, who entered the war against France on 10 June 1940. It was a short-lived episode, for France surrendered only twelve days later. The goums returned to their police duties, which the French used as an explanation for their existence – they did not count against the manpower ceiling for the African Army which had been agreed with the Germans. The Germans were prepared to accept this deception, although the Italians – who had briefly fought against them – were not: to them the goums were soldiers. The Germans' opinion prevailed, however, and the goums were not counted among the military strength of the French colonies. The German decision may have been based upon their racial prejudices, which failed to recognize such untrained tribesmen as having the potential to be soldiers in the *Wehrmacht* sense of the word, or it may be that they did not wish to devote any effort to monitoring what the goums actually did. A further factor was that the Germans had no wish to take on the duties of internal security and policing a defeated enemy's colonies. Whatever the reason, the door was open for the French to build up a useful addition to their overseas army. In remote areas goumiers were trained in the use of modern weaponry – or at least what weaponry was available. The numbers grew, and after the TORCH landings regimental groups were formed, each of four tabors. In December 1942 the *1e Groupe de tabors Marocains* joined the Moroccan Division in northern Tunisia. A second *groupe* arrived a few weeks later. With later additions, the *groupes* provided mountain troops who would prove their worth in Italy at a later date. Unfortunately, they were also to leave a lasting scar on the Italian memory because of the outrages they committed on the civilian population, so much so that the word '*marocchinate*' entered the Italian language to depict the mass rape and murders committed by the goumiers after the breakthrough of the Gustav Line. Trained in modern weapons they may have been, but they did not leave their historical methods of war-fighting or of exacting revenge on a defeated enemy behind them.[4]

The original formations drawn from the French North African Army were the 1st and 2nd Armoured Divisions (*1ere* and *2e Divisions Blindées*; the *2e Division* was reactivated as *5e Division Blindée* in July 1943); 2nd and 3rd Moroccan Infantry Divisions (*2e* and *3e Divisions d'Infantrie Marocaine*; the *3e Division* was redesignated 4th Moroccan Mountain Division in June 1943); and 3rd Algerian Infantry Division (*3e Division d'Infantrie Algerienne*). These were later joined by other forces from the Free French, including the *1e Division Française Libre* (1st Free French Division) which had the *13e Demi-Brigade de la Légion Etrangère* (DBLE: Half-Brigade of the Foreign Legion) and French colonial units such as the *Bataillon d'Infanterie de Marine du Pacifique* (BIMP: Marine Infantry Battalion of the Pacific) in its ranks. There was also an artillery regiment from the Levant and units of French sailors among the French forces which eventually arrived in Italy.

To prepare them to make a full contribution to the fight against the Axis, they needed training and re-equipping. At first General Eisenhower was unconvinced of their combat effectiveness, a view formed from the reports he received during the first weeks of their operations with the Anglo-American forces. He questioned their offensive spirit and was doubtful of their potential, a view which inclined him to relegate them to garrison duties, but in an attempt to encourage them to take a more aggressive role he recommended that small arms, anti-tank and anti-aircraft weapons be supplied to the French. Before long reports from Tunisia indicated that the French had recovered from the series of psychological blows which they had suffered following TORCH: the token resistance which some units had been ordered to offer to the invaders, the conflicting orders they had been given, the shift of allegiance from Vichy, and finally being thrown into battle against the Germans unprepared and ill-equipped. Faced with evidence that the French were capable of more than garrison tasks, Eisenhower had now to decide how best to use them. His priority was to have them properly equipped for the immediate future, a priority which came before preparing for whatever might face the French later on.

Some equipment had already been reserved in the United States, but as yet no date had been set for its shipment to the French. General Giraud had assigned some 7,000 men under General Juin to Eisenhower for the Tunisian operations, a figure which would increase to 40,000 in the following months, but these troops could not fight effectively against German tanks. They could only act as a holding force until either equipment or Allied reinforcements were available. The only equipment close to hand was that held by Allied forces already in theatre, and Eisenhower authorized first the Commanding

General, Eastern Task Force, and then the Commanding General, Western Task Force, to supply whatever the French needed. This was to be on temporary loan, and was to constitute only items surplus to Anglo-American requirements. He also ordered the Fifth Army to assist in training the French to use the weapons and other supplies provided.

With the Tunisian situation worsening before Christmas 1942, Eisenhower again contacted the Combined Chiefs of Staff about the re-arming programme. On Christmas Eve they replied to the effect that rifles would be despatched from the United Kingdom within two days, and anti-tank and anti-aircraft guns would follow from America by 6 January. However, shipping limitations prevented anything more being sent at the moment; as it was, equipment bound for the American forces in North Africa had to wait because of the French requirement. Eisenhower was going to have to make his mind up about his priorities.

General Giraud was also giving consideration to his force's needs. His concern went wider than just those who were engaged in Tunisia, for the whole of his strength needed equipping. To this end his staff prepared an update of the Mast Plan which was presented to Eisenhower's Armed Force Headquarters. A second copy was later given to the United States War Department by General Béthouart, the chief of the French military mission in Washington. This revision envisaged a total of eleven French divisions, one more than the Mast Plan.

For the Combined Chiefs of Staff the French demands had to be balanced against the global strategy which the Allied powers were set upon. The industrial output of the United States was a finite entity, and decisions had to be taken on where armaments were to go. Would the investment in the French be worth more, say, than sending matériel to another ally, or even to US forces? The amount of worldwide shipping available to deliver equipment was a critical factor – Béthouart's shopping list for eleven divisions – if met – would require 325 cargo vessels to deliver to North Africa. This amount of shipping was simply unavailable. Another factor came into play, as it had to when considering international relations and the effectiveness of a coalition: politics. Giraud was preparing the French to re-enter the war, and he needed the moral advantage of not only getting equipment for his troops, but he also had to demonstrate that it was he who was able to get it. Generals Giraud and de Gaulle were discussing the unification of their forces, a matter which was far from straightforward, as has been previously noted. Giraud had to be seen to be getting not only matériel but also support from the United Nations if he was to prosecute an effective war, to set French minds at rest, and to establish himself firmly as the head of French military forces. And it should be remembered that Giraud was the man favoured by the Americans for the task.

In their decision-making during the Casablanca Conference (14–26 January 1943), the Combined Chiefs had to weigh up the concerns of short- and long-term assistance to the French. The first step was to determine what use they meant to make of the North African forces, which in turn depended upon the trust that they felt they could place in them. The British appeared reluctant to place too much faith in an army which had been extremely loyal to Vichy until only a few weeks previously; the Americans had more belief in the French. On the one side Admiral King, head of the US Navy (and an Anglophobe) urged that his American colleagues 'insist' that maximum use was made of the French despite the anticipated British opposition; on the other, General Sir Alan Brooke, the CIGS, regarded the usefulness of the French as being largely to provide garrison troops.[5] Roosevelt wanted a French army of 250,000 men equipped with the best equipment; Brooke offered to provide them with used tanks which the British had replaced. Marshall was prepared to modify the supply programme to the American Army to produce more modern equipment than the British had offered, which would be carried to North Africa in French shipping. The debate was swung by the appearance of Giraud, who explained that he was confident of raising thirteen divisions (three armoured and ten motorized infantry), and also an air force which would require a total of 1,000 aircraft. Despite the difficulties that this would impose on United Nations resources and planning, he was sure that France would make a great contribution to victory.

On 24 January in a meeting with Giraud, Roosevelt committed America – in principle, at least – to re-arming France. General Giraud returned to Algiers happy that he had obtained American promises, but his joy was short-lived. Hardly had the ink dried on the agreement, to which the British had not been a party, than its consequences began to come under scrutiny. Once Churchill heard of it he made clear to the American delegate in Algiers, two weeks after the end of the Casablanca Conference, the military and political ramifications of the agreement in which he had played no part. Not only had Churchill been left out of the negotiations between Roosevelt and Giraud, but so had de Gaulle, which would have consequences for French unity. The British reservations led to a re-drafting of the agreement, to include reference to the possibility that other priorities might have to be considered when re-arming the French. Another sticking point emerged when American officials began considering the agreement in the context of worldwide strategy and of other commitments, of the availability of shipping, and of production issues. The overarching question was what 'in principle' meant. The French saw it as a binding agreement, the Americans as expressing the spirit of the agreement rather than the letter of the text. It was possible that Roosevelt had not realized that the words he had written in the margin of the document, 'Oui en principe', meant more in French than the less binding 'yes in principle' translation. It was yet another of the misunderstandings and difficulties the coalition was to encounter.

When General Béthouart called on Marshall to discuss the implementation of the re-armament plan both individuals were taken by surprise at the other's interpretations of the agreement. The American had not been informed by Roosevelt of any specific agreement with General Giraud apart from that the United States would re-arm the French as quickly as possible, but that details of what particular equipment and the priorities for shipping it had yet to be decided. Worldwide commitments would have to be taken into consideration before the French would get their matériel. Availability of cargo space – again assessed against global requirements – would be decisive, regardless of what Giraud believed to be the urgency of the French case.

Giraud went to Eisenhower on 16 February with his complaints: the Americans seemed now to be delivering only minimum assistance as compared to what he had understood Roosevelt to have promised. Moreover, a rumour was circulating that American policy was not to equip the French for overseas operations, but to give them only enough matériel to defend North Africa; if this were so, then he, Giraud, would resign as French Commander-in-Chief. Eisenhower was spurred into action and sent both a report on the meeting to the War Department and a personal message to Marshall. America was being accused of being 'long on promises and short on performances', and there was a danger that French morale would be further damaged and that General Giraud's control of his army would be weakened.[6] Already, French forces in Tunisia were claiming that they faced a repeat of the situation in 1940, when they had been sent into battle without proper equipment, and they were suffering losses unnecessarily. This did not equate to the promises Giraud had made them after his return from the Roosevelt meeting in Casablanca.

Marshall referred the matter to the President. Roosevelt's immediate reaction was to instruct the American political representative in Algiers to inform the French that at no time did he (Roosevelt) or General Marshall promise firm dates for the delivery of equipment; what had been agreed to was 'the principle of rearming them … as soon as possible from the shipping point of view'. He added,

> Tell your good friends in North Africa that they ought not to act like children. They must take prompt steps to deny the silly rumours that they have been let down in equipping an expeditionary force to go into France or that slowness in supplying armament is delaying political progress. . . . They must remain calm and sensible.

The communications difficulty appeared to be more a case of Giraud being carried away by his eagerness to have his forces re-equipped, and of allowing his wishful thinking to sway his interpretation of his earlier discussions with Roosevelt, than a deliberate attempt to force the Americans' hand. On the other side of the discussions there is at least a possibility that Roosevelt had not given the agreement sufficient attention and had allowed the possibility of misinterpretation to creep into its wording. It was a lesson for the future, especially when language nuances might bring serious problems to Allied relationships.

In the United States some progress had in fact already been made on assembling matériel for the French, although the timetable for its delivery had not yet been established. This had been done in anticipation of a decision from the Combined Chiefs of Staff on how far the re-armament programme was to go, taking into account other commitments and the availability of shipping. Equipment for two infantry divisions, sufficient Sherman tanks for two armoured regiments, three tank destroyer battalions, three reconnaissance battalions and twelve anti-aircraft battalions had been stripped from United States divisions and plans were in hand to ship it to North Africa in a convoy (known as UGS 6½ and consisting of fifteen cargo ships) due to set sail and anticipated to arrive around 11 April; it awaited the CCS decision on long-range policy. Further shipments were planned, which in all would allow the French to equip another infantry division, a third tank destroyer battalion, two more reconnaissance battalions, two extra anti-aircraft battalions, a dozen truck companies and 200 aircraft. The news of UGS 6½ reached Eisenhower as he was about to tell Giraud of Roosevelt's message, complete with its condescending air about remaining calm and sensible; Eisenhower was able to reassure Giraud about the United States' commitment without causing resentment. All that was needed was the approval of the CCS.

The reaction of the British Chiefs of Staff to the Americans' proposal to delay equipping United States divisions in favour of the French was unfavourable. It was not, they maintained, in accordance with the Casablanca agreements on future strategy – the French could not be rearmed sufficiently quickly to take part in the Tunisian operations, and there had as yet been no decision taken on French participation in future plans; they were not likely to be required for those operations that had been decided on for post-Tunisia. To divert shipping to cater for the French would necessarily deny its use for other operations such as those in the Indian Ocean, which would inevitably have a knock-on effect. British reservations about the agreement were prompted by a fear that the French would take precedence for matériel that was in short supply for US or British forces. In short, the American decision to support the French should be re-examined in the context of strategic priority. The COS argument was parried by the American response that the decision had been made 'at a higher level' than the CCS – that is, by the President – and that the topic before them was not whether or not the commitment should be made, but how it should be implemented. With an American acceptance that any delay to British assignments would be made good at a later date, eventually the agreement was re-worded as follows: 'Munitions of war will be assigned to the French Forces up to the limits and at a speed to be decided by the CCS . . . without prejudicing other commitments.'[7]

It appeared that, all protestations to the effect that the United Nations would act in full accord with each other notwithstanding, there were occasions when some voices were louder than others. Roosevelt had directed that the loading of the special convoy be continued, despite Churchill's claim that he and the President had not discussed French re-armament at Casablanca (a claim which ran contrary to Roosevelt's version of events). Inter-Allied disputes apart, a major factor in bringing the issue to a close was the American argument that whereas there was no shortage of matériel (despite the US divisions which would have to wait their turn while the French were equipped) there was a possible United Nations manpower shortage. The French forces were available to fill this particular gap at shorter notice than was the US Army, still under training and thousands of miles away from the battlefields, and the shipping problem was a major shortage of troopships rather than cargo vessels.

The Anglo-American debate continued, both sides reiterating their viewpoints – the Americans that the French had performed well in Tunisia and were worthy of the investment of re-equipping them, the British that the initial requirement was to ready them for static operations, which would free Anglo-American formations for offensive operations. On 18 May 1943, during the TRIDENT Conference, the CCS suddenly agreed a compromise wording which broke the deadlock:

The rearming and re-equipping of the French Forces in North Africa should be proceeded with as rapidly as the availability of shipping and equipping will allow, but as a secondary commitment to the requirements of British and U.S. Forces in the various Theatres.[8]

This was a major surrender to the British, but the Americans had confidence that there were no shortages in either equipment or shipping that might interfere with arming the eleven French divisions as agreed. They also felt that the French had demonstrated their worth and that there was ample justification for re-arming them.

While this might have poured oil on the Anglo-American disagreement, the French were less content. About twenty-four per cent of the French North African forces who fought in Tunisia (9,600 from a total of 40,000 men) had become casualties, and the inadequate equipment they had been compelled to use played a significant part in this statistic.[9] The end of the Tunisian campaign placed the re-armament problem in a fresh light. By the time it closed in May 1943, the first United States equipment began to arrive and a ceremony was held in Algiers on 8 May which jointly celebrated the Axis defeat and the formal handing over of new American matériel to General Giraud; but it was too late to be of immediate use to the French. The promise made by Roosevelt on 24 January had taken over three months to materialize, and the French had yet to be fully trained to use their new weapons. The timescale was probably as fast as it could have been, but for those French forces which had fought in Tunisia armed with weapons of French origin and matériel that had been supplied by the American and British forces in the region – a miscellaneous collection of small arms, outdated tanks and an assortment of vehicles – it was not fast enough. Nor was it enough to equip more than the formations provided for in the first phase of the plan drawn up in Casablanca: three infantry divisions, two armoured regiments, and four tank destroyer, five reconnaissance, fourteen anti-aircraft and three ordnance battalions, and twelve truck companies.

The arrival of equipment was only the first step towards fitting the French for whatever role they were to assume in the months and years ahead. Allied Forces HQ (AFHQ) recognized that left to their own devices the French would struggle to assemble, distribute and maintain tons of equipment, much of which was unfamiliar to them. If maximum use was to be made of the French forces they had to be trained in the use of the equipment – and for that to happen, their partners in the alliance would have to provide support, especially in the form of administrative and technical staff. Even before the equipment from the United States arrived, locally-sourced matériel from

American and British sources had been slow to get to Tunisia once the French had received it and had taken responsibility for sending it to the troops in the field; on one occasion it had taken a month for equipment delivered in Algiers to be delivered to Tunisia because of chaotic French administration. Setting up an entire command and service organization was a major problem, not helped by apparently simple difficulties such as obtaining typewriters. Few were available in theatre, and they had to be sent from the United States, with all of the delays that were entailed in shipping by convoy. Assistance in overcoming the inevitable difficulties was forthcoming from the American and British forces, whose staff officers worked with their French counterparts to prepare for the arrival of UGS 6½. A detailed programme was established for the reception of the equipment, including the provision of an American-managed assembly line with sufficient tools to assemble some 200 vehicles daily. It was capable of putting together one 2½-ton truck every three minutes, apart from carrying out similar functions on other equipment. During the first week of operation 1,900 vehicles were assembled by a French team, the Chantiers de Jeunesse, which had been created in North Africa in 1941. They were incorporated into the French Army in late 1943 as the 7th Chasseurs d'Afrique Regiment.

The French intention had been to group the first formations to be equipped into an expeditionary corps, but as they did not include engineer, signals and chemical warfare units, the corps could not act independently. Appropriate equipment for these units would have to be provided in later convoys. Another obstacle to the French ambition was the lack of trained drivers (an estimated 50,000 were required for the target of eleven divisions) and the technical troops for ordnance, engineer, signals and medical units. The majority of these specialists would be Frenchmen. For an overall army of 300,000 men, Giraud estimated that 100,000 Frenchmen would be required, the remainder being natives from the various colonies, but where such a number might be found was uncertain. A possible solution to the problem, suggested by AFHQ, would be to put a small independent task force in the field, operating within a British or American formation which would supply the specialists. This proposal would not meet the French aspiration of raising a full army, and the subject was to be debated with some heat for months.

Availability of Frenchmen aside, growth of the force was limited by the speed at which it could be equipped from the United States. Despite attempts to have the tonnage of cargo raised from 25,000 to 100,000 per month, the shipments could not be increased without penalties to other Allied requirements. The French would have to re-examine the structure and composition of their expeditionary corps. After further negotiation it was agreed that a second phase of rearmament would bring the force strength up to one armoured division which incorporated the two armoured regiments that were currently being equipped; the nucleus of a second armoured division; one mountain division; headquarters for one armoured, one infantry and one expeditionary corps; corps artillery; additional service units; and 18,000 tons of naval equipment. Air force units to the strength of 300 aircraft would be considered at a later date. Having agreed this, it would inevitably be some time before the reality emerged on the ground. It was nearly four weeks before the requisitions were placed, partly because at this time AFHQ was preparing for Operation HUSKY, the invasion of Sicily, and because of the CCS decision that French re-armament would be secondary to British and American needs, which were also tied to HUSKY. Not since March had any initial equipment been sent to the French, and despite the requirement to bring them up to the agreed strength, the current situation did not augur well for this to happen quickly. It was a period of great frustration.

As this debate was proceeding, General Giraud was on his way to Washington. His intention was not only to press for increased matériel shipments, but he also wanted Roosevelt's support on the political concern currently facing the French. Giraud was the supreme civil and military authority in North Africa, but de Gaulle – based in London – was president of the French National Committee and head of the Free French Forces. Before the Casablanca Conference the two generals had agreed in principle that the two factions should merge; the close of the Tunisian campaign presented an opportunity for this to happen. On 30 May de Gaulle flew to North Africa with the intention of establishing a central executive body with Giraud, which would govern all French areas not controlled by the Axis. There were obstacles in the way, however. The two generals and their followers had differing opinions on the status the respective parties held. For de Gaulle, his argument was that he and the Free French had been the sole representatives of French resistance, who had refused to surrender their arms, and that consequently it was they who had the right to lead the French forces to victory. Giraud and his associates had received the recognition of the Anglo-American allies in November 1942, and in their eyes this gave them the entitlement to command the French forces. In politics, too, the groups held differing views: de Gaulle wanted a new, progressive government in France after the liberation; Giraud was in favour of a slower return to political freedom, a more conservative approach. Three days of heated discussions produced a French Committee of National Liberation (the *Comité Français de la Liberation Nationale*—CFLN) on 3 June 1943, which was composed of members of both factions, and with the two generals as co-presidents. The uneasy French agreement may have indicated some progress towards reconciliation, but the United Nations considered that it did not go far enough to merit official recognition as being the de facto government of France. This was delayed largely because of President Roosevelt's mistrust of the Gaullists.

His reservations were not unfounded. As soon as the CFLN had been established, the Gaullists challenged Giraud's authority on the grounds that he should not hold two positions, those of co-president and Commander-in-Chief of the French forces. They began manoeuvring to ensure that de Gaulle assumed control of the armed forces. Once President Roosevelt heard of this he directed Eisenhower not to permit de Gaulle, or any other body not under the complete control of the Allied C-in-C, to assume command of the French armed forces. The United States would not continue to arm any French force in which they did not have complete confidence. Consequently, Eisenhower summoned both Giraud and de Gaulle and informed them that the former must remain as French Commander.

It was inevitable that the sharing of power would increase friction. In July 1943 the situation deteriorated. Both individuals and whole units defected from one faction to the forces of the other, a situation which raised alarm in Washington. Attempts by the Free French headquarters to establish links with AFHQ to obtain equipment were met with coolness until French political and military unity had been achieved; until then arrangements would continue to be made only with General Giraud.

In Washington, Giraud started a ten-day series of visits and conferences with the President, General Marshall, and other officials. He reported that the expeditionary force was now ready for deployment; its strength was between 70,000 and 75,000 men, and included two infantry divisions and one mountain divisions, and half of an armoured division. To this force he proposed adding some 13,000 goumiers. A second corps was being prepared, for which equipment was required – by 1 August – to complete the first armoured division and to equip a second, together with two infantry divisions and supporting troops.

While Giraud was in Washington Eisenhower proposed a solution to the problem of French co-operation. He recommended that all French forces be controlled through AFHQ; that until the CCS made a decision on the matter, no further arms would be supplied to the Free French by the British; and thirdly that General Giraud should include the Free French forces in the eleven divisions that were to be re-armed under the Casablanca agreement. The CCS endorsed these points. Meanwhile the French had also come to the conclusion that the two-headed organization was unworkable and that another solution must be sought. After several weeks of tension agreement was reached on 31 June that all armed forces would come under the overall command of General Giraud. As far as the two-presidency nature of the CFLN was concerned, Giraud would preside over debates on military matters, and de Gaulle when political or economic affairs were discussed.

All was still not settled, however. When Giraud was informed of the CCS decision on incorporating the Free French into the eleven divisions, he was also told that the British would cease equipping the Free French; moreover, they were to return all matériel to British depots, including arms of all descriptions, equipment and clothing. Giraud was to get 13,000 extra men, but without equipment – and with no corresponding increase from American sources. Following a great deal of argument and negotiation, which included the French re-organizing their order of battle and the British reversing their decision to recall equipment (they had decided that it was now unserviceable anyway, and not worth having), the French voyage towards modernization continued.

On 18 June General Giraud had notified AFHQ that he had appointed General Juin as commander of the expeditionary force which was expected to participate in the forthcoming invasions of Sicily and Italy. Corsica was another objective which had been assigned to the French, at a date to be decided once the Sicilian operation was over, but on 21 July AFHQ had called for French forces to be employed in the invasion of the Italian mainland. In the absence of Giraud, still in Washington, Juin was asked to consider sending those French forces not committed to Corsica to serve with the Fifth Army in Italy. With these requirements on the horizon the urgency of completing the rearmament programme was stepped up. Eisenhower's recommendations for this included a detailed plan agreed with Giraud himself for an army of four corps (three infantry and one armoured) consisting of seven infantry and four armoured divisions. This proposal reached Washington on 12 August. Once considered by the Joint Staff Planners it was submitted to the CCS on 18 August, as they were meeting in Quebec for the QUADRANT Conference. The British again expressed their concern that the French rearmament programme might interfere with other commitments, a concern which was met – again – by adding a proviso to the effect that the plan would proceed 'in so far as this does not interfere with operations scheduled previous to the QUADRANT Conference'. At the same time, the CCS agreed that those

French forces that were equipped and fit for war would be employed in the Mediterranean.[10] The United States, British and Canadian governments also agreed to a limited recognition of the CFLN as the representative body for all Frenchmen fighting against the Axis, until such time as mainland France was liberated and its people free to make their own choice of government. Twenty-three other members of the United Nations had followed suit by 3 September.

It had taken nearly ten months since the TORCH landings for the first definite rearmament commitment, including scope and date, to be made by the Anglo-Americans. The original aim was to complete the eleven-division programme by the close of 1943, but this target became watered down progressively, primarily because of French disagreements. Once again the Gaullists questioned Giraud's authority. This time the argument was based on the concept of civil control of the military; Giraud claimed that he had the right to speak for the armed forces – in his view the United States had provided arms to him in his personal capacity as the supreme French military commander. The Gaullists held the view that Giraud's powers (except insofar as they were concerned with control of the expeditionary forces) should be given over to the civil authorities, i.e. the CFLN. The disagreement was strong.

Roosevelt's first inclination was to halt all equipment supplies, but he held back from this action which would have forced a showdown and instructed Marshall to monitor the situation. It was to resolve itself in October when the CFLN did away with the two-headed arrangement and appointed de Gaulle as sole representative. Giraud was thus removed from the political sphere; as C-in-C he would now report to the Commissioner of National Defence. AFHQ decided to deal directly with him on military matters, despite the fact that he would have to refer decisions to the CFLN.

Meanwhile, on 13 September 1943, Operation VESUVIUS began – the first major engagement of French forces outside North Africa, the liberation of Corsica. Apart from one US Ranger unit (and later, elements of the Italian Army) the 15,000-strong force was entirely French. The campaign against some 10,000 Germans was completed on 4 October.

For the remainder of the French forces in North Africa, the re-equipment programme was still incomplete. The requirement for service troops, and who was to provide them, became the next bone of contention. No more than a nucleus for any engineer unit was to be established until early in 1944, and there were no French plans in place to establish transport, petrol supply or base depot service units for the foreseeable future. Only three ordnance depot companies were planned for the rest of the year, those that had already been equipped by the Americans. From AFHQ's standpoint, the French would have to address the problem, lack of suitable French manpower notwithstanding. The option of finding the necessary numbers from the planned establishments of the eleven divisions was one which the French did not want to consider: the implications of this were that the number of divisions would have to be reduced, and it was readily apparent to AFHQ that the French wanted the maximum number of combat units with which to redeem their honour on the battlefield. To many of the white soldiers who had escaped from France to fight for its liberty, the idea of serving in support units which dealt with administration or maintenance functions was unacceptable: there was little glory in being a vehicle mechanic. The French solution was to rely on their Anglo-American allies, who had the technological expertise and the manpower to man the service units while the French got on with the fighting. There was another reason behind the French thinking: many of their senior officers were technologically illiterate; they had no grasp of the importance of such knowledge in modern warfare and did not understand that this form of support was essential. It was a reflection on French performance in 1940, and it was a shortcoming that was to endure for the remainder of the war. Even when fighting in North West Europe in the ensuing years, the French had to be supported by United States service units.

With no immediate agreement forthcoming on how the support elements were to be found – the French refused to address the problem, preferring instead to propose that the planned eleven divisions be increased to twelve – Eisenhower threatened not to commit French forces 'even in Metropolitan France'[11] unless they were completely self-sustaining. While this dispute continued the Americans halted shipments of matériel until a decision was taken on whether combat or support units were being equipped. Eisenhower proposed recommending to the War Department that equipment for two armoured and one infantry division be removed from the programme; manpower for the French service units could be found from these formations. His hope was that Giraud would be forced to address the problem. He then learned, informally, that the French had come up with a counter-proposal to eliminate only two divisions – one armoured, one infantry – which would produce the support elements for the remaining nine. There was, however, a disagreement within the French camp on the numbers of specialists that could be found from these sources. The French General Staff thought that it would be virtually impossible to find enough for eleven divisions (147,500 Frenchmen would be required); General Giraud's staff anticipated that there would be a pool of 189,250 men available, once restructuring had been implemented. The essential difference between the two viewpoints was that one was based on quality, the other on quantity.

AFHQ had come to a decision regarding the future employment of the French corps. They were to be used in self-sustaining increments as soon as they were ready, serving with other Allied forces. On 8 December 1944 an American-equipped formation, the 2nd Moroccan Infantry Division together with the 4th Group of Tabors (a regiment of goumiers) was committed to combat in Italy. It was to reinforce VI (US) Corps. The 3rd Algerian Infantry Division was en route to join the Moroccans. Despite the debate about service troops the French were being pushed forward, partly because it had been agreed that they should gain battle experience in Italy before the campaign began to liberate France. The fact that French divisions were now being brought into action demonstrated the success of the rearmament programme: it had taken just seven months from the first shipments of matériel arriving to equip and train the Moroccan Division, and more formations were in the pipeline.

The question of service units aside, there were other factors affecting the modernization of the French divisions. It has already been noted that supplies had not arrived in sufficient quantity for all of them and the situation was exacerbated when the French decided to divert some of the matériel to units that were not part of the re-armament programme. These included four Moroccan tabor groups which were preparing for deployment to Italy, and which represented a total of some 13,000 troops. In addition, there was an assortment of other units – a brigade of spahis, a commando battalion, and so on. These had eaten into the amount of equipment sent from the United States, leaving the 'programme' formations even shorter of the necessary matériel to ready them for war. If this was not enough, there was still one division – the 1st Motorized Infantry Division – which was not part of the programme. The *1e Division Motorisée d'Infanterie* (1e DMI) was a Free French formation which had been, and still was, equipped by the British. It was included in the French order of battle, but was not part of the re-armament programme. However, Giraud wanted to send this division to Italy, as much for reasons of French politics (its presence there would help build unity with the Gaullists) as for its military qualities (it contained a high percentage of Foreign Legion units). AFHQ had requested a third division be nominated for Italy, and this was it. However, neither General Alexander nor General Clark were prepared to accept its service with the Fifth Army unless it was equipped with American matériel (although such constraints were not applied when British formations came under Fifth Army command; these, however, were generally whole corps rather than individual divisions, and the British had a support system for them). Alexander requested Giraud to nominate an alternative. His choice, the 9th Colonial Infantry Division, was in turn rejected by the French National Defence Committee, which took de Gaulle's side in the debate about which faction's troops would be represented in Italy. Franco-American relationships became even more strained; the time taken to re-equip and train the 1e Division would inevitably delay its departure for several months. Giraud ordered that the division would henceforth be included in the re-armament programme, but the time taken to prepare it meant that it could not go to Italy when requested; the third division to do so was the 4th Moroccan Mountain. 1e DMI would not join the *Corps expéditionnaire français* (CEF) until April 1944. The failure to despatch a third division until the end of February and the lack of reinforcements for a period of six weeks meant that General Juin was unable to exploit the successes his forces had achieved north of Cassino. It was the consequence of national and factional pride and the positioning of the two parties as they manoeuvred to gain power once France was liberated.

An question that had not been addressed since November 1942 was control of the French forces. During the Clark-Darlan negotiations it had been agreed that they would operate under French direction; there was no authority for AFHQ to issue orders, and Eisenhower had to rely on the French accepting his proposals voluntarily. The Americans may have re-armed the French but this did not automatically give them the power to use them as they saw fit. The incident of the selection of a third division for Italy highlighted the problem. Giraud's choice was over-ruled by the CFLN, so who was AFHQ to deal with on matters concerning the French forces? The delay in sending the third division to Italy had important military ramifications, and Eisenhower could not be forced to wait while his allies' internal differences held up the prosecution of the war. The CFLN had effectively removed Giraud's powers of negotiation. He had been appointed by the CFLN, but he only controlled the expeditionary forces, and once they had been committed overseas he lost command of them. AFHQ admitted that Giraud's authority was now 'negligible'.[12]

During the Cairo Conference the CCS had agreed that OVERLORD would be supported by landings in southern France (ANVIL, later DRAGOON); the majority of French forces would contribute to the latter operation. This reassured the French that they would participate in the liberation of their nation and removed concerns about the future employment of their armed forces; consequently they expressed themselves content to place these forces at the disposal of the CCS to be used by Eisenhower in consultation with the French High Command. The French reserved the right to appeal to the American and British governments, and the right of the French High Command to appeal to the Allied Commander-in-Chief, to ensure that French interests would be taken into account as completely as possible.

The situation regarding the service units to support the French divisions had still not been resolved. AFHQ became convinced that Giraud was avoiding the matter of reducing the eleven-division target to produce the required manpower, a conviction that was reinforced when they discovered that he had made a direct approach to General Marshall. The United States Chief of Staff had demonstrated his support for French rearmament, and it was to him that Giraud now turned with his preferred option of having the Americans man the support units. To break up three perfectly good French fighting divisions would, he argued, severely affect French morale and was unlikely to produce efficient service units considering the lack of skills and aptitude available. Meanwhile Eisenhower had taken the problem to de Gaulle, who appeared to be more sympathetic to the former's point of view.

As the new year approached, the time for a decision was becoming critical – it would take time to put into action a programme to provide service elements, regardless from whence they came. The urgency of the situation prompted Giraud to confirm that two divisions were to be deactivated to provide manpower for service units, a decision that the French National Defence Committee confirmed on 11 January 1944. It had come to this decision rather than deactivate one armoured and one infantry division, following the realization that it was only by these means that the demand for technical personnel could be met. The manpower thus released would provide service units and fill shortfalls in other infantry divisions, as well as staffing headquarters and base functions. French wishes notwithstanding, the Americans had no foreseeable employment for another armoured division (the fourth in the French order of battle). The terrain in southern France was not favourable for armour, and they could anticipate using only two there; a third, if required, could be used in the cross-Channel invasion. After some discussion, it was agreed that these infantry and armoured divisions would be retained at cadre strength only, the remainder of their manpower being dispersed as previously stated.

The establishment and training of French supply and service units were still well behind schedule to meet the planned operational dates of

ANVIL/DRAGOON, let alone for the Italian campaign. From the time matériel began arriving from the United States the problem had not been addressed by the French, and US equipment piled up in North African ports because the system could not cope. Ordnance units could not obtain the required spares, and much unfamiliar equipment was arriving that the French could not identify. They just did not know what to do with it, they did not have sufficient storage facilities, and their organization was inadequate. To assist, the Americans provided a small group of experts to set up and operate a stock control section but there was still no interest shown by the French, who appeared to expect the Americans to carry out the functions on their behalf. For the United States, the philosophy of American management following American equipment was a sensible development and the French were happy for the Americans to get on with it, particularly if it minimized the reduction of their combat forces. With as much as three-eighths of the combat strength of the Fifth Army expected to be French, the Americans were of the view that the same proportion of French service troops should be employed. Not only would their presence assist the American support services in Fifth Army, which had to cope with their own shortages, but the experience would prepare the French for their future employment during and after ANVIL.

In Italy the two French divisions were performing well, and the provision of service support became increasingly urgent. Despite discouraging reports, it was becoming apparent that the CEF had begun to recognize the problem and was taking its own steps to address it. Keen to participate in the fighting as much as possible, the French were equally keen to ensure that mistakes that hindered this ambition were rectified. Nonetheless, this bugbear was to continue.

In early January 1944 Eisenhower and some of his staff left the Mediterranean and the Allied command in the theatre was reorganized. With the hypersensitivity of the French high on the agenda, the new Supreme Allied Commander, General Wilson, called on de Gaulle, le Troquer (the Commissioner of War and Air), and Giraud. He later discussed ANVIL with General de Lattre de Tassigny. Wilson was not the only Allied officer giving attention to French matters. Reports had reached Marshall that Franco-American relations had deteriorated: the French claimed that United States officers were impatient, intolerant, officious and discourteous to the French, and belittled their efforts. The Deputy C-in-C and commanding general of NATOUSA, Lieutenant General Jacob ('Jake') Devers, reported back that, while misunderstandings existed, the complaints had been exaggerated and that examples of discourtesy were not widespread. French officers who had worked with the Americans on the re-armament programme agreed with Devers that Americans had generally been sympathetic with the French, although mutual misunderstandings because of language difficulties and national idiosyncrasies had sometimes led to impatience. If there was a complaint, Devers suggested, it was because the French were frustrated by the convoluted system through which their equipment requests had to pass. A second irritation was that the French felt that Washington promised more than Americans in theatre were prepared to give. The third complaint was that the Americans, while wanting the French to do more to build up their service units, had not provided equipment for them; and finally, the French forces in Italy were not receiving enough food. The last point, Devers reported, was down to inefficient planning by the French themselves. AFHQ would henceforth ensure that the CEF would receive the same rations as the Americans, and he had taken steps to rectify the other complaints.

The French forces that fought with the Fifth Army in Italy from early 1944 until they were withdrawn for ANVIL/DRAGOON had gone through a series of transformations since the outbreak of war in 1939. They had been defeated in 1940, then divided between those loyal to de Gaulle and those who kept their allegiance to the government in France. They had engaged in warfare between the two factions (and Vichy units had also fought against their current Anglo-American allies), and they were now – sometimes unhappily – working together to achieve the liberation of their homeland. With new equipment they were attempting to fit into a coalition led by the United States, in which they would serve alongside troops from a large number of countries, some of which they had considered to be enemies in the recent past.

They brought with them a mixture of ethnic groupings, customs and military strengths and weaknesses; as they had all been French-trained they had common procedures, in much the same way that British Commonwealth forces had. However, while this training had prepared them to work together, it had not prepared them to work with their allies from outside the French colonies. Whereas they had new equipment and had received training on how to use it, some of their senior officers (as in the armies of other nations) had yet to become acquainted with the changing nature of modern warfare. For the French, there were two weak spots: the emphasis that they placed on the fighting arms at the expense of developing the support services that were essential to maintaining them in the field; and the time that the majority of them had spent away from the modern battlefield (apart from some of the

Free French) while their allies and opponents had been learning new skills. Underlying these points ran the mutual suspicion between the Gaullists and the ex-Vichy commanders that was to endure throughout the war.

A final point. Eisenhower was criticized both during and after the time he spent as Commander-in-Chief in the Mediterranean for the amount of time he spent concentrating on political, rather than military, affairs. The problems of integrating the French into the Allied order of battle illustrate why this was so. The French Expeditionary Corps was to prove a valuable part of the Allied campaign to defeat the Germans in Italy, particularly during the breakthrough of the Gustav Line and the pursuit to Rome, but its path from 1940 had been far from smooth.

Notes

1. Schmitt, *The Bechuanaland Pioneers and Gunners*
2. Scheck, *Hitler's African Victims: The German Army Massacres of Black French Soldiers in 1940*
3. Vigneras, *Rearming the French*
4. Bimberg, *Augustin-Leon Guillaume's Goums in a Modern War*
5. Vigneras, op cit.
6. Ibid
7. Ibid
8. Ibid
9. Ibid
10. CCS 317, 18 Aug 43, QUADRANT Conf, quoted in Vigneras, op cit.
11. Vigneras, op cit.
12. Ibid

PART II – THE COALITION AT WAR

There is only one thing worse than fighting with allies –
and that is fighting without them.
Winston S. Churchill (1874–1965)

CHAPTER 6

The Commanders

Mark Clark

For its time in the Italian campaign the Fifth Army's history is inextricably linked to that of one man: Lieutenant General Mark Wayne Clark, who was its first Army commander and then Commander of 15th Army Group, of which the Fifth Army was part. While every general will leave his mark on the army he commands – for good or bad – Clark ensured that Fifth Army's successes were attributed to him: press reports were to be issued using the phrase 'Mark Clark's Fifth Army', and his name was firmly cemented to that of his army. One of the more controversial senior officers of the war, of all nationalities, Clark's actions and personal qualities still cause debate.

In trying to gauge Clark's abilities and personality, one encounters a widespread perception of him which is less than favourable; yet he achieved high rank, and must be rated as one of the top American commanders of the Second World War if only because he commanded his nation's forces in one of the theatres of war. Throughout his career, observers commented on his penchant for self-publicity, which was driven by his personal ambition. In his book, *Calculated Risk*, he portrayed himself as an agreeable self-deprecating man, and much the same impression is gained from his biographer, Martin Blumenson. The latter writer does not, however, shy away from reflecting the point made by many of Clark's senior officers who in their performance appraisals of him repeated the charge made by Bradley, that he was 'Very ambitious and somewhat inclined to seek publicity'.[1] Blumenson was not afraid to quote from Clark's contemporaries, including General Jacob Devers (Chief of the Army Field Forces, 1948, rating Clark in his appointment at that time as Commander of the Sixth US Army) who described him as 'A cold, distinguished, conceited, selfish, clever, intellectual, resourceful officer who secures excellent results quickly. Very ambitious. Superior performance.'[2] Winston Churchill once wrote that 'History will be kind to me, for I intend to write it'; Clark was of a similar frame of mind. Not only did he produce his own version of his life and career, he encouraged Martin Blumenson, who wrote his biography while he held the post of 'Mark W. Clark Visiting Professor of History' at the Citadel Military Academy in Charleston, where he spent no small amount of time talking to Clark and studying his personal papers. Many of Blumenson's comments could well have come, in fact they probably did, from the lips of Clark himself, particularly when referring to descriptions of some of the British officers with whom he served during the North African and Italian campaigns. General Harold Alexander was, for example, 'a peanut and feather duster', Brian Horrocks was 'somewhat patronizing'.[3] The inclination to place what today would be termed 'spin' on his actions extended to the introduction which Clark wrote for the *Fifth Army History*, which he caused to be written while the Italian campaign was still underway, in which he said that 'The American soldiers of Fifth Army who went ashore at Salerno on 9 September 1943 were the first Americans to plant themselves on the soil of Europe in this war. Our invasion virtually destroyed the Rome-Berlin Axis ...'[4] The point is made that – apart from the fact that American forces had been fully engaged in Sicily, which geographically and as part of the Italian state is surely part of Europe – the Italians had negotiated a separate armistice with the Allies on 3 September, the announcement of which was made to the world the evening before the Salerno landings. To claim that the Fifth Army was instrumental in destroying the Axis in Europe was disingenuous; it had already disintegrated.

The *Fifth Army History* throws very little light on the difficulties of coalition warfare, or indeed of the problems of leading and managing an international force. It is, as with Clark's own memoirs, largely focused on the actual fighting, with only a skim across the surface of what happened behind the front line: planning issues are not addressed in other than a superficial manner. No explanation is given, for example, of why the Army's two corps employed different tactics when landing at Salerno (the British X Corps went in under cover of a naval barrage, while the American VI Corps attempted a silent approach – as if the bombardment just to the north of their beaches would not arouse the defenders). Nor is any mention given of the reasons for two successive commanders of VI Corps, Major General Ernest J. Dawley at Salerno and Major General John P. Lucas at Anzio, being relieved of their commands. And no justification is given for Clark's deviation from the plan for the breakout from Anzio, when he ordered a change of priorities and advanced on Rome rather than sticking with the plan to cut the German withdrawal from the Gustav Line as drawn up by

Alexander's staff. The *History* does, however, throw light on a multitude of statistics on troop numbers, orders of battle, losses – of every conceivable piece of equipment, as well as of casualties – and it gives a broad overview of events and copies of the principal operations orders. It is the proverbial curate's egg, 'good in parts'. It is definitely uncritical of the Army's commander, Clark.

The controversy over Mark Clark (who was known to friends and family as Wayne) arises partly because of his personality and character, but also because some of his decisions were questionable and are still the subject of debate nearly seventy years after he made them. Born the son of an army officer in 1896, he went to West Point in 1913, graduating in April 1917, when he was commissioned into the US Infantry. On 1 May 1918 he arrived in France with the temporary rank of captain and in command of a company of the 11th Infantry. Six weeks later he was Commanding Officer of that regiment's 3rd Battalion, having assumed that appointment when the CO became ill. One year after being commissioned, his career was already showing promise. Clark's battalion command and his combat experience were brief, however: on 14 June he suffered wounds from shrapnel as his battalion was entering the front line for the first time and he was hospitalized until the end of July. Deemed unfit to return to the infantry, he was transferred to supply duties as a staff officer. Like many American officers who were to reach high rank during the Second World War, Clark had little combat experience to fit him for the positions he was to achieve later in life.

It was his skill as a staff officer that was to further his career. During the inter-war years he spent time in a number of administrative and command appointments appropriate to his rank until, as a major, he was posted to the Command and General Staff College at Fort Leavenworth in August 1933. In October 1935 he was Assistant Chief of Staff G-2 (responsible for intelligence) and G-3 (operations) in VII Corps Area Headquarters; a year later he became a student at the Army War College in Washington DC. After ten months, he was again an Assistant Chief of Staff G-2 and G-3, this time with the 3rd Division. Here he came into contact with Brigadier General George C. Marshall, who commanded the Division's 5 Brigade. The two men worked together and Marshall became Clark's mentor, the latter seeking advice from the senior officer as he developed his plans for the preparation of the Division's personnel and units for war. It was a relationship which was to stand Clark in good stead.

One of the exercises planned by Clark during this time involved Marshall's brigade, in which it was to make a night manoeuvre to turn the 'enemy's' flank, after which it was to mount an attack on its positions. Marshall chose not to wait until daybreak to launch his assault, which would have been the orthodox practice. Clark, acting as an umpire for the exercise, praised Marshall's decision despite the opinions of others who faulted it for not complying with current doctrine. The two officers maintained contact thereafter. Another officer who was to become closely associated with Clark also reappeared on the scene: Eisenhower, at that time a lieutenant colonel serving in the Philippines, was interested in Clark's thoughts on tactics and renewed his acquaintanceship. He had first met Clark at West Point where he was two years senior to Clark, and his company's cadet sergeant.

It would be unfair, and untrue, to claim that the senior ranks of the American Army during the Second World War were simply filled by a clique of officers who had all worked together in the inter-war years. Given the size of the Army before it went through a rapid programme of expansion as war approached, and the training and promotion system that sent select groups of officers to courses at the Command and General Staff College and then to the Army War College to prepare them for high command, it was inevitable that the majority of commanding generals during the war years knew each other. This familiarity naturally allowed officers the opportunity to form opinions on each other's capabilities as they worked and studied together, for good or bad, and these opinions were to play a part in selection for appointments once war broke out. Apart from this background knowledge, the comparatively small size of the pre-war US Army was to expand enormously, an expansion which was to demand a corresponding increase in the number of general officers to be given command appointments. It was not unreasonable for those who had spent their earlier years being selected and trained by the Army for such roles to get the key jobs – there was little alternative. 'Clique' is too strong an expression for the group that emerged, especially when one considers the animosity that was to become apparent between some of them during the war, such as Patton and Bradley.

The outbreak of war in Europe in 1939, followed by the fall of France in June the following year, led the United States' Government to address the question of the nation's military readiness. Under the command of General George C. Marshall, now the Chief of Staff of the US Army, a General Headquarters was activated which controlled the four armies in the continental United States. Amongst a number of additional responsibilities GHQ covered the training of field forces for combat, a task which Marshall assigned to his Chief of Staff, Major General Lesley McNair, who had been Commandant of the Command and General Staff College. McNair was faced with the problem of preparing thousands of soldiers for war: the authorized strength of the US Army increased from 227,000 to 375,000 at the end of June 1940; a year later it was 1,326,577-strong, and by the end of the war its manpower was 8,157,386. From being, in 1939, the seventeenth largest army in the world (ranking below Romania) it was to grow by a factor of forty-four by the end of the war. The intent was to activate three to four new divisions every month from March 1942. It was an enormous task. Ninety-one divisions were mobilized during the war: sixty-eight infantry, one mountain, sixteen armoured, five airborne, and two cavalry divisions.[5] The difficulties produced by such an explosion of numbers were considerable: not only did training of fresh recruits and new formations have to proceed in tandem with the preparation of existing formations for service overseas, there was a dearth of experienced junior officers and NCOs to carry out the training. In 1940, the year of mobilization, the army had only 14,000 professional officers, and many of these were over-age. The average age of majors was nearly forty-eight, and in the National Guard nearly a quarter of first lieutenants were older than forty. Consequently, training officers and NCOs were drawn from units already earmarked for duties outside the continental United States, a practice which placed an additional strain on those formations. Many of the soldiers lacked confidence because they lacked experience; at the senior levels the problem was the lack of skill in commanding large formations. National Guard officers (and some Regulars) were sometimes overage and unqualified, and among the first group's ranks were political appointees of dubious military competence. No serving officer had commanded a formation as large as a division during the First World War, and among some senior officers there was an unwillingness – or inability – to learn from the past and to introduce both fresh thinking and tactics to the battlefield on which American servicemen might be expected to fight. In 1941, despite the lessons of the First World War, let alone those from *blitzkrieg* that were emerging from Europe, the head of the US Cavalry maintained in evidence to Congress that four horsemen could gallop unscathed across open countryside to destroy a machine-gun nest.[6]

The evolutionary process through which the organization of the United States Army was passing compounded these difficulties. The move from 'square' to 'triangular' divisions, mentioned earlier, reduced the strength of riflemen in an infantry division by twenty-five per cent and also removed two brigade headquarters. The manpower saved by this reorganization only went part of the way towards meeting the requirements for the new divisions which were being raised, and the challenge of finding sufficient soldiers while also ensuring that American industry moved to a war footing was no small one.

The principal architect for the plan which put the process in place to achieve this was Clark. Having been promoted lieutenant colonel on 1 July 1940, he was given the job of a staff officer in General Headquarters, Washington. Less than a year later he became Assistant Chief of Staff G-3 GHQ, and on 4 August 1941 he was promoted to the rank of brigadier general, becoming Deputy Chief of Staff for Training in December.

This rather bland-sounding list of promotions and appointments conceals the reasons that led to them. Clark was fortunate enough – and skilled enough – to come to the attention of General McNair. While a student at the Army War College, in a class with Mathew Ridgeway, Walter Bedell Smith and Geoffrey Keyes, all of whom he was to work with in the future, Clark was tasked with examining the structure of infantry divisions and with making recommendations for improvements. The paper produced by Clark and his syndicate recommended reducing the size of the division and doing away with the brigade command level. These recommendations were seen by McNair, and foreshadowed the reorganization that eventually took place.

An extremely able administrator Clark may have been, but his performance in other military skills was questioned by some. While Clark's promotion to the rank of brigadier general reflected the high opinion of his superiors it was to rankle with some of his contemporaries and also with officers who saw him leapfrogging over them up the promotion ladder. Eight months later Clark was promoted again. The new major general was appointed Chief of Staff of Army Ground Forces working for General McNair in one of three new commands into which General Headquarters had been reorganized.

June 1942 saw Clark and Eisenhower, now head of the War Plans Division, in England liaising with the British on staging US forces there in preparation for taking the war into continental Europe. During this trip they met Churchill and his advisors and discussed options for an invasion, as well as plans for standardizing training for both nations' armies, a necessary factor for co-ordination in the coalition. Churchill was to take a liking to Clark, and dubbed him the 'American Eagle'. In Churchill's view Clark was the epitome of the United States soldier in his looks and martial bearing; Churchill, however, was noted for his inclination to judge generals' abilities on outward appearances. He considered Alexander the 'beau ideal' of an aristocratic general in the mould of Marlborough, despite the reservations others, such as Brooke, had about his abilities. Clark's and Alexander's careers were to come together in Italy; the combination of the two men's skills as generals and leaders was to prove both interesting and controversial.

Clark's relationship with Eisenhower was to develop further during the ensuing months. While Clark held the appointment of COS Army Ground Forces Marshall asked him his opinion as to which officer should go to the United Kingdom as Commander of a new headquarters, European Theatre of Operations, United States Army (ETOUSA). His response was to nominate Dwight D. Eisenhower, a choice which Marshall had already decided upon, unbeknownst to Clark. In his turn, Eisenhower had recommended Clark for the position of Commanding General of the United States II Corps, the formation which was to command all American ground forces in the United Kingdom. Both appointments were confirmed.

As Commander II (US) Corps, Clark was responsible for training American forces and for planning the invasion of mainland Europe, tasks for which his previous career fitted him well. However, Roosevelt's decision to support the British proposal for landings in North Africa increased the planning element of Clark's work and led to him relinquishing the Corps command to focus on Operation TORCH. The majority of the forces to be employed in the operation were to be American, and it appeared logical that the commander in chief should also be American. Eisenhower was given the job. The pattern was established whereby the Combined Chiefs of Staff appointed theatre commanders according to the numerical strength of the nationalities involved, with deputies of the other nationality. For TORCH, however, because of the political sensitivities involved in landing on French territory, the CCS also appointed an American as Deputy Commander-in-Chief: Clark. This structure was not followed subsequently, and Allied Force Headquarters, which commanded formations from both the United States and Great Britain, had staff officers from both nations working together, with section heads from one nation and their deputies being from the other. Clark's appointment as Deputy was explained by Eisenhower, who wrote that it was made in case he, Eisenhower, should be incapacitated for some reason and that his immediate subordinate had to take command. This would maintain the fiction that TORCH was a 'practically exclusively American operation'.[7]

Among the officers with whom Eisenhower and Clark worked was Major General George S. Patton, designated Commander of the Western Task Force for the landings. Patton was a friend of Eisenhower, but had a more jaundiced view of Clark. The relationships between Clark and his fellow officers, both American and Allied, are worth considering when measuring his status as a commander, again of both American and Allied forces. Clark's *Calculated Risk* repays careful reading and comparisons made with writings of those who knew and worked with him. It is readily apparent that Clark's view of his own abilities and his relationships with others, or at least his portrayals of them, do not always mirror their perceptions of him. His description of Alexander mentioned earlier does not equate to that which he gave in his own book, where the British general is described as an outstanding leader whose friendship Clark valued. In similar vein, Patton was someone with whom Clark got on 'splendidly'. Patton's stance on this was rather different, although he was careful not to let Clark realize it. To Patton, Clark was 'Too damned slick', and 'made my flesh creep'.[8] He was also someone who was 'more preoccupied with enhancing his own future than with winning the war'. Some of this may be written off as personal and professional jealousy, with one American general envious of another's success. However, the accusation that Clark was obsessed with his own career was one that recurs; Patton was not alone in his judgement, and it is one which resurfaces as the story of the Fifth Army continues.

For Operation TORCH to succeed the cooperation of the Vichy French was essential, but their relationships with Britain were at best strained following the attacks on the French fleet earlier in the war at Mers El Kebir and Dakar, attacks which had been ordered by Churchill to prevent the fleet falling into German hands after the fall of France. It was therefore decided that initial approaches to the French in Morocco would be made by American officers who were familiar with the invasion plans. This task was entrusted to Clark, who with four staff officers landed in Algeria by submarine on 22 October 1942. Their adventures read more like a thriller than an episode of diplomacy which helped secure Vichy support, for Clark had to hide in a cellar to avoid detection by authorities whose sympathies may not have been assured; he later made his escape by folding canoe back to the submarine – but at the price of losing his trousers and the money he had been given for emergencies. While the meeting was a success, the lengthy report which Clark sent back (and which must have been a trial to encrypt!) was somewhat melodramatic. It included irrelevant information about hiding in an 'empty repeat empty wine cellar', and even Marshall became irritated by what he called the 'cheap details' of Clark's expedition: 'There was more about his loss of pants and of his money than there was of the serious phase of the matter.' This comment might be a fair criticism of Clark's whole book, *Calculated Risk.*

With the promise of French support achieved TORCH went comparatively smoothly despite resistance from some French forces.

Clark's work in planning TORCH and in securing French assistance played its part in convincing Eisenhower that Clark was worthy of an army command. On 11 November 1942 he was promoted to lieutenant general, the youngest man to reach this rank in the American Army. Reports in the press at home of his submarine mission and the subsequent achievements gave him prominence – which again earned him the animosity of some of his colleagues, but which suited him well. He had travelled to Algiers to negotiate with the French and on 22 November had signed an agreement with Admiral Darlan, the de facto Vichy leader in North Africa, which secured the armistice in Algeria and French Morocco.

At AFHQ Clark had to tackle the practical difficulties of coalition warfare at the operational level. Clark found working with British staff officers, who followed their own procedures, too slow. As at the Chiefs of Staff level, the British devoted effort to time-consuming analysis and preparation which was at variance with the American practice. He also objected to some American forces being placed under the orders of Lieutenant General Kenneth Anderson, the British commander of the Tunisian theatre, a situation which was eventually rectified when the Americans were returned to the United States' chain of command. These issues did not promise well for coalition cooperation or for Clark's later role in commanding an army which included large numbers of troops from other than American nationalities. On 4 January 1943 Clark was appointed commander of the newly-established US Fifth Army, created to prepare for contingencies in the theatre's rear areas, and for the future invasion of Europe. It was an appointment that he believed he deserved; Eisenhower recorded that Clark wanted the job more than the one he held as Deputy Commander in Chief. Despite Fifth Army initially being a training organization, and there being the probability of commanding a corps which would be in combat in the near future, Clark held out for the command of an army – he had already commanded II Corps. The choice for the job was between Clark and Patton; Clark already held the rank of lieutenant general, whereas Patton was still a major general, and if Fifth Army was, indeed, destined to be a training formation, then Clark's background was ideal.[9] Given foresight, commanding the Fifth Army with what lay before it as the American contribution to a campaign that the Joint Chiefs of Staff in Washington did not wholeheartedly support, may not have been the choice Clark might have made. Whereas he recognized that the decisive blow against Germany would come via the cross-Channel invasion, the date for this had yet to be set and was some distance into the future; command of the Fifth Army was an immediately achievable target for the ambitious officer. Taking it, however, meant that he missed the opportunity of an alternative job – that of being sent to London to prepare the OVERLORD landings. Had he gone to London, he would have been in the ideal position to move on to a key position in the North West Europe campaign, which was to be where the United States' Chiefs of Staff channelled their main effort. The London job went to Bradley, who moved on to command the First US Army for the invasion. Instead, Clark had relegated himself to what was later to be called 'The Backwater War'.

Clark had risen rapidly. Only two years earlier he had been a newly-promoted lieutenant colonel working at a desk in Washington. However, the twenty-two years between his command of an infantry company during the First World War and his appointment as Commander II Corps had been largely spent at staff duties: his command experience at company, battalion – for two or three days – and corps levels came to less than eighteen months out of a total career which stretched back twenty-six years. Now he was an army commander. On the positive side, he was a professional officer whose planning and organizational duties had been sufficiently well performed to earn him his appointment.

Clark did not waste time before pursuing his own ends. On 4 January 1943 General Sir Alan Brooke, Chief of the Imperial General Staff, noted in his diary that Clark – 'very ambitious and unscrupulous' – had apparently been 'egging on Giraud (the high commissioner of French North and West Africa) to state that French troops could not fight under British'. This he did in an attempt to be appointed commander of the Tunisian front. In a post-war reflection, written in 1950, Brooke went on to observe that once Eisenhower came to hear of this manoeuvring, he relieved Clark of his appointment as his Deputy Commander and sent him to command reserve forces in Morocco; this raised Eisenhower in Brooke's estimation, but Clark was to continue to fail to impress him.[10]

Clark's first real experience of combat came at Salerno, where he commanded Fifth US Army. He was not alone, particularly amongst American generals, in finding himself facing the enemy for the first time while in command of an army engaged in a major operation.

Alexander

Clark's dealings with his superior, the Commander of 15th Army Group, Sir Harold Alexander, play a central part in any analysis of Fifth Army's performance. Like Clark, Alexander's career had been meteoric. But whereas

Clark's had been founded on staff work, Alexander had built his reputation on the battlefield – or more accurately, the plural: battlefields – of the Western Front, the Baltic, India, Burma, North Africa and, most recently, Sicily. Unlike Clark, whose experience of leading forces from nations other than his own (and that experience, as we have seen, was limited), Alexander had worked with, and led, multinational forces for some time.

In August 1914 the then Lieutenant Alexander had departed for France with his regiment, the Irish Guards, and was soon involved in the Battles of Mons and First Ypres, being wounded during the second battle. On returning to duty during the autumn of 1915 Alexander progressed to command at every level from a company to a brigade in the ensuing four years, becoming temporary and then permanent battalion commander, leading the 2nd Battalion of the Irish Guards at the Third Battle of Ypres at the age of twenty-six. He took charge of 4 (Guards) Brigade during the British retreat of March 1918 when its commander was gassed, before being posted to command X Corps School in May 1918.

In 1919 and 1920 Alexander, with the temporary rank of lieutenant colonel, led the Baltic German *Landeswehr* in the Latvian War of Independence. He commanded German and Baltic soldiers (with a German chief of staff) in the successful fight to drive the Bolsheviks from Latgalia. His experience of working with foreign forces grew as he served in Turkey and Gibraltar, and he was made substantive lieutenant colonel in 1922 at the age of thirty-one; the average age for this promotion at that time was forty to forty-two. In 1926 he went to the Staff College, was promoted colonel in 1928 and appointed commandant of the Irish Guards and its regimental district, and in 1930 went to the Imperial Defence College as a student. Here two of his instructors, Alan Brooke and Bernard Montgomery, were unimpressed with his performance, the latter claiming that Alexander 'had no brains'.[11]

If Alexander displayed no enthusiasm for staff work he more than compensated for it with his practical abilities and common sense. He also had the natural ability to instil loyalty and affection in his subordinates, an ability which was strengthened by his self-deprecating and patrician attitude. He was the pre-war ideal of a British Army officer, the aristocratic Guardsman. He was cool, immaculately dressed, always urbane and gave the impression of being the amateur who nonetheless produced the professional solution to whatever problem occurred.

From the Defence College and an appointment as GSO1 Northern Command Alexander moved to India as commander of the Nowshera Brigade on the North West Frontier. He took part in two frontier campaigns in 1935, and in 1938 was appointed GOC 1st Division. His career could hardly have been better tailored to fitting him for his later role as commander of multinational forces.

The outbreak of war in 1939 meant that 1st Division deployed to France with I Corps, part of the British Expeditionary Force. For the defence of Dunkirk Alexander took command of I Corps, which was responsible for the perimeter defences. In this appointment, despite Churchill having given his permission for the rearguard to surrender if necessary, Alexander announced his intention to extricate his command and to surrender no part of it. In this endeavour he displayed a firm control of the situation and of his forces, despite earning the disapproval of some of the French when the evacuation proceeded. It was an action which they felt was in the interests of Britain but not of the Anglo-French Alliance. It was, nevertheless, a success which earned him a reputation as a field commander of no small ability, and he was confirmed in the rank of lieutenant general in July 1940 and appointed GOC Southern Command, responsible for the defence of south-west England. He still failed to impress Brooke, who openly criticized his performance during an anti-invasion exercise in 1941.

From England Alexander went to the Far East as GOC Burma, where once again he had to deal with a retreat, having to salvage the disaster that had befallen the British following the fall of Singapore. The task of halting the Japanese was well-nigh impossible, but Alexander made the best of a bad job. While in Burma Alexander had to deal with the touchy American General, Joseph ('Vinegar Joe') Stilwell, yet more experience of the difficulties of international cooperation which he dealt with in his customary patient and diplomatic manner. He returned to the United Kingdom in the summer of 1942 where he had been selected to command the First Army in Operation TORCH. However, this appointment was overtaken by events in the Western Desert, where both Churchill and Brooke felt that General Auchinleck's double-hatted role as Commander-in-Chief Middle East and GOC Eighth Army (he had replaced General Richie and personally commanded the Army to stop the *Panzerarmee Afrika* at the First Battle of El Alamein) was not producing the results they wanted. Auchinleck had annoyed Churchill by maintaining that it would take six months to prepare the Eighth Army to mount an offensive after it had exhausted itself at El Alamein; Churchill wanted an early British victory before TORCH. Alexander became GOC Middle East, with Lieutenant General Gott nominated as GOC Eighth Army. The latter was killed when his aircraft was shot down before taking up the appointment, and Montgomery became Eighth Army Commander.

Alexander's appointment owed much to his ability to bring conflicting personalities together into an effective team. Brooke felt that Alexander would allow Montgomery sufficient freedom to perform at his best, but was later to urge Alex to increase his 'grip' on his subordinate generals to ensure that they were more proactive.

After the Eighth Army's victory at the Second Battle of El Alamein and its advance into Tunisia to meet the Anglo-American forces which had landed for the TORCH operation, Alexander was given the appointment of Ground Forces Commander in North Africa and then, in February 1943, GOC 18 Army Group, the unified command under which the Allied forces were to operate. In this role, and as Deputy to the Supreme Commander, he reported to Eisenhower at Allied Forces Headquarters.

The immediate task facing him was to resolve the difficulties encountered by Lieutenant General Sir Kenneth Anderson, who commanded the First (British) Army in advancing from the west. Here the landscape was mountainous and a different problem from that of the Western Desert, and the difficulties were exacerbated by the American antagonism towards Anderson whom they found to be cold and detached. On 14 February II (US) Corps was routed by Rommel at the Kasserine Pass. Alexander was unimpressed with what he found of the American forces – in his opinion their training was too defensive and little urgency was displayed when attacking. In a confidential letter to Brooke he noted that unless something was done about it, then little assistance would be forthcoming from the Americans in the future. Nor did he find the American generals – Eisenhower, his Chief of Staff Bedell Smith, and Patton – professional. He did, however, warn British officers against assuming a superior attitude towards their ally, but they should adopt an attitude which would encourage greater cooperation and professionalism. Warnings aside, the Americans became suspicious that they were being patronized, a feeling which was to persist for some time. It was fed by a latent Anglophobia among some United States officers, including Bradley and Patton – and Clark. On the other side of the alliance, the suspicions held by some British commanders that their American brothers in arms were not quite up to the mark also lingered for longer than was strictly accurate. The American ability to learn and improve was underestimated, to the detriment of relationships. Alexander's efforts to speed up the pace of American operations by giving a succession of orders to Patton – which the latter regarded as overly detailed and contradictory, in that Alexander's plan kept changing – proved frustrating, and the decision to give American formations supporting roles to gain experience was resented by their commanders. The criticism of Alexander for becoming too involved in giving orders to American forces is interesting, for he was later to attract censure from Brooke for failing to 'grip' his army commanders in Italy. Whether or not his 'hands-off' style of generalship in Sicily and Italy was as a result of his Tunisian experience is debatable, but he certainly adopted a different style with the Americans after it.

With friction developing in the Allied camp Alexander and Eisenhower found themselves having to intervene to calm Anglo-American tensions in their respective headquarters. While Eisenhower worked hard to build Anglo-American relationships, his efforts were not always appreciated by his colleagues. Patton noted in his diary that Eisenhower was more British than the British[12] and he and Bradley were incensed that the Alexander was planning that the British should capture both Bizerta and Tunis, excluding II (US) Corps (apart from 9th Division) from participating in the final defeat of the Axis forces in Africa. The two officers made representations to Eisenhower, which led him to urge Alexander to make use of II Corps right up until the campaign's conclusion. A fresh plan was produced which increased the American role: part of II Corps and half of the 1st US Armored Division would participate in the capture of Bizerta.

The Tunisian fighting left one aspect of coalition warfare unresolved: the French were, as yet, unable to unite in a common cause. Gaullist troops refused to participate in the victory parade in Tunis alongside those who were loyal to Giraud.

The comparisons between Alexander and Clark are evident. One, the aristocratic, confident, well-travelled officer who had commanded troops from many nations in battles at locations which stretched across the globe; the other, the ambitious American who had minimal command and combat experience, but who was a highly professional staff officer. Each had formed opinions about the other, and about their fellow officers and armies; both were to find, if they had not already experienced the fact, that commanding coalition armies was far from straightforward.

Notes

1. Blumenson, *Mark Clark*
2. Ibid
3. Ibid

THE COMMANDERS

4. Starr, *Fifth Army History* Vol I

5. Greenfield, Palmer & Wiley, *US Army in World War II, The Organization of Ground Combat Troops*

6. Atkinson, *An Army at Dawn*

7. Eisenhower, *Crusade in Europe*

8. D'Este, *Patton – A Genius for War*

9. Blumenson, op cit.

10. Danchev & Todman (Eds), *War Diaries 1939–1945, Field Marshal Lord Alanbrooke*

11. Holden Reid, 'Alexander'. In Keegan, *Churchill's Generals*

12. Quoted in Atkinson, *An Army at Dawn*

CHAPTER 7

The Fifth US Army

The Fifth US Army was constituted on 1 December 1942 by a letter to General Eisenhower in his capacity as Commanding General of the European Theatre of Operations. The Army's original composition came from troops available in North Africa: the Western Task Force, which had sailed directly from the United States for the landings at Casablanca on 8 November 1941, was disbanded and contributed I (US) Armored Corps. II (US) Corps, which had landed at Oran on the same date, minus those reinforcements that it had taken under command for the TORCH landings, was also re-assigned. More troops came from 'any other available sources', which included XII Air Support Command.[1] Command of the army was to go to Lieutenant General Mark W. Clark, who was to surrender his appointment as Deputy Commander in Chief, Allied Forces.

From its inception, Fifth Army was involved with French forces. Its first missions were to make ready a 'well organized, well equipped and mobile striking force' trained for amphibious operations, and to work with the French to ensure the security of the areas of French Morocco and Algeria that fell within its responsibility. Fifth Army was also to assist in the organization, equipping and training of French forces. Clark established his headquarters in a girls' school in Oujda, Morocco, where he activated the army at one minute past midnight on 5 January 1943.

With training featuring so prominently in its initial tasks, the Fifth Army established a number of schools in which to inculcate the lessons learned from TORCH. These included Invasion, Airborne, Leadership and Battle Training, Field Officers' Training, Tank Destroyer Training, Engineer Training, and Air Observation Post Training Centres; plus the French Training Section. This last unit (which did not come into operation until May 1943) had to train the personnel of five French divisions to handle American equipment and to provide first- and second-line maintenance.

In addition to its training tasks, Fifth Army had to prepare to occupy Spanish Morocco should Spain enter the war on Germany's side, or if Spain failed to resist a German occupation of its territory. This latter possibility was considered to be a viable threat, the German purpose in carrying it out being seen as a move to seal the Straits of Gibraltar to prevent Allied access to the Mediterranean. During the time that much of the coast of North Africa had been in Axis hands the movement of Allied shipping had been greatly restricted; once the German and Italian armies had been cleared from Tunisia the route to Suez was virtually free of interference by their air and naval forces, and introducing German forces to Spain would re-impose the Allied shipping difficulties. The Fifth Army planners were also involved in preparing operations against Sardinia (BRIMSTONE), and the Italian mainland (Operations BARRACUDA, GANGWAY, MUSKET and AVALANCHE). Only the last of these, the codename for the Salerno landings, was to come to fruition. As is often the case, much effort was put into planning operations that never took place.

Although the invasion of Italy followed closely on from the conquest of Sicily and may be regarded historically as a sequel to it, from the point of view of the Grand Strategy of the war there is a great division between the two operations. The conquest of Sicily marked the conclusion of the North African campaigns which cleared the Axis forces from the southern shores of the Mediterranean Sea. The invasion of Italy was part of the next phase of Grand Strategy, which was targeted at removing Germany from the war by way of the cross-Channel invasion. Italy would no longer be high on the priority list for men and matériel; operations here would be subsidiary to the preparations for OVERLORD, and the armies which had been successful in Africa would be broken up and selected divisions would be removed from the Mediterranean theatre and redeployed to the United Kingdom. Those formations that remained to carry out the campaign included many that were understrength or not fully trained or equipped.

The clear break between the Sicilian and Italian campaigns is reflected in the differences in the objectives that the Combined Chiefs of Staff had for the two operations. For the former the intention was clear cut and definite – firstly, to make the Mediterranean line of communications more secure; secondly, to divert German pressure from the Soviet front; and thirdly, to intensify pressure on Italy.[2] The possibility of removing the enemy forces which defended Sicily from the Axis order of battle by cutting their escape route to mainland Italy was not seriously attempted. For Italy the CCS informed Eisenhower that the major strike against the Axis would be made in North West Europe, and that he should plan to remove Italy from the war and to tie down the maximum number of German divisions with the purpose of keeping them away from Normandy. Taking Italy out of the war would play its part in this, for Italy had about two million men under arms in some sixty divisions; these were not necessarily first-class troops, but they were deployed in garrisons in southern France (seven divisions) and the Balkans (thirty-two divisions), as well as in many anti-aircraft and coastal defence units in both areas. Their removal would force the Germans to replace them with their own forces, which could now not be employed against OVERLORD.

The CCS also set forth a general pattern of Mediterranean operations for 1943–44, dividing it into three main phases: (1) the elimination of Italy from the war and the establishment of air bases as far north as the Rome area, and, if feasible, including the Ancona area; (2) the capture of Sardinia and Corsica; and (3) the eventual entry of Anglo-American forces and the bulk of the re-equipped French forces into southern France.[3]

The CCS orders to remove Italy from the war could only be achieved by invading the mainland. The intelligence staff believed that capturing Sicily would not be sufficient.[4] Nor would taking Sardinia guarantee Italy's capitulation – it had to be the mainland itself. In any event, even should Italy surrender once its islands fell, it would be necessary to occupy Italy to prevent the Germans moving into the country in strength. For Alexander the obvious way forward was to invade, and to do so in such a way that the Allied force was as concentrated as possible – the forthcoming withdrawal of formations to the United Kingdom, together with the requirement to tie down yet more for garrison and defensive purposes elsewhere in the Middle East, left the Allies with less than the optimum force levels for Italy; as Alexander pointed out in his report on the campaign, the Allied forces 'never at any time enjoyed any but the slenderest margin of superiority over the Germans, and usually not even that, and, above all, the invasion of the West was never deprived of any resources in men or materials by the needs of the operations in Italy'. To compound the difficulties, the CCS were unable to define any geographical objectives because the campaign in Italy would be defined by the outcome of Sicily – the factors which would shape the later campaign were not yet clear. The very geography of Italy was ready-made for defence with its long 'leg' bearing difficult mountains running down its length, rivers running across its width, and many places where nature could be reinforced to produce defensive lines which would prove to be almost unbreakable. What man had been able to make in the years before the invasion to improve communications by building roads through the mountains could be undone in a matter of less than a day with the aid of modern explosives.

From Alexander's perspective as commander of 15th Army Group, operations in Italy would be determined by geography – which was ready-made for defence. Where nature had not provided readily defensible positions, the enemy was sure to reinforce their lines by demolishing the communication system which previous generations had striven to put in place. The roads and bridges that had taken years to build could be removed in a matter of hours by explosives, and it would take far longer to replace them in order to facilitate an Allied advance; certainly not swiftly enough to guarantee keeping the Germans on the back foot and unable to construct fresh defences farther back.

On the positive side, the Allies were permitted a measure of flexibility by their amphibious capabilities – so long as they remained available and were not withdrawn for OVERLORD. There was a constraint on their use, however – that of the range of air cover. Having regard to the vulnerability of naval vessels, evidenced by the losses of the *Prince of Wales* and the *Repulse* to Japanese aircraft off Malaya earlier in the war, Alexander was not about to risk a repeat in the Mediterranean. Whereas in the Pacific large numbers of American aircraft carriers were able to provide cover, no such situation pertained in the Mediterranean: carriers were few. The Fleet Air Arm capability could provide a maximum of eighty sorties on the first day of an operation. The sortie numbers dropped each day thereafter, and after three days were negligible.[5] Spitfire range (with 90-gallon tanks) was 180 miles from north-east Sicily, once airfields had been constructed in that region. At the time of planning, the Sicilian operation had not been completed, and there was only one small airstrip known to be available there. The arc of operations drawn from Sicily extended to the island of Capri, just north of Salerno, and included the Italian provinces of Calabria and Basilicata. Nowhere here were any targets of major strategic importance; the area was the poorest in Italy and was one of mountains and difficult communications. Just beyond fighter range were two targets worth taking – the city and port of Naples, and the Italian naval base of Taranto – but a direct assault on either of these heavily defended locations, especially without air cover, was out of the question.

Calabria appeared to be the only route into Italy, with a relatively safe passage across the Straits of Messina, but this way led into a narrow region with mountains rising to 6,000 feet in height, which offered the defender a number of points on which to base his resistance. The danger of focusing the invasion solely at this point was that the Allies could find themselves stuck in a barren region as winter approached, unable to advance sufficiently far to tie down significant German forces. It was evident to Alexander that an effort must be made to identify somewhere – risky that it might be – at the extremes of fighter cover but closer to strategic objectives. Detailed planning started in Allied Force Headquarters on 3 June 1943, but much would depend upon the progress of the operations in Sicily. The first few days there gave promise for the future: the Italian forces on the island, which might have strongly resisted the landings on their homeland, had little heart for the fight. Many units, especially the coastal defence formations, put up virtually no fight at all, and mass desertions were frequent. The civilian population seemed welcoming, seeing the Allies as liberators. These indications, together with the comparatively light Allied casualties and the limited damage imposed upon the landing craft employed during the invasion, contributed to a more ambitious plan for Italy than would otherwise have been the case.[6]

On 17 July Alexander met Eisenhower and the naval and air commanders, Admiral Cunningham and Air Marshal Tedder, and together they drew up an initial series of objectives for the invasion of Italy. These included a swift exploitation of the anticipated success in Sicily to launch an attack across the Straits of Messina by the Eighth Army, which would be followed by a move up the 'toe' of Italy to Cotrone, on the ball of Italy's foot, where an amphibious landing would be made. Should sufficient landing craft be available, then Fifth Army would mount an operation against Taranto and – in the fullness of time – once the Allied advance had secured Naples, reinforcements would be sent to Italy via that port. Five days after this meeting, on 22 July, Fifth Army was ordered to prepare plans to seize the 'heel' of Italy and to secure the area east of a line running from Taranto to Bari. The target date was 1 October 1943.

It was hoped, with the rapidly-collapsing Italian Army and the Germans retiring northwards, that a small mobile force could advance swiftly across the mountains and seize Naples. On 15 July Fifth Army had been directed to prepare plans for an unopposed landing in Naples, but now Taranto was given priority. Naples was too good a target to ignore, however – its occupation would give the Allies a base from which to maintain an army which would be well placed for an advance northwards to Rome and the presence of Allied troops there would force the Germans to withdraw from Calabria. However, any force that landed in Naples had to be capable of being supported by troops advancing from the south, especially as the port lay beyond air cover.

News came from Rome on 25 July that Mussolini had fallen, which led the Allies to reconsider more adventurous options. Although there was, as yet, no indication that the Italians were about to surrender, the prevailing expectation was that it would be only a matter of time. The discontent of a number of senior Italian officers was well-known, and already some cautious approaches had been made to the Allies. With an enhanced possibility that Italy would collapse, General Clark was again ordered to prepare plans to seize Naples. The target date was 7 September, the earliest that the availability of troops allowed. All of these were currently involved in Sicily, including the two reserve divisions: 9th (US) and 78th (British). The end of the Sicilian campaign was hopefully to come in mid-August; the first week in September would mark the date when sufficient landing craft would become available; and the moon would be at its most suitable for the operation between 7 and 10 September.

Operation AVALANCHE, the landing to seize Naples, was to be carried out by VI (US) Corps and X (British) Corps, each of which theoretically comprised one armoured, two infantry and one airborne division. In practice they could not all be used because shipping was only available for an assault force of little more than three divisions, and there were sufficient aircraft for only one airborne division. Additionally, because the plans for operations in Calabria were still under consideration – for which General Montgomery wanted X Corps – that formation had to be prepared for both AVALANCHE and Calabria; the final decision would be taken once the situation clarified.

The AVALANCHE landings were to be made in the Gulf of Salerno for several reasons. To sail directly into the Bay of Naples, which was well-defended by minefields and coastal batteries, as well as being an area in which the Germans would concentrate their forces, was out of the question. The decision, therefore, had to be taken on landing to the city's north or south. To the north the Plain of Campania lay between Naples and the mouth of the Volturno river, and offered landing sites which were not dominated by mountain ranges. The opportunity here existed for a swift landing and deployment of forces which would permit Allied armour to be used to its best advantage to cut enemy communications from the south. It appeared that the Germans expected a strike to be made in this area, for they had moved two divisions there. However, the beaches were less suitable for landings than the alternative, Salerno, and had sandbanks lying offshore. They were also beyond the range of air cover.

South of Naples there lay a twenty-mile stretch of suitable landing beach with clear approaches and gradients which permitted landing craft to come close inshore; the coastal defences were comparatively weak; there was an airfield less than four miles from the coast which could be seized to accommodate four fighter squadrons; and the landing area was within air cover from north-east Sicily. On the debit side, the beaches were overlooked by a semicircle of mountains which were located at distances of between two and ten miles from the shore, and which gave the defenders positions from which to both observe and locate artillery. Furthermore, between the landing area and Naples there ran a spur of the Monti Picentini which ran down to Sorrento, and through which there were only two, easily defensible, passes. The question of air cover was the deciding factor, and Salerno it was to be.

The question of X Corps' participation in AVALANCHE was decided when Alexander ruled that Montgomery would have to make the crossing of the Straits of Messina with the resources he had. Neither X Corps nor the landing craft required to carry it to Salerno would be available to him.

On 16 August the Commanders-in-Chief conference in Carthage made the final decisions on the Italian invasion. With the Sicilian campaign virtually over, the Germans being able to evacuate their troops from the island more successfully than the Allies had anticipated, and German forces moving into Italy from the north in great numbers, it was expected that there would be as many as eighteen enemy divisions in the country by the end of the month. The Allies could not anticipate being able to match that strength until December. Nonetheless, it was agreed that the invasion should go ahead as soon as possible. XIII Corps would cross into Calabria between 1 and 4 September, and AVALANCHE was timetabled for the 9th.

Fifth Army came under Alexander's command on 17 August, only three weeks before it was to land at Salerno. It had prepared its plan for the invasion, which was presented two days earlier. With a few modifications, largely concerning the use of 82nd Airborne Division, the plan was accepted and the Operation Order was issued on 26 August. The plan called for an initial assault by three divisions, supported by a floating reserve of one Regimental Combat Team. To the left, X Corps (46th and 56th British Divisions) was to land between Salerno and the Sele river. Its task was to seize Salerno and the airfield at Montecorvino, to establish a firm base and to take control of the passes which led to Naples. Having done this, the Corps was to advance to Naples and the airfields at Capodichino and Pomigliano. For the landings themselves the Corps would be supported by three US Ranger battalions and two Commandos, all operating on its left flank; and on D+4 reinforcements in the shape of 7th Armoured Division would be landed.

On the right VI Corps would land with 36th (US) Division and one tank battalion. Its task was to secure the right flank and to establish a firm beachhead. The Fifth Army reserve was one Regimental Combat Team from

45th Division, under the divisional commander. Once the initial landings were made and sufficient shipping became available, the rest of 45th, and later the 34th Divisions, would be brought across. In the initial plan 82nd Airborne Division would provide a Regimental Combat Team to drop north of Naples in the Volturno valley. Its task was to capture bridges at Cancello, Capua and Triflisco and prevent enemy reinforcements moving into the region from the north, but this operation was later cancelled.

The forces assigned to AVALANCHE were not great, but they were all that could be carried to the Bay of Salerno by the numbers of landing craft available. With priority now being given to preparations for OVERLORD, the Mediterranean theatre was left with limited resources, and landing craft which had been used in Sicily had to be refitted in Bizerta before being re-employed for this operation. Some Landing Ships Tank (LSTs) were taken away from the Messina crossing as soon as they had finished ferrying their loads across the Straits, and sent to be loaded for their next task later on the same day.

To highlight the constraints which shipping and aircraft limitations imposed on the invasion, it is worth comparing the strengths of Allied forces that formed the initial assault waves during Operation HUSKY, the landings in Sicily (seven infantry divisions, one infantry brigade, elements of two airborne divisions, three Ranger battalions and three Commandos, with an armoured division as floating reserve) and AVALANCHE (three infantry divisions, a tank battalion, three Ranger battalions and two Commandos). The Italian campaign was firmly relegated to a secondary position when resources had to be assigned to OVERLORD, and the commanders had little option but to make the best of what they could pull together.

With initial discussions being held about surrender terms, there was hope that the landings could be made without facing resistance from the Italians. However, the Allies believed that in addition to the German divisions that were withdrawing from Sicily there were another ten or twelve in Italy. Two of these were situated close enough to Rome to occupy it should the Italian government declare a unilateral surrender. Understandably, the Italian government feared reprisals from the Germans once news of their dealings with the Allies broke, and wanted reassurances that the Allied landing would be made north of Rome with a strength of not less than fifteen divisions. As has been illustrated, this was completely impossible. The best that could be done was to offer to send an airborne division to land on airports that had already been seized by the Italians. The combined Italian-American force (the Italian forces in the area, together with the 82nd Airborne Division which was nominated for the task) would then defend Rome against the Germans until the seaborne force reached it. This, of course, meant that 82nd Airborne would not be available for AVALANCHE.

At 0515 on 3 September, thirteen hours after Eighth Army opened its assault across the Straits of Messina, General Castellano on behalf of the Italian Government, and General Bedell Smith on behalf of General Eisenhower, signed the Italian Surrender Terms in a tent in an almond grove near Cassibile in Sicily.

The Germans in Italy, 1943.

At the beginning of the year the German High Command was faced with a defeat in south Russia and the probability of a second one in North Africa. To lose Stalingrad would open a gap in their Eastern Front; to lose Tunisia would lay southern Europe open to Allied attack. While having confidence that they could hold Tunisia, Russia was more of a danger to the Germans and therefore the available reserves went there. Some nineteen divisions were sent to Russia from France during January and February 1943[7] but in Tunisia elements of the British 6th and 7th Armoured Divisions entered Tunis and 248,000 Axis troops capitulated, over 130,000 of them German, to add to the twenty divisions lost at Stalingrad. German reaction was to reinforce the Balkans, but attention was also given to Italy. The loss of that country would not only signal the break-up of the Axis but would also remove Italian forces from the Russian front and their garrisons in the Balkans, and would open airfields to the Allies from which they could directly attack southern Germany. The loss of Italy would also mean the loss of Italian industrial and agricultural resources.

On 3 September *Army Group B* under command of Field Marshal Rommel was situated in the north of Italy above a line running from Grosseto to Rimini. It consisted of ten divisions, two of which were armoured, and one-and-a-half of which were stationed in Sardinia and Corsica. These forces controlled the north of the country from their headquarters on Lake Garda, and had established a very big staging and maintenance area around Verona. There had also been a major effort to improve the lines of communication throughout the area, which would serve the Germans well in the forthcoming months. Germans and Allies alike anticipated that the Italian population in this region would present the Germans with a significant security problem, should Italy defect from the Axis.

German dispositions in south Italy under Kesselring were positioned to resist any invasion attempt. They included the four divisions which had been evacuated from Sicily. Of these, *29th Panzer Division* was in Calabria, *15th Panzer Grenadier* and the *Herman Göring Divisions* were refitting in the Naples area, and the bulk of *1st Parachute Division* in Altamura. Two other divisions, both newly-formed, were south of Naples: the *26th Panzer* in Calabria and *16th Panzer* covering the Gulf of Salerno, having been moved there at the end of August. The *2nd Parachute Division* was near Ostia and *3rd Panzer Grenadier* was around Viterbo, both in the area of Rome. These eight formations were under the command of Colonel General von Vietinghoff's *Tenth Army*, and organized into *XIV Panzer Corps* in the north and *LXXVI Panzer Corps* in the south.

The lesson that the Germans had taken from Sicily – although not every German general subscribed to it, as was evidenced by the response to OVERLORD the following year – was that an invasion should be defeated on the beach. The difficulty was in identifying on which beach the Allies would land, and ensuring that there were sufficient forces in its proximity to deal with whatever came ashore. The odds on pinpointing the correct stretch of coastline was not as unscientific as sticking a pin into a map, however, because the Germans were well able to weigh up the factors which the Allies would consider when making their choice – range of air cover, closeness to a sizeable port, and so on. They were also sufficiently suspicious of the Italians to have prepared contingency plans to take over their defences should it prove necessary to do so. German dispositions covered the Naples, Rome-Civitavecchia, and Genoa-Spezia areas, although the distances involved meant that the defenders were spread relatively thinly. In the Salerno area four infantry and one tank battalions, supplemented by the divisional engineer and reconnaissance battalions, covered over thirty miles of coast. General Alexander did not believe that this indicated that the enemy had correctly identified the AVALANCHE beaches.[8]

With the Italian surrender agreed, albeit not made public, planning proceeded for the 82nd Airborne Division to drop on the Rome airports. There were not sufficient aircraft to use the other airborne division available to Alexander, 1st (British) Airborne, in the role for which it had trained; neither were there spare landing craft for it to participate in an assault landing. The Italian surrender opened another possibility, however: to land the division at Taranto. If the Italians were not going to oppose the operation, then 1st Airborne could be carried to the port aboard Royal Navy warships and disembarked in the harbour. The opportunity to capture a port which was well-placed to support Eighth Army's future operations on the Adriatic was too good to be missed. With only five days' notice Operation SLAPSTICK was mounted and 1st Airborne Division was to arrive in Taranto on 9 September. Alexander's intention was that the division should secure the port, the neighbouring airfields and other installations, and prepare for the arrival of 78th Division once landing craft became available to transport it thence from Sicily. The force would be reinforced by 8th Indian Division from the Middle East, and V (British) Corps Headquarters would take command. The Corps would come under Eighth Army as soon as it had made contact after advancing through Calabria.

The AVALANCHE convoys set sail from their various ports of departure each day from 3 to 7 September. The proposal to drop 82nd Airborne Division on Rome was still under consideration, however, and because of the uncertainty surrounding Italian intentions and capabilities to support the operation, it was decided to send Brigadier General Maxwell Taylor, the division's artillery commander, to the city to gauge the situation there. With AVALANCHE scheduled for only two days later, he and Colonel Gardener USAAF sailed from Palermo on a British motor torpedo boat on 7 September. Because of the laws of war both officers carried out the mission in American uniform despite the possibility that such dress could lead to their immediate capture. Transferring to an Italian corvette off Ustica Island they were received by Rear Admiral Maugeri, head of Italian Naval Intelligence. After landing in Gaeta they then proceeded to Rome, travelling part of the way in an Italian ambulance, where they found that all was not what had been promised. Marshal Badoglio was not able to guarantee that the airfields which had been intended for the 82nd would be secure – according to General Carboni, commander of the Italian Corps in the Rome area, the Germans were too close and too strong – some 12,000 (mainly parachutists) were in the Tiber valley and a further 24,000 *Panzer Grenadiers* nearby. The proposal for the airborne operation (codenamed GIANT II) was greeted with dismay by Badoglio, who had no plans in place for an Italian uprising against the Germans. Faced with this disarray, Taylor made the decision to cancel the operation. His message to do so arrived as American paratroops were preparing to depart – according to the Divisional History the aircraft were loaded and the engines being warmed up. The tightness of the schedule meant that not only was the 82nd Airborne not dropped on the Rome airfields, but they were unavailable for their original task (GIANT I), which had been to seize crossings over the River Volturno as part of the AVALANCHE operation.

The date for AVALANCHE was selected because of the moon cycle, and because it was hoped that by then the Eighth Army would have progressed far enough towards Salerno to support the landings. The available numbers of landing craft limited the invasion force to two British and one American divisions: 46th British Infantry Division was made up of two North Midland brigades and a third which had three battalions of the Royal Hampshire Regiment; 56th (London) Infantry Division, which included 201 Guards Brigade; and – for the Americans – 36th (US) Infantry Division. In addition, there were three US Ranger battalions and No. 2 Army and No. 41 Royal Marine Commandos. The chain of command descended from Eisenhower at Allied Forces Headquarters, through Alexander at Headquarters 15 Army Group, to Clark at Headquarters Fifth Army. Below this level came Lieutenant General Richard McCreery, commanding X Corps, and Major General Ernest J. Dawley, commanding VI Corps. In terms of nationalities the sequence ran American-British-American, and then British and American at corps level. The length of time that some of these officers had to get to know and to learn to work with each other was not long, particularly when they came from different nationalities. Alexander had first met Eisenhower and Clark in 1942. Eisenhower and Clark had known each other since being at West Point and had worked together since June 1942. Alexander had worked with McCreery before Dunkirk when the former had commanded 1st Division with McCreery as his GSO1. He had later appointed McCreery as his Chief of Staff Middle East Command in 1942, and then his Chief of Staff when Alexander took command of 18 Army Group. McCreery was given X Corps in July 1943 when its commander, General Horrocks, was wounded, but the corps was only confirmed as being part of Clark's Fifth Army when AVALANCHE was given the go-ahead. Until then X Corps had prepared both for AVALANCHE and BAYTOWN so as to be capable of being employed in either operation, as the situation demanded, and there was no real time for Clark and McCreery to get to know each other, let alone work together. Clark had appointed his other corps commander, Dawley, with reluctance. He had wanted a younger officer for the job, but Dawley had seen service in Mexico and France and was both older and senior to Clark. Their relationship was not helped when Clark felt that he had to reprimand Dawley about the appearance and behaviour of his soldiers, which Clark considered to be lax.[9]

The links, as might be expected, were strongest along national lines. If it can be accepted that mutual trust and understanding based upon shared experiences help to ensure effective and efficient working relationships, then the senior officers involved with the Salerno landings were largely missing that advantage. Although some of these officers had learned to trust each other, the reverse was also true. Past experience could breed dislike or distrust. Clark, because of his appointment as Army Commander, is particularly important in this respect, and several of the officers who worked in subordinate positions for him during the campaign – including Americans – held him in poor regard. Dawley, Truscott (3rd Division, then VI Corps and later Fifth Army Commander), and Walker (36th Division) were among these officers. British officers would join their ranks.

Salerno

During the early hours of 9 September the invasion fleet for AVALANCHE drew close to the Salerno beaches. Its arrival was not entirely unannounced, for German aircraft had detected and attacked the British Task Force twenty-five miles south of Capri, but Kesselring could not be sure where the landings would occur nor did he have sufficient forces to cover all possibilities. The Allies anticipated that there might be as many as 39,000 Germans in the area on D Day, which could be reinforced to bring the figure to 100,000 within three days. To face these forces Clark hoped to land 125,000 men.[10] His men, but not the senior officers, were in optimistic spirits, for Eisenhower had released the news of the Italian surrender on the preceding day and many soldiers expected that there would be no resistance to the landing; the generals were less optimistic. Instead of unsteady Italian troops facing them, there would probably be Germans. With nine hours between the time of Eisenhower's broadcast and the time at which the landings were to be made, the Germans had time to take over the Italian coastal defence positions and to be ready for the invasion force.

The first Allied troops ashore were the Rangers, who landed at 0310 hours, twenty minutes before the main landing force was timetabled to arrive. They moved inland swiftly and were in their planned positions by daybreak, while the Commandos captured the town of Salerno, which was only lightly defended. X Corps' landing was preceded by a heavy naval bombardment, whereas VI (US) Corps did not announce its arrival. The British felt that as their convoy had been attacked en route to the beaches there was no possibility of surprise and that a supporting bombardment would assist; the Americans hoped to take advantage of stealth, regardless of the fact that the barrage just to their west would have awoken anyone for miles around. Admiral Hewitt had recommended a bombardment, but both Clark and the commander of the 36th Division, General Fred Walker, had rejected his advice in the belief that there would be no serious resistance. There was only one identifiable target anyway, a three-gun artillery battery which was reported to be obsolete and unmanned.

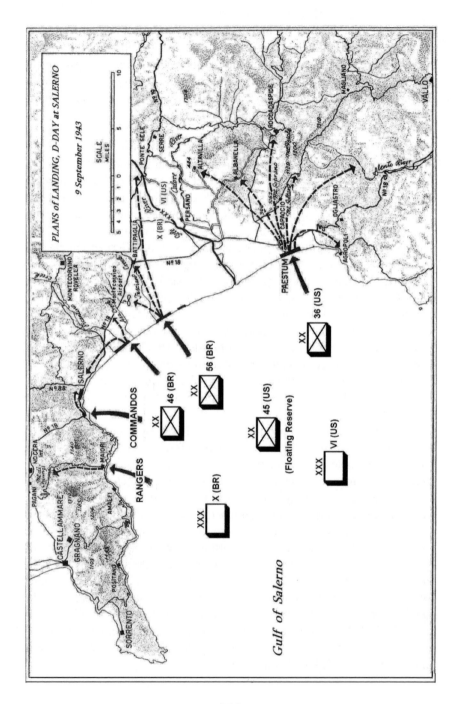

PLANS of LANDING, D-DAY at SALERNO

9 September 1943

SCALE
MILES

Mark Clark and Winston Churchill. Two men whose ambition and vision shaped the Italian campaign.

French troops in Algeria being instructed by American artillerymen. Modernizing the French Army was essential before it could play a full part in the coalition.

Salerno casualty evacuation. The landings highlighted the lack of experience of Fifth Army planners and nearly led to a defeat.

7th Armoured Division: infantrymen of 1/6th Queen's on a Scots Greys' Sherman in Torre Annunziata on the outskirts of Naples, 1 October 1943.

British infantry of X Corps house-clearing in a village on the slopes of Monte Camino.

Canadian Lieutenant Kostelec and American Lieutenant Wilson, First Special Service Force Casualty Clearing Station, Venafro, January 1944. The FSSF was perhaps the most integrated formation in the coalition, but the selection process and intensity of the training meant that its example could not be used as a blueprint.

36th (US) Division: stretcher bearers taking cover near the Rapido river. The attempt to force the river crossing was a costly failure which called Clark's judgement into question.

New Zealand: Lieutenant General Sir Bernard Freyberg VC. Not only commander of the New Zealand Corps, his role as his country's national representative meant that his superiors in the Mediterranean theatre had to treat him with sensitivity.

New Zealand: 'hoping to accomplish results by use of heavy bombers ... without risking too much infantry' (Brooke). Bombing Cassino town on 15 March 1944 in preparation for the New Zealand Corps' second attempt to capture it. The earlier bombing of the Monastery was one of the most controversial events of the war.

Rations: Clark stated that the diets of Fifth Army's various nationalities presented administrative difficulties. Here a 4th Indian Division cookhouse prepares chapattis near Cassino.

Rations on the hoof. Goumiers of the French Expeditionary Corps with a takeaway.

Rations: Thanksgiving 1944. Whenever possible soldiers were given food appropriate to their national and religious traditions to support morale.

Anzio: General Lucas' headquarters was located in wine cellars in Nettuno, which he was reluctant to leave to visit the front lines. His relationship with the British forces under his command was to cause friction.

Anzio: an American field hospital after German bombardment. Despite red crosses being displayed prominently, hospitals came under frequent attack. There was no rear area in the beachhead.

Goumiers leading a mule train past a French M5 tank in the Aurunci Mountains. The French Expeditionary Corps' capability in mountain warfare was a valuable asset which would be sorely missed when the Corps left Italy to take part in the invasion of southern France.

Italian Co-Belligerent Forces manning a railway gun on the Gustav Line. Italians fought for both the Allies and the Germans throughout the campaign.

General Alexander, commander of the 15th Army Group, with Italian soldiers. The major general in the foreground is Lemnitzer, Alexander's American Deputy Chief of Staff.

Photo opportunity number one: Clark at the meeting of II and VI Corps' troops at Borgo Piave on 25 May 1944, when the isolation of the Anzio beachhead came to an end. Clark had numerous cameramen and war correspondents standing by to record the event – and his part in it.

Photo opportunity number two: Clark, Keyes (II Corps) and Frederick (FSSF) with cameramen very much in evidence. Other versions of this photograph were cropped to show only the generals.

Photo opportunity number three: Clark, Keyes (II Corps) and Truscott (VI Corps) in Rome, where Clark's speech lauded the American Fifth Army at the expense of the other Allied contingents.

Americans waiting to enter Rome. Clark refused to hold a victory parade in the Eternal City in which all Allied nations would be represented.

Nisei (Japanese-American) of 552nd Field Artillery, 442nd Regimental Combat Team, and Italian muleteer, Castellina, July 1944. The Nisei served with distinction in Italy and France.

South Africa: Rhodesian Sherman on Monte Vigese, 1944. Rhodesian sub-units served in several South African regiments.

British anti-aircraft gunners protecting US engineers constructing a Bailey Bridge across the River Reno. Pioneers from Bechuanaland and other Commonwealth countries were re-trained as anti-aircraft gun detachments to serve alongside the Royal Artillery.

South African armour firing across the River Reno, November 1944.

Brazil: the first troops arrive in Naples. A commitment for political reasons, the presence of the Brazilians assured them a place at the victors' table.

Brazil: German General Otto Fretter-Pico, Commander of the *148th Infantry Division*, and General Mario Carloni surrendering to Brazilian officers, 1945.

Major General Almond inspecting his troops of the 92nd (Negro) Division. In common with many white officers, Almond had doubts about the division's morale, a fact which did little to improve matters.

Winter in the mountains: American repairs, Indian mules, Italian mud.

34th Division in Bologna, 1945. The end of the campaign approaches.

X Corps met significant resistance as its advance troops pushed inland. On the American beach 36th (US) Infantry Division, in action for the first time, came under fire as it approached the shoreline. The leading troops suffered heavy casualties, but all of the first waves were ashore by 0610 hours, forcing the two German companies which had been defending the area to withdraw. Enemy resistance during the first hours of the invasion was piecemeal while the local commanders reacted to events as they developed in their immediate areas, and it was not until 0700 hours that an effort was made by fifteen tanks of the *16th Panzer Division* to mount a counterattack which was driven back by naval gunfire together with artillery, infantry and engineers from the forces that were now ashore. The *16th Panzer* had been ordered to the area only two days earlier, but it had been busy laying mines and improving the Italian defences. They also shot the commander of the local Italian coastal division for resisting their operations.

 Luftwaffe fighters put up the strongest aerial resistance of the campaign, bombing and strafing the invaders. Facing the aerial attacks and under fire from mortars, machine guns and artillery, the landings became disorganized and units were put ashore in the wrong places; a battalion of the Hampshire Regiment (46th Division) landed in the 56th Division area and had to cross the Asa river to take up their proper positions; in the course of doing so they came under panzer attack, which wrought devastation. In the 36th Division area the first experience of combat for the Texans was also horrendous.

General Walker and his staff landed at 0730 hours and established a command post, but they had difficulty in comprehending what was happening in the chaos that existed on the beaches. Nevertheless, by the end of the first day 36th Division had managed not only to repulse the Germans' initial counterattack but had also made gains, capturing the town of Paestum and some high ground about five miles inland. X Corps was three miles inland and had reached Montecorvino airfield. The initial landings had been relatively easy and the remainder of D Day had been spent seeing off small-unit German resistance. While the situation looked favourable, the two corps were still separated by a seven-mile gap through which ran the Sele river and were acting independently of each other. The beachhead was as yet narrow and was facing increasing numbers of enemy forces as the Germans rushed reinforcements to the area. Moreover, Clark was still afloat on Admiral Hewitt's flagship, the *Ancon*, and had only an imperfect picture of the situation. He appeared to play down the importance of the gap between his two corps, a consideration which was not shared by Eisenhower who was far less optimistic. He was not alone in this opinion, for General Patton – who had been briefed on the landing plans so that he might assume command if Clark were to be killed or wounded – had immediately forecast that the Germans would try to exploit the Sele river gap. The plan was essentially flawed, a product of an inexperienced commander and his staff.

From the German perspective, when AVALANCHE occurred Kesselring was in the process of withdrawing forces from southern Italy as he had earlier planned; *29th Panzer Grenadier* and all but one battle group from *26th Panzer Grenadier*, plus one regiment of *1st Parachute Divisions* from *LXXVI Panzer Corps* would soon be available in the Salerno area from Calabria, and until such time as it arrived he concentrated *16th Panzer Division* against X Corps. The *Hermann Göring* and part of *15th Panzer Grenadier Divisions* were rushed from the northwest to oppose X Corps, followed by *3rd Panzer Grenadier Division*. Resistance to the advance of Eighth Army was to be left mostly to natural features, but Montgomery's command was about to halt its advance to allow its logistic tail to catch up and to replenish its supplies. The late decision to invade Italy had left Allied logistic facilities poorly positioned to support the fighting formations; hospital capacity in North Africa, for example, was less than half the number of beds that the Surgeon General recommended to care for the wounded evacuated from Italy, and service units were insufficient to perform all of the tasks that would normally fall to them. Combat troops had to carry out general labouring, guard and port duties.[11]

The position now facing the Allies at Salerno was that they were unable to reinforce the invasion force as quickly as the Germans could bring in overwhelming strength to push it back into the sea. The AVALANCHE plan had only two brigades designated to make the breakout from the beachhead from the nine brigades which were theoretically available. Both of these were infantry and therefore moved on foot. Of the three divisions put ashore on D Day, 36th and 56th Divisions were given defensive roles protecting the southern flank and Montecorvino respectively. The remaining division, the 46th, was too far away from its objective of Salerno to be certain of achieving its mission. Poor planning went farther than this, for lessons from the Sicilian landings regarding loading matériel onto sea transports were not heeded and unnecessary equipment arrived before vital supplies. General Walker felt that the Fifth Army planners were incompetent.[12] They were certainly inexperienced.

Major General Dawley arrived on the beachhead at 1300 hours, ordered ashore by Clark earlier than scheduled, and began to take command of the VI Corps troops, which at this stage were mostly from 36th Division. For a period the American forces had a corps commander with only a single division to command, and without his staff to assist him. On 10 September the 157th and 179th Regiments of the 45th (US) Division came ashore and bolstered the southern positions. The 157th was deployed across the Sele into the X Corps sector to capture high ground around a tobacco factory near the village of Persano. This was vital ground which overlooked the weakest point of the beachhead, but the Germans were not to be driven off it easily; seven Shermans were lost in the attempt. General Clark visited both corps on the 10th. Concerned by the resistance against X Corps and the weakness in his centre, he narrowed the British front by moving the American boundary four miles to the north. To achieve this he had to move two regiments from the 45th into the front vacated by the British, a redeployment which stretched VI Corps even further. By 13 September 36th Division was covering a thirty-five mile front, a distance much farther than a division was expected to defend even when at full strength – and the 36th had suffered losses. To add to the disarray Clark had returned to the USS *Ancona* after his first visit ashore and was unable to get to his troops again until late on 12 September. The command ship with all of its communications equipment was the sensible place to be until such time as headquarters could be established ashore, but it was a highly visible target to the *Luftwaffe*. Radio intercepts indicated that the ship was about to be attacked, so Admiral Hewitt put her out to sea – taking the Army commander with her until it was judged safe to return inshore. When he did get back Clark established his headquarters with VI Corps and proceeded to devote his attention to that part of his command. X Corps was left to fight its own war while Clark personally directed Dawley's forces, which even now were not at full corps strength.

On D+3 the *Luftwaffe* hit again, using glider bombs and radio-controlled rockets against the Allied shipping. Thirteen vessels were sunk, including a hospital ship, HMHS *Newfoundland*, which had been transporting American nurses to the beachhead.

With German forces arriving in strength the Allied position continued to worsen. Major attacks were made on 13 September: X Corps was assaulted by the *Hermann Göring* and *3rd* and *15th Panzer Grenadier Divisions* and pushed out of the village of Battipaglia. Elements of the *26th* and *29th Panzer Grenadier* and the *16th Panzer Divisions* struck against VI Corps and the lightly defended area along the Sele river. That afternoon the Germans overran a battalion of the 36th Division and began to threaten the Allied rear. Dawley had no reserves to counter. As he reported to Clark: 'All I've got is a prayer.'[13] Clark felt that the situation was so severe that he ordered his staff to prepare orders to evacuate the VI Corps beachhead and to land its troops on the British position. An alternative plan was to be drawn up in which the British would be evacuated to the American beachhead.

What Clark did not do, however, was to take into account the opinions of his corps and divisional commanders, all of whom were angered by his intentions. Middleton, commander of the 45th Division, refused to take the suggestion to evacuate seriously. McCreery was horrified, and signalled Clark to state that there was no question of such an operation being carried out. Nor were Clark's superiors impressed. Alexander supported McCreery, and Eisenhower wondered if Clark's nerve had gone. Any such evacuation would have had enormous consequences which the Germans proceeded to exploit as soon as they had got wind of the plan. Axis Sally, a German-American woman who broadcast Nazi propaganda, was swift to inform the beleaguered troops that transports were on their way to bring them to safety – but that they would not succeed.[14] The crisis, if such it was, has been described by Graham and Bidwell[15] as a 'flap' which was caused by no more than four enemy battlegroups, each no larger than a reinforced battalion. The entire German strength involved was little more than a British brigade or an American regimental combat team, but it had been sufficient to cause a sense of panic in the mind of the inexperienced Fifth Army commander.

Clark saw the state of affairs as becoming increasingly desperate but there was no way of moving reinforcements into the area by sea, given the shortage of shipping and the distances involved which had already dictated the strength of the assault waves. There was one possibility of improving the odds: Eisenhower had made 82nd Airborne Division available, and Clark asked for it to be parachuted onto the beachhead. During the night of 13/14 September 1,300 men dropped and immediately moved to support the 36th Division defences. That it happened so swiftly was a tribute to the 82nd's commander, General Ridgway. He received the order, delivered by a fighter pilot, less than twelve hours before the drop was to be made; the 504th Parachute Infantry Regiment was to jump and help man the line along the Sele river gap, and it did so.

The next day, 14 September, German attacks were made along the whole front. Their attempts to break through were unsuccessful, and further Allied reinforcements began to arrive: the British 7th Armoured Division to the X Corps sector and the third of 45th (US) Division's regiments, the 180th Infantry, to VI Corps to become the Fifth Army reserve. To supplement the British infantry, anti-aircraft gunners formed companies which were deployed with the Queen's Brigade. Another 2,100 paratroops from the 82nd dropped that night, and the crisis had passed.

Whereas the two night drops into the beachhead itself had gone smoothly, a third operation was less successful. The 509th Parachute Infantry Battalion dropped about twenty miles north of X Corps during the evening of 14 September to disrupt enemy lines of communications. Their orders had been to stay at the task for about five days and then to link up with advancing ground forces or to infiltrate into the beachhead as the situation dictated. However, only fifteen of the forty aircraft involved in the operation delivered their loads within four miles of the drop zone. Of the 640 men who jumped, only 400 got through to Allied lines after raiding the enemy rear.

Kesselring's final attempts to dislodge the Allies took place on 15 and 16 September. Once it had become evident that the Fifth Army was not to be removed, the Germans began an orderly withdrawal northwards; the Allies commenced their pursuit as soon as they had consolidated their positions. Many units had been considerably reduced in strength (2nd Battalion of the 143rd Infantry had almost ceased to exist, for example) and nearly all needed time to rest and reorganize. It took McCreery's X Corps another ten days to push their way through the passes to Naples, hindered every step of the journey by enemy resistance.

Allied casualties came to over 13,500 killed, wounded and missing, of whom 7,398 were British, 6,189 American. It was a bloody initiation for the Fifth Army.[16] German casualties amounted to 3,472.

By 17 September elements of the Fifth and Eighth Armies met at Auletta, twenty miles east of Eboli. The question was posed then, and since: why had it taken Montgomery so long to get to Salerno? British and American historians have different viewpoints: Graham and Bidwell[17] maintained that the Eighth Army could not have reached the beleaguered Fifth Army any sooner than they did, whereas Carlo d'Este[18] was less forgiving. He was of the opinion that it was a straightforward operation which Montgomery could have managed had Alexander pushed him harder. Alexander was also criticized for not committing the 82nd Airborne earlier.

While it is unarguable that Alexander should not have accepted Clark's plan for AVALANCHE because it repeated the weaknesses of the original proposals for the Sicilian landings, by putting the invaders ashore on beaches that were too far apart for mutual support, d'Este's other criticism appears harsh. The Eighth Army had been launched across the Straits of Messina only six days before the Salerno landings, and if it was a valid point that the Salerno beaches were too far apart, then the same can be said – writ large – of the intention to support AVALANCHE with the forces from BAYTOWN, almost 300 miles away and separated by unfriendly terrain across which all routes had been thoroughly disrupted by the Germans. It was certainly a weakness that worried Montgomery, who saw little point in the Italian campaign anyway. Like the American Chiefs of Staff, he believed that it led nowhere.[19] He constantly demanded a clear plan and objectives for the campaign, which he was not to receive.

The Eighth Army's XIII Corps had crossed the Straits of Messina six days before the Salerno landings and had proceeded to push into mainland Italy from its toe. While there was little enemy resistance to the advance, the Germans had certainly done everything possible to slow the British by demolishing every bridge, culvert and road that would have made their progress any easier. By 8 September they had advanced more than 100 miles in five days, but then they had run out of bridging material. The logistic support that had been put in place for the Sicily campaign was woefully unsuitable for the extension into Italy, and there had been no time to build it up. XIII Corps' lines of communication were three times the length that the system had planned for, and the Eighth Army was maintained from ports in North Africa, Sicily and the United Kingdom. From late August 1943 most matériel would come directly from the United States and the United Kingdom; detailed loading of maintenance convoys had to be settled ten weeks before they sailed, an impossible task when it had not been decided what formations were to be supplied, what their locations or missions were, and what ports (and the facilities available in them) were to be used, until 16 August. Furthermore, the decision had been taken in June that full base installations were not to be established in Sicily. This was sensible when Sicily was seen as a limited operation, but now that the campaign was to be extended into Italy it did not work. Many installations necessary for the fresh campaign were in Egypt or North Africa, and could not easily be uprooted and moved forward.

By 9 September the 5th British and 1st Canadian Divisions, in XIII Corps, had supplies for only one day. The 5th Division had fuel for 225 miles, the Canadians for 150.[20] It was on this date that Alexander asked Montgomery to extend his operations towards Salerno. Given the state of the roads after the Germans had demolished them, without bridging material, and with the logistic state of Eighth Army, it was a tall order to expect it to get to Salerno swiftly, let alone to have the fuel to manoeuvre and to fight once it had arrived. The best that Montgomery could offer was to send light forces ahead to threaten the enemy, and to resume the main advance on 13 September, hoping to arrive on the 17th. On 16 September 5th Division's Reconnaissance Regiment made contact with VI Corps' troops about thirty miles south of the beachhead. At the time, and since, much was made of the fact that a small party of war correspondents made the journey to the Fifth Army without hindrance – but that is a rather different matter from moving a corps which was bound to attract the enemy's hostile attention.

As for Alexander sending reinforcements to the beachhead, the first echelon of 7th (British) Armoured Division and the third regiment of 45th (US) Infantry Division reinforced the beachhead by 15 September, landing as originally planned. On 16 September another 1,500 men arrived on Royal Navy warships from a transit camp in Tripoli; these had been assembled on Alexander's orders to fill the gaps in the British ranks caused by the fighting.

The Germans had held the Allied invasion force at Salerno for eight days with limited resources despite their opponent's overwhelming supporting naval gunfire and air superiority; Kesselring had come away from the conflict reassured that he could employ a defensive strategy in Italy which would reduce the Allied advance to a crawl, if not halt it completely. To Kesselring, Salerno proved that one German soldier was the worth of three Anglo-Americans. With the topography of Italy on his side he could fight the campaign that he had promised Hitler.

Salerno was important because it set the coalition agenda for much of the remainder of the campaign. Anglo-American differences had been exacerbated and become more entrenched as a result of the experience: Clark's Anglophobia was to become an obsession as he convinced himself that the British were determined to get to Rome before him. From the British perspective, the view that their allies were green was strengthened by the performance of American commanders at Salerno who had appeared to panic, and the removal of Dawley from command of VI Corps was the price they paid. When visiting the beachhead Alexander had observed to Clark that Dawley was 'a broken reed' who was demonstrating signs of nervousness and who had failed to give his staff confidence; he was duly replaced by General John P. Lucas. Hearing of Dawley's situation Patton, at that time waiting idle in Sicily, requested Eisenhower to give him command of VI Corps. This would have been a step backwards for Patton, who had commanded the Seventh (US) Army in Sicily, and Eisenhower refused the request because of the antipathy between Clark and Patton anyway – but it is worth reflecting on the difference Patton's presence might have made to future operations in Italy.

American staff work was also suspect, for the Fifth Army plans for Salerno had been made without proper consideration of the ground and without anticipating that the distance between the two landing beaches would cause difficulties. The assumption had also been made that Salerno was to be a defensive battle (hence two-thirds of the landing force on D Day were given roles in which they protected the beachhead rather than exploiting the anticipated surprise by pushing rapidly inland). It was an assumption that was to come into play again at Anzio, for right or wrong.

Alexander's leadership was questioned by the Americans because they felt that he influenced the battle in a negative way; he failed to press Montgomery sufficiently to get to Salerno in time to assist during the crisis, a move which many Americans believed was possible.[21] They failed to explain, however, what Monty might have sought to gain by deliberately and unnecessarily dawdling. Alexander was also criticized for not giving the beachhead the support it needed by ordering the 82nd Airborne to drop at an earlier stage of the battle, but Clark could have done this himself – and eventually did. Whereas one might quibble about the validity of these observations, a more serious criticism must surely be that Alexander accepted Clark's AVALANCHE plan without identifying its weaknesses. Not only that, he did not protest at the strategy that placed the Fifth and Eighth Armies so far apart that they were unable to support each other at short notice. Underlying these errors was the Allied assumption that they would face only limited opposition; it was this assumption that led them to make mistakes which would show Kesselring that he could adopt the defensive strategy he wanted.

Salerno established Clark as a man of personal courage but he had a great deal to learn about high command. He mistakenly believed that he had saved the invasion by his leadership, whereas it was precisely his inexperience that precipitated most of the problems. His relationship with Alexander, while always cordial on the surface, never went beyond the formality of a senior commander-subordinate relationship and frequently led him to ignore Alexander in the same manner as Montgomery did. The difference was that Monty had considerable personal rapport with Alexander based on several years of acquaintance, whereas the Alexander-Clark relationship was essentially adversarial. The relationships between Clark and other British officers were as bad: McCreery held Clark in utter contempt, while Clark referred to the X Corps commander as a 'feather duster'.

There were other episodes in the saga of Salerno which did damage to Anglo-American relationships. The first was when the Americans discovered that the press department in Alexander's headquarters had suggested that the Salerno situation should be played down in news reports and that Eighth Army's movements should be highlighted. While this might be explained by the propaganda need to emphasize Allied successes while drawing as much of a veil as possible over their difficulties, it appeared to Clark that his army was being pushed into a subordinate role in which the British were claiming to have come to his rescue, which was certainly not the case. The affair was one factor which led him to publicize both the Fifth Army's achievements and his own throughout the remainder of the campaign, although it must be acknowledged that he was well aware of the usefulness of the press in furthering his career well before Salerno.

The exchange of messages between Clark and Montgomery after the two armies made contact did little to improve matters. Monty, by his own admission sometimes a tactless man, came across as patronizing; Clark told Montgomery, 'I want to tell you of our deep appreciation for the skilful and expeditious manner by which you have moved your Eighth Army to the north', and later, 'The Fifth Army is just a young army trying hard to get along, while the Eighth Army is a battle-tried veteran. We would appreciate your teaching us some of your tricks.'[22] American observers classed these as respectful and courteous statements which served to build bridges; the British might well have regarded them as sarcasm given Clark's view of the time it took Eighth Army to arrive.

There was a further incident which would not have given the Americans a good impression of their ally. On 20 September 192 British soldiers had refused to obey orders, an action which caused them to be charged with mutiny. They were part of a group of 1,500 reinforcements which had been sent from a transit camp in Libya, where they had been assembled after recovering from wounds or illness, but the mutineers believed that they were to be reunited with the formations in which they had served: the 50th (Northumbrian) and 51st (Highland) Divisions, both of which had been due to return to the United Kingdom in preparation for OVERLORD. Instead of this, the urgent requirement for reinforcements at Salerno found them sent to the 46th Division. Placed under arrest, the men were sent to Algeria and court-martialled. Although the three sergeants involved in the affair were sentenced to death this punishment was later commuted to twelve years' hard labour and then suspended. The remaining mutineers were given varying sentences according to rank, which were also later suspended, and the men were posted to units in the Mediterranean theatre.

Notes

1. Starr, *Fifth Army History*
2. Matloff, *Strategic Planning for Coalition Warfare 1943-1944*

3. Ibid
4. Alexander, *Alexander's Despatch*
5. Ibid
6. Ibid
7. Ibid
8. Ibid
9. Blumenson, *Salerno to Cassino*
10. Ibid
11. Ibid
12. D'Este, *World War II in the Mediterranean*
13. Ibid
14. Ibid
15. Graham & Bidwell, *Tug of War*
16. D'Este, op cit.
17. Graham & Bidwell, op cit.
18. D'Este, op cit.
19. Carver, 'Montgomery', in Keegan (ed), *Churchill's Generals*
20. Malony et al *The Mediterranean and the Middle East* Vol V
21. Ibid
22. Blumenson, *Mark Clark*

CHAPTER 8

Naples to Cassino

On 23 September X Corps pushed northwards towards the two passes which led to Naples, a journey that was to involve them in repairing numerous bridges (on one seventeen-mile stretch of road twenty-five major bridges had been blown by the Germans). Progress was inevitably slow, but by 30 September McCreery's forces were through the eastern outskirts of Naples and moving northwards. The following day 82nd Airborne and Darby's Rangers entered the city, and by the end of the first week in October the Fifth Army was at the Volturno river in strength. The 56th and 7th Armoured Divisions had marched through Caserta and both X and VI Corps were on the river. The cost of AVALANCHE, of capturing Naples, and of advancing to the Volturno was over 12,000 British and American casualties (some 2,000 killed, 7,000 wounded and 3,500 missing).[1] Naples had been systematically destroyed by the combined efforts of Allied bombers and German demolitions; transport, communications, water and power installations had been ruined. Harbour facilities, railways, bridges and buildings had been rendered unusable by dynamite, mines and booby-traps, and the German artillery continued to play on the city for several days after its capture. Half of the city's civilian population had escaped into the surrounding countryside and for some ten days those remaining had little food. It would take the Fifth Army Base Section three months to restore Naples to a semblance of normality, a task which required it to expand from a headquarters strength of 600 men to an administrative force of over 33,000 personnel attached and assigned to carry out the restructuring. Among the tasks was the removal of the hulks of more than 100 vessels scuttled in the harbour. Two weeks after Naples had been captured the Allies were able to unload 3,500 tons of matériel daily, less than half of the port's pre-war capacity; by the end of October the figure had risen to 7,000 tons daily by employing about 600 DUKWs. All American, and some British, supplies were delivered through the port and smaller local harbours at Salerno, Castellamare and Torre Annunziata were used for some of X Corps' requirements[2].

The entry into Naples had illustrated Clark's desire to be seen at the forefront of events, preferably with cameramen available to record them for posterity. As the British 23 Armoured Brigade with the attached 505th (US) Parachute Infantry Regiment approached the city with orders to clear it, one of Clark's staff officers presented the paratroops' commander, Colonel James Gavin (later to become General Gavin), with an order to halt until Clark arrived to make a 'triumphant entry'. Gavin had little alternative but to obey and a procession was duly organized in which Clark was driven to the Piazza Garibaldi for the enthusiastic welcome the Fifth Army staff had predicted. Unfortunately for Clark's ego the Piazza was empty, for the Neapolitans had gathered in the Piazza del Plebiscito, the traditional location for greeting conquerors.[3]

The Allies had a number of possible courses to pursue after the fall of Naples, and much depended upon the effect that their actions would have on OVERLORD. The more German forces that could be tied down in Italy, the fewer would be available to counter the cross-Channel invasion. The decision to invade Italy had been taken to exploit the success of Sicily and to drive Italy out of the war while containing as many German divisions as possible; Italy had ceased to be an enemy, but the objective of containing German forces was vague in the extreme. The Combined Chiefs of Staff had failed to stipulate geographical objectives, a factor which gave the campaign no defined structure. Without such objectives there was no indication of how far up the Italian leg the Allies should press, and to attempt to fight as far north as possible – up to the Alps, say – would require a great deal of resources which might arguably be better used for the North West European theatre. The implications of fighting a major campaign in Italy were immense for both the teeth and tail organizations.

The balance of Allied/German strength was of concern. While there were Allied formations departing from the theatre for the United Kingdom and OVERLORD, and others beginning to arrive, the number of divisions available was expected to be fifteen by mid-October, seventeen a month later, and then sixteen in mid-December. The estimate for German divisions was twenty-six.[4] Allied air power would have to improve the odds, and with the *Luftwaffe* in decline the RAF and USAAF could expect a relatively free run at the enemy. At sea, although German naval power in the Mediterranean was now negligible, Allied resources were being steadily leeched away in anticipation of OVERLORD and options were becoming more limited.

For the United States planners at the Joint Chiefs of Staff level, gaining air bases north of Rome near Ancona from which to step up the bombing of

German-held areas in North West Europe would be sufficient justification for continuing to push onwards. In early August Marshall informed Eisenhower that at least twenty-four American, British and French divisions would be available to him for future operations; these should be sufficient to occupy Italy as far as north of Rome, to seize Sardinia and Corsica, and to make a landing on the Mediterranean coast of France to support OVERLORD. No attempt was to be made to move into the Balkans, and operations on the Italian mainland would be halted north of Rome.[5] Eisenhower's response was that as far as operations on the Italian mainland were concerned a situation in which the Allies held the south of the country and the Germans the north, with a no man's land lying between, was unsustainable. One side or the other would be driven out, depending upon the resources each could muster, and Allied capabilities would be limited by shortages in men and equipment rather than by numbers of divisions. He re-emphasized the argument that a particular limiting factor would be the amount of shipping and landing craft which could be drawn upon for Mediterranean operations, commodities which were in high demand for OVERLORD.

With a belief that the Germans would fall back as least as far as Pisa to shorten their lines of communication, the planners envisaged a rapid advance northwards, an advance which would facilitate the landings in southern France. In AFHQ the planners felt that it was probable that the Germans could be forced back as far as the Piave river and the foothills of the Alps by the spring of 1944. Both American and British intelligence indicated that the enemy was preparing to withdraw, possibly covering their move on a line running through Cassino. As the Germans had evacuated Sardinia and Corsica they had exposed their flank on the western coast of the mainland and would have to pull back or risk having Allied forces land behind them. Eisenhower believed differently. He considered that the German strength in Italy would impose a painstaking and methodical advance on the Allies, a view supported by fresh evidence that the enemy's withdrawal would be slower than previously thought. The German move would be paced to allow time for defensive lines to be completed, to give time to stabilize the internal security in northern Italy, and to inflict as much damage on the Allies as possible while denying them access to airfields from which missions might be flown against targets in German-held territory farther north.

Eisenhower's view was seconded by Alexander. Although German morale might have been lowered by the Italian surrender, their numerical superiority in ground forces, the absence of any significant internal security problem in

German-occupied Italy, the strongly defensive nature of the terrain south of Rome, and – on 12 September 1943 – Mussolini's rescue by the Germans and the establishment of the Italian Social Republic eleven days later, from which Fascist sympathizers could continue to support the Axis cause, led him to expect increased resistance. Apart from these reasons, the fact that the Germans had been retreating since El Alamein in November of the previous year spelt out to him that there would soon be a decision to make a stand.

Nearly a month after the Allies landed in Italy Hitler made the decision that Alexander anticipated. He had been presented with two possibilities: Rommel, commander of *Army Group B* based at Lake Garda, believed that the south of Italy could not be defended and should be abandoned; Kesselring, as Commander-in-Chief South (*Oberbefehlshaber*, or *OB*, *Süd*), disagreed strongly. To him, failing to fight in the south meant that Allied bombers would gain bases from which to strike into Germany; Rome could and should be held until the summer of 1944 (as indeed it was). He also believed that resistance in the south was necessary to deny the Allies a stepping-stone to the Balkans, an option which the German High Command (*OKW*) considered to be the Allied intention. In October Hitler summoned Rommel and Kesselring to his headquarters to hear their views. By this date he had already received Admiral Dönitz's estimate of the situation: the Commander-in-Chief of the German navy recommended that southern Italy should be held to prevent it being used as a bridgehead to the Balkans. A few days later the Foggia airfields fell into Allied hands, which weakened his argument unless they could be retrieved by a counterattack. Rommel and Kesselring were asked for their views on the possibility of such an action. Although their responses have not been recorded, it is probable from their attitudes to defending Italy that the former was less positive than the latter; Kesselring's stance was beginning to prevail, and Hitler ordered him to build up and to hold the Bernhardt Line. Rommel was ordered to prepare a defensive line in the northern Apennines and to send two infantry divisions and some artillery units as reinforcements to Kesselring. In the discussions about the future shape of German strategy in Italy, Kesselring's opinion was taking the greater prominence, and by 6 November Hitler had the drafts of two sets of orders before him, one appointing Rommel, the other Kesselring, as supreme commander in Italy. Kesselring got the job, and received orders that the Bernhardt Line would mark the end of withdrawals in Italy. Two weeks later Rommel was transferred out of the theatre and *Army Group B* ceased to exist as an active command. Kesselring's appointment was redesignated Commander-in-Chief South-west (*OB Südwest*) and *Army*

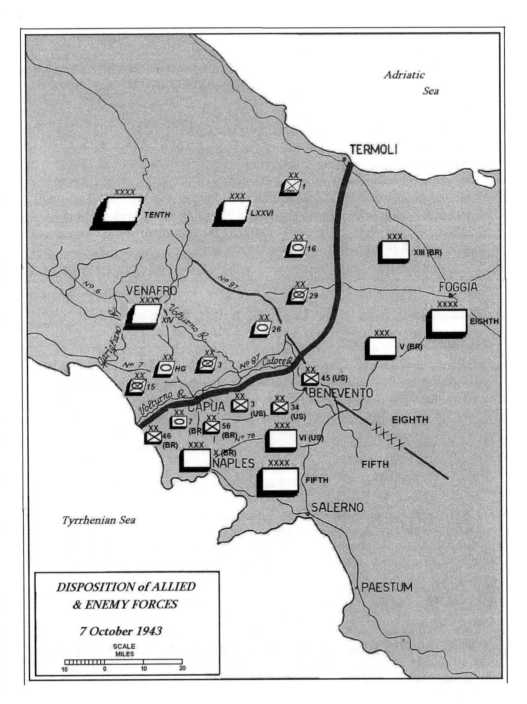

DISPOSITION of ALLIED
& ENEMY FORCES

7 October 1943

SCALE
MILES

Group C, which included the *Tenth Army* (*AOK 10*) in the south and the *Fourteenth* (*AOK 14*) in the north.[6]

The options for the Allied advance to and through the stiffened lines of defence were dictated by the geography and communications system of Italy.

The highway running up the east coast was connected to a number of lateral roads crossing the peninsula, on which the enemy's flank might be turned – but the highway itself could only carry a limited number of divisions and it crossed numerous steep-sided river valleys, which gave the Germans many opportunities to delay Allied operations. On the west coast there was the possibility of greater freedom of manoeuvre on the plains and of making better (although still limited) use of armoured forces; but here an advance was again going to be a laborious process against well-prepared defences. On balance, the western side looked to offer the best alternatives once the Volturno and Biferno river line had been secured.

The Fifth Army's left flank lay on the western coast with its right on the Matese Mountains, part of the Apennine chain. These mountains formed a barrier astride which the Fifth and Eighth Armies would advance independently of each other. In front of the Fifth the ground between the Volturno and Garigliano river valleys was mountainous, crossed only by narrow, twisting roads running through steep-sided passes and across fast-flowing streams which favoured the defender. Attackers were forced onto routes which became clearly defined killing zones, the most obvious of which lay along the two highways leading northwards to Rome. Route 7 followed the line of the coast from Naples to Rome; it ran across the Campanian Plain and into the olive-tree covered hills beyond, where terraces supported the agriculture but slowed the advance. Inland the terrain was rocky, with deep gorges and steep cliffs, and the second highway, Route 6, passed through this countryside from above Capua to Rome via the mountains and through the town of Cassino.

General Alexander had given the Fifth Army the mission of capturing the heights which overlooked the Garigliano and Rapido rivers, which formed obstacles farther upcountry, a task which first meant clearing the enemy defences along the Volturno river line. Facing the two Allied armies were some 60,000 men of the German *Tenth Army*. The *XIV Panzer Corps*, about 35,000 strong was on the north bank of the Volturno, with the *15th Panzer Grenadier*, the *Herman Göring* and the *3rd Panzer Grenadier Divisions*, the last of which was supported by the reconnaissance battalion from the *26th Panzer Division,* defended the line opposite the Fifth Army. The *LXVI Panzer Corps* with the rest of *26th Panzer Division*, the *29th Panzer*, the *1st*

Parachute and the *16th Panzer Divisions* covered the remainder of the front to the Adriatic. These formations were of different qualities, both in manpower and equipment: the *Herman Göring*, for example, had more self-propelled assault guns and anti-aircraft artillery than normal, whereas the *26th Panzer* was understrength.[7] The *Tenth Army* commander, General Vietinghoff, believed that the weaknesses in his defence were the lack of air support and his inability to make good any losses in both men and matériel; there was little in reserve. On the positive side, from his perspective, was the strength of his positions. The Volturno was in a state of flood and easy to defend, although in some places the south – Allied – bank overlooked the north, and deeply-cut river banks offered shelter to the attacker. The sixty-mile lower stretch of the river made a serious obstacle, beyond which the hills provided mutually supporting positions from which the Germans could bring fire to back up the demolitions and minefields with which they planned to delay the Allied advance.

With winter and more bad weather approaching, speed was of the essence for the Fifth Army. On 2 October Clark ordered McCreery to cross the Volturno at the earliest opportunity, and not to wait for Lucas' VI Corps – which was making slower progress – to come up alongside X Corps. McCreery's advance was, however, delayed by the weather, enemy rearguard action and the inevitable demolitions. The flooded ground hindered the concentration of troops and supplies for the assault, and McCreery estimated that his attempt to cross the river could not take place earlier than 9 October. Lucas was now ordered to go ahead on the night of 9/10 October with 3rd Division, which was in place for a crossing near Triflisco; X Corps was to force a crossing the following night.[8] A combination of weather, problems in moving troops and enemy action caused the operations to be delayed until the night of 12/13 October but 56th (British) Division failed in its attempt to force the river at Capua. The next day it made a feint attack, but the strong resistance it encountered illustrated that heavy losses would be taken if the division tried to breach the defences at this point and McCreery refused to push it forward for another try; its failure also left the left flank of the 3rd (US) Division dangerously exposed. Clark altered the inter-corps boundary to give the 56th Division the use of the 30-ton bridge which had been constructed in 3rd Division's area at Triflisco[9] and it joined the 7th Armoured Division and the 46th Infantry Division, which had more success in their attacks, north of the river. But it was, again, the 56th Division, X Corps and McCreery that Clark felt had failed him.

They would soon do so again. On 6 November 56th Division was ordered to clear Monte Camino, a three-peaked feature defended by five German battalions against which the division could only muster four. The contest lasted until the 14th, at which stage McCreery advised Clark that a halt should be called and the surviving infantrymen withdrawn. Clark agreed, but the episode gave more fuel to his resentment. As Graham and Bidwell point out, he was probably not interested in the fact that by the third week in November X Corps' infantry battalions had suffered an average of 400 casualties. Regardless of this, McCreery put 56th Division into the battle for Camino again at the beginning of December. This time he used a brigade from 46th Division to secure a firm start-point for the attack, which was supported by an artillery barrage which delivered 1,329 tons of ammunition in seventy-five minutes. This time the Germans withdrew.

Advancing northwards progress was slow, hindered by enemy roadblocks and demolished roads and bridges. Churchill had stressed to Alexander that Rome should be captured before the end of the year, but it was becoming increasingly obvious that this was not going to happen. In twenty days across a front measuring some forty miles, the Fifth Army advanced only fifteen to twenty miles. It did, however, break through the poorly-defined Barbara Line, the first of the German defences; behind it lay the Bernhard Line along which the enemy had laid 45,000 mines with another 30,000 on its approaches.

The Fifth and Eighth Armies were at the point of exhaustion. They had maintained pressure on the Germans incessantly, their lines of communication were stretching ever farther, and the weather was deteriorating as they pushed into increasingly difficult countryside. With OVERLORD ahead there was no question of rotating units in the front line for rest and rehabilitation: there were no fresh ones to replace them for they were being withdrawn to the United Kingdom, although the headquarters of II (US) Corps, under Major General Geoffrey Keyes, arrived from Sicily and took command of the American 3rd and 36th Infantry Divisions. Fresh reinforcements were not scheduled to arrive until December and January, and although Italy had declared war on Germany on 13 October Italian forces were not at that time ready to offer substantial assistance. By the beginning of December, however, the Italian 1st Motorised Group was attached to II (US) Corps and serving alongside American troops. On 8 December the Corps engaged enemy defences in the San Pietro area, the Italians attacking Monte Lungo while the Americans assaulted Monte Sammucro and the village of San Pietro. Despite having the support of a heavy artillery bombardment the 36th (US) Division and the Italians took large numbers of casualties: the Italians lost eighty-four killed, 122 wounded, and a further

170 men missing. The week-long battle for San Pietro cost the 36th Division 150 killed, 800 wounded and 250 missing, and casualties were also high in supporting airborne, Ranger and armoured units. The Germans withdrew on 16 December, and a blizzard then brought the fighting to a close at the end of the year.

Co-Belligerents

When the Italian armistice was being negotiated the Badoglio government had argued that an Italian surrender would be conditional on the Allies securing Rome; they had hoped for a force of some fifteen divisions being landed to achieve this aim, but – although they did not advertise the fact – the Allies knew that this was plainly impossible. In the event, as recounted earlier, they were only able to offer the 82nd Airborne, which in itself proved impossible given the lack of Italian forces to join them. At the forefront of Badoglio's mind was the awareness that the Germans would exact retribution for what Hitler would undoubtedly regard as treason. The Italians wanted assurances that they would be protected from whatever measures their former ally might take against them; as a minimum they needed prior warning of the news of their surrender being broadcast so that they might evade imprisonment. Eisenhower's announcement on 8 September took the Italians by surprise and left both Badoglio and the royal family scrambling to escape from Rome. On 9 September they fled to Brindisi, taking only a small number of staff officers with them despite their plan to re-locate army headquarters out of Rome. In their haste to leave they did not have sufficient time to issue detailed instructions to the Italian armed forces on what action they should take, and many units were unaware of the fact that they were supposed to deny facilities to the Germans, by force if necessary. Moreover, Italian troops were to take possession of all German-occupied points. Mussolini and his associates were to be handed over to the United Nations, another arrangement which Badoglio had no time to finalize. Mussolini was rescued from his captivity in the Abruzzo Mountains on 12 September by a small force of German paratroops led by Otto Skorzeny, and was able to establish his Social Republic based in Salo on Lake Garda, around which those military units which retained their allegiance to the Fascist cause rallied. With political interests and military forces actively supporting both the United Nations and Mussolini, Italy entered a state of civil war.

On hearing the news of the Italian surrender the Germans had been swift to disarm and intern Italian servicemen, sometimes having to use force to do so. In the coastal town of Nettuno, near to Anzio, for example, the Germans rounded up Italian soldiers and drove them away into captivity on 9 September. Active resistance broke out and some soldiers who had evaded capture forced the Germans out of the town; they returned soon afterwards, in strength and supported by Stuka dive-bombers. Retribution and firing squads quickly followed. The Germans occupied Rome on 10 September inflicting over 1,000 casualties for a loss of more than 600 of their own men, and on the island of Cephalonia over 1,000 Italian soldiers died during ten days of fighting the Germans, who then executed nearly 5,000 of those who had surrendered. Of those who survived this massacre, more were to be killed when the ships that were transporting them to Germany had been sunk by mines and those who attempted to swim to safety had been machine-gunned. Italian soldiers were also executed on Corfu and Kos. In all, over a million Italian servicemen (about half of the army) were disarmed and imprisoned by their former ally. Some of these prisoners, particularly those who were members of the Fascist Republican Party, elected to accept the offer to continue fighting against the Allies.

The first unit of the Co-Belligerent Army was formed in late September from soldiers, some of whom had narrowly avoided being interned, who were gathered in tented camps near Lecce awaiting reorganization. The 1st Motorised Combat Group (*1 Raggruppamento Motorizzato*) included elements of two divisions from the old Italian Royal Army and numbered some 295 officers and 5,387 men. Its participation in the fighting at Monte Lungo did much to remove the distrust felt by the Allies, who were understandably suspicious of their former enemy, the second nationality – after the French at the time of TORCH – which had until recently been trying to kill them.

The reputation of Italian troops was not high. Allied propagandists tended to dismiss them unquestioningly, especially after their disastrous attempts to invade Greece in October 1940 and then the defeat of the Italian Tenth Army in Egypt in February 1941, after a six-month campaign in which they faced a British force only a fifth of its size. The Italian losses were heavy: about 3,000 were killed and 115,000 captured. In the words of Anthony Eden: 'Never has so much been surrendered by so many to so few'. The Italian forces had to cope with an incompetent leadership and inadequate equipment, much of which was of Great War vintage, and British propaganda, particularly in 1941 when morale at home was low, made the most of playing up their enemy's shortcomings. The message stuck, despite occasions when Italian troops displayed courage. Their reputation was not enhanced by their ally, Germany, which made much of the performance of the *Panzerarmee*

Afrika despite the fact that Italian forces contributed greatly to its success in North Africa, a role which Rommel recognized. Against British and Indian formations in the Battle of Keren, Italian forces were acknowledged as being outstanding. Their courage in manning outdated tanks and guns against a technologically superior army at El Alamein was also noted.

By 1943 Italy was growing tired of a war that Mussolini, but not large numbers of the population, wanted. Nevertheless some Italian units continued to fight doggedly: in Sicily some of the *Sixth Army* divisions resisted strongly, although many of the locally-enlisted coastal defence formations chose to return to their families rather than oppose the Allied landings.

On 17 April 1944 the 1 Raggruppamento Motorizzato was renamed the Italian Liberation Corps (Cor*po Italiano di Liberazione*). With an increasing number of volunteers the Co-Belligerent Army expanded, and by the end of the war in Italy there were six combat groups (each having one or two infantry regiments comprising three battalions, with supporting artillery and engineer units; the strength of each group was the equivalent of a weak division) and eight auxiliary divisions which were generally employed in support duties. In late April 1945 the Legnano Combat Group, which had served under II (US) Corps, was expanded and became Fifth Army Troops.

Equipping the Co-Belligerents was to present problems. In his attempts to fill the manpower gaps in 15 Army Group during July 1944, Alexander pressed for greater use to be made of the Italian forces. The Americans refused to become involved in providing matériel or training, but Churchill agreed to arm and equip four new Italian divisions, each of 12,000 men.[10]

The First Special Service Force
In an account of coalition forces in the Italian campaign one formation stands out as being an exemplar of the level of integration which could be achieved between two allies: the Canadian-United States First Special Service Force. Its debut in Italy came in November.

Formed in August 1942 the Force was unique in that officers and soldiers from the United States and Canada served in units and sub-units without segregation; men of both countries, although retaining their own nationalities, were distributed throughout the formation initially on an equal basis. The Force's origin was in preparation for Operation PLOUGH (the object of which was to land a force of parachutists into the Norwegian mountains from whence they would carry out guerrilla operations against the occupying Germans; the plan never came to fruition). Although the undertaking was the brainchild of a British scientist working for Mountbatten's Combined Operations Command, it was offered to the United States during the Chequers Conference of March 1942, largely because the British were already heavily committed elsewhere. Marshall agreed to have the project examined, and in due course it was reported on by Lieutenant Colonel Robert T. Frederick, who was working in the Operations Division of the US General Staff. Frederick's report identified a number of weaknesses in the plan; his reward was to be given the task of raising and training a force to carry it out.

Because of the winter-warfare nature of the operation it had been envisaged that a mixed United States-Canadian-Norwegian force be assembled, all of whom would be familiar with working in the climate and terrain in which the task would be carried out. Difficulties in finding suitable Norwegian troops for the mission resulted in the US-Canadian mix that was to form the basis for the formation. The American volunteers were originally drawn from officers serving at Forts Belvoir and Benning and from soldiers who preferably had experience as lumberjacks and hunters or with similar backgrounds. The Canadian element (initially forty-seven officers and 650 other ranks) was raised under the cover story that they were to become the 2nd Canadian Parachute Battalion, a name which they retained until the spring of 1943, when their title became the 1st Canadian Special Service Battalion. Whereas the Canadians were of above-average quality in comparison to other soldiers, being recruited under higher standards which included being of non-commissioned officer material, already qualified as infantrymen and having volunteered for parachute duties, the first Americans to join the formation included many who were regarded by their commanding officers as troublemakers and who were best got rid of. A large number of these individuals – and indeed some Canadians – were rejected during the training process, although some remained. Their presence contributed to the formation's nature of tough individualists. The Canadian requirement that soldiers be potential NCO material was based on the intention that the lowest rank in the Force would be that of sergeant.[11]

Reasons for personnel being rejected included refusal to make the required number of parachute jumps (by far the highest category: 193 Canadian soldiers requested a return to other duties), suffering broken bones during training or for other medical reasons, and being regarded as 'undesirable'. The gaps in establishment were made up by posting in qualified parachutists from 1st Canadian Parachute Battalion – ninety-seven men came from that source in December 1942, much to the dissatisfaction of their original unit, where it was felt that its own preparations for war had been set back. A later attempt to raise more men for the FSSF from the 1st Parachute Battalion attracted only twelve other rank – and no officer – volunteers, the unit having built up its own esprit de corps prior to deployment across the Atlantic. Once the FSSF had departed from the United States it was intended that no further reinforcements would be made available from either country, although this decision was later reconsidered.

The Force was activated on 9 July 1942, nearly a year before the Canadian element became officially recognized. It comprised three small regiments, each of some 600 men divided into two battalions, supported by an all-American Service Battalion, again numbering 600 men who provided non-combat functions including headquarters, communications, the medical detachment and vehicle and weapons maintenance. Apart from the Service Battalion, Canadians and Americans were mixed evenly throughout the Force, with Canadians occupying about half of the command appointments and less than half of the combat units' manpower. Most battalion commanders and senior sergeants were Canadian; most junior officers American, which reflected the greater experience of the former soldiers who were generally older than their colleagues from south of the Canadian border. The average age (twenty-six) of the FSSF during its first year was higher than other units; this comparative maturity may have been a contributory factor to its success.

Forming a unit of this type made up of broadly equal numbers of men from two countries, each with its own military traditions, procedures, structure and code of discipline, was not as straightforward as might appear. It had been necessary for the respective governments to draw up a succession of agreements on their areas of responsibility, which included finance (including pay and transportation costs), provision of quarters, clothing, medical and dental services, matters of discipline and equipment. The division of responsibility for financial support was thrashed out in detail, with the Canadian government accepting pay and pension allowances, parachute pay, transportation to the initial training facilities in the United States, and payment for rations – for the Canadian contingent only. The Americans covered quarters, equipment, clothing, transport and medical services. A particular area of contention was that of pay, for the Americans received a considerably higher rate than the Canadians; despite Frederick's recommendations for parity, the Canadian Minister of National Defence took the view that this would discriminate against those Canadian paratroops who were not serving with the FSSF (i.e. the 1st Canadian Parachute Battalion) and all other servicemen who happened to be stationed with allied forces. An eventual agreement to pay Canadian FSSF other ranks the princely daily sum of seventy-five cents, and officers two dollars, parachute pay brought little satisfaction – Canadian staff sergeants earned less than the American privates who served under them. The rates, and the discontent, remained.

The unit underwent a stiff training programme at a fast pace – for example the parachute course was completed in six days as compared to the normal three weeks – with the training day starting at 0530 and not finishing until 1630 hours, and with evening lectures on four evenings each week. Training included skiing, climbing, survival techniques, physical training, demolitions and infantry skills, including the use of enemy weapons. All officers took a full part in the training, a factor which contributed to unit esprit and cohesion.

Operation PLOUGH may be included in the great number of plans which never came to fruition, and the Force's role was thrown into doubt while representatives of the two nations considered the alternatives for its future. A pertinent question was posed by the Canadian Minister of National Defence: 'whether from the Canadian viewpoint the 1st Special Service Force was anything more than just a stand-by Force, "its principal virtue being that it gives us the opportunity to say the Canadians and Americans are co-operating".'[12] Apart from this political consideration, so necessary in coalition warfare, the Force's capabilities in sabotage, raiding, and winter- and mountain-warfare saved it from being disbanded and, in April 1943, it undertook amphibious training in preparation for an operation to re-take the Aleutians from the Japanese. On 15 August the FSSF landed on Kiska Island, to find that the Japanese had departed some days earlier; shortly afterwards it departed for the Mediterranean, where Eisenhower had requested its presence to carry out reconnaissance and raiding missions in Italy, or to support resistance groups in the Balkans.

By 20 November 1943 the Force had assembled in Naples and was moved north by road convoy to Santa Maria, just south of the Volturno, where it came under command of II (US) Corps. The first mission undertaken by the FSSF was to take the German positions on the supposedly impregnable Monte de la Difensa, part of the Camino complex. These positions were key features on the Bernhardt Line, the first series of defences of the Winter Line, the purpose of which was to delay the Allies until the positions farther to the rear – the Gustav Line – could be completed. The Camino feature guarded the approaches to the Mignano Pass, through which the Liri and Gari river valleys lay, and beyond them the route to Rome up Highway 6. By now the weather had steadily deteriorated from the conditions at the time of the Salerno landings, and unusually heavy rain had been falling since the middle of September. Flooding rivers threatened the bridges hastily erected by the

Allies to replace those demolished by the enemy, and roads were regularly washed out with their verges a sea of mud sometimes a foot or more deep. Manpacks, mules and porters replaced vehicles for much of the re-supply operations to the front lines. The cold, the wet, and the mud affected morale and effectiveness, and not only on the Allied side: many German troops still wore the lightweight uniforms which had seen them through the fighting in Sicily and southern Italy in the summer and autumn months.

The Fifth Army was dispersed with the VI Corps on the right, on the Eighth Army's flank, II Corps in the centre opposite Camino, and X (British) Corps to the left, to the coast. German counterattacks in the latter half of November had stalled II Corps' advance, producing a situation of stalemate on that part of the front, and on the 29th of the month orders were issued for an attack in the Mignano area. German forces occupied positions on Monte Camino and Monte Maggiore, from which their artillery observers were able to bring fire onto the lower-lying ground to the west. In cooperation with X Corps, II Corps was to capture the Camino-Maggiore feature; 46th (British) Division was to attack the southern end of the Camino position and 56th (British) Division the Camino peak; 36th (US) Division, reinforced by the FSSF, was to capture Monte Maggiore, Monte de la Difensa and Monte la Remetanea. The 36th Division employed its 142nd Regiment against Maggiore and the 2nd Regiment of the FSSF was to take de la Difensa and then la Remetanea. The other two FSSF regiments were to stay out of the conflict for the immediate future: the 1st Regiment in divisional reserve, the 1st Battalion of the 3rd Regiment as FSSF reserve. The 2nd and 3rd Battalions of the 3rd Regiment were to assist the Service Battalion in supplying the assault unit.

Throughout the day and night of 2 December, the heaviest concentration of indirect fire thus far seen in the war in the west was delivered on the Camino massif by 820 guns and Allied aircraft. Some 22,000 rounds of high explosive, smoke and phosphorus were directed at the summit of la Difensa. At 0100 hours on 3 December the FSSF's 2nd Regiment commenced its attack up the steep slopes of the feature, stretching some 2,500 feet above the Mignano valley. By 0700 hours the Regiment's 1st Battalion had captured the summit, but had taken heavy losses in doing so; it was relieved by the 2nd Battalion later in the day. Having a shortage of ammunition and being uncertain of the German strength, further advances were called off until such time as reinforcements were brought forward. The 2nd Battalion held the position until 6 December, reinforced from the other two FSSF battalions, when the 1st Battalion advanced on la Remetanea under mortar and machine-gun fire from Camino, still held by the enemy. By midday the objective had been taken, and after a heavy artillery barrage from the whole of II Corps' guns on 8 December, the 1st Battalion of the 2nd FSSF Regiment drove the Germans into the valley west of the mountain. The success of the sequence of operations was muted by the casualty list: nine officers and seventy-one men killed or missing, and eleven officers and 339 men wounded. Casualty evacuation was a slow and laborious process – each stretcher had to be carried by six men, and it took between eight to ten hours to bring each of the wounded down the slopes of la Difensa. Eight Canadian NCOs were temporarily commissioned to fill some of the gaps in the officer ranks, appointments which were later confirmed.[13]

Clark recognized the achievement of the FSSF in a Fifth Army commendation, highlighting the fact that this was the formation's first action against the enemy, and was carried out in poor weather conditions against well-equipped defences.

II (US) and X (British) Corps had established firm footholds in the mountains between Mignano and Cassino, but a formidable barrier remained in the shape of Montes Chiaia, Porchia and Trocchio, which lay east of Cassino.

The Nisei

It has been noted that there were forces from the British Commonwealth and France that were recruited from the indigenous populations of overseas properties, and the United States Army was no different in this respect. After Pearl Harbor Americans of Japanese ancestry who were serving in the Hawaii National Guard or other local military units were regarded with suspicion and disarmed. The impending threat of a Japanese invasion of Midway Island and doubts about the loyalty of these soldiers prompted the authorities to send them to mainland United States as the Hawaii Provisional Infantry Battalion, later to be re-named the 100th Infantry Battalion (Separate). The battalion's performance during training convinced the government to reverse its decision on Japanese Americans serving in combat, although they were generally forbidden to fight in the Pacific theatre (those proficient in Japanese were an exception). On 1 February 1943 Roosevelt authorized the formation of a Regimental Combat Team (the 442nd) made up of Japanese Americans. In Hawaii nearly 10,000 men applied, from whom 2,645 were selected, but the response from Japanese Americans on the mainland was less enthusiastic; some 1,300 volunteers were selected. The reason for the reluctance of mainland Japanese to enlist may be found in the fact that on 19 February

1942 President Roosevelt signed an Executive Order requiring all Japanese Americans to be held in internment camps. The reason given for this action was to prevent spying (despite the fact that German and Italian Americans, who at least looked American and who would presumably have had less difficulty merging with the general population, were not interned), although there was also an element of revenge following Pearl Harbor and racist motivation; over 110,000 Japanese Americans were re-housed to the camps. Despite their treatment, some 17,000 men from both mainland USA and Hawaii enlisted into the US Army, where they served in segregated units.

The Japanese Americans, or Nisei, were permitted from the outset to serve in combat units, unlike Negro soldiers who were initially restricted to support units in the Italian campaign until the 92nd Infantry Division arrived in 1944. The 442nd RCT was to become the most highly decorated unit of its size and period of service in the US Army; twenty-one of its soldiers earned the Medal of Honor during its time in North Africa, Italy, France and Germany, all but one from the 100th Battalion of the 442nd. Apart from one, all the Medal of Honor recipients had originally been awarded lesser decorations because of the prejudices of the time; these were reviewed and upgraded in 2000.

After a brief stay in Oran the 100th Infantry Battalion was assigned to the 34th Division. It landed at Salerno on 22 September 1943 and its first combat experience was at Castelvetere six days later, after which the battalion was engaged in the Volturno crossings. It was to go on to fight at Cassino and Anzio, becoming known as the 'Purple Heart Battalion' because of the number of wounded the unit suffered in this time – over 1,000 medals were awarded.

The 442nd RCT provided thirty-one officer and 524 enlisted men replacements for the 100th Battalion from December 1943. This drain on its manpower meant that when it was sent to Italy in June 1944 it could only muster two infantry battalions rather than its full establishment of three. The 100th Battalion was attached to the 442nd to restore it to strength. The RCT served as part of 34th (US) Division until September 1944 when it was re-assigned to the 36th Division in southern France. In March 1945 it was to return to Italy at the request of Clark, to serve with the 92nd Infantry Division.[14]

Notes

1. Blumenson, *Salerno to Cassino*
2. Ibid

3. Gaham & Bidwell, *Tug of War*

4. Blumenson, op cit.

5. Ibid

6. Mavrogordato, *Hitler's decision on the defence of Italy*

7. Blumenson, op cit.

8. Fifth Army Operations Instruction No 6, dated 7 October 1943, in Starr, *Fifth Army History*

9. Starr, *Fifth Army History*

10. Holland, *Italy's Sorrow*

11. Canadian Department of National Defence, *Report No 5*

12. Ibid

13. Combat Studies Institute, *CSI Battlebook 14-A, Monte La Difensa*

14. McNaughton, *Japanese Americans and the US Army*

CHAPTER 9

Cassino to Rome

If inter-Allied working relationships in Italy appeared strained after Salerno, they were to sink to a new low in the period from January to June 1944. It would be possible to focus on these months alone as an illustration of much that is positive and negative about fighting a war as a member of a coalition. At all levels from the global strategic down to battlefield tactics, and including national and personal interest-furthering strategies wherein politicians and generals alike sought to achieve their own objectives, examples abound of the advantages and difficulties of working with allies.

In January 1944 the Allied command structure changed, with General Sir Henry Maitland Wilson replacing Eisenhower as Supreme Allied Commander, Mediterranean theatre. The American Lieutenant General Jacob L. Devers became his deputy. The direction of Mediterranean operations passed from the United States Joint Chiefs of Staff to the Chief of the Imperial General Staff, Sir Alan Brooke. Churchill immediately began attempts to revitalize the Italian campaign; for him the stagnation that had set in with the winter weather was unacceptable, and he wanted Rome captured as a priority. The Eighth Army also had a new general: on 23 December Montgomery departed from Italy and command passed to Lieutenant General Sir Oliver Leese.

Relationships between the new commanders were not destined to improve the conduct of operations. According to d'Este[1] Alexander held a low opinion of Wilson and generally chose to ignore any suggestions he made, unless they happened to coincide with his own ideas. Devers was equally ineffectual. Before arriving in the Mediterranean as Marshall's choice to oversee American interests, he had been stationed in England as commander of US ground forces, a position which he had surrendered to Eisenhower as OVERLORD approached. Neither Alexander nor Clark had much respect for Devers, and Clark regarded him as a 'dope' who failed to influence any command decisions. Devers saw Clark as a man obsessed with his own

169

career; Clark thought that Devers had no concept of tactical matters.[2] The two officers failed to get along with each other, but there were exceptions to the relatively poor working interactions between some of the US generals. Alexander's deputy chief of staff was the American General Lyman L. Lemnitzer, an able officer who was to rise to command NATO after the war.

As the Fifth and Eighth Armies made their attempts to break through the Winter Line operations broke down into regimental- and battalion-sized actions. In the Italian mountains, with their range after range of peaks which gave dominating observation points, there were just too many key features, each of which seemed to be overlooked by another. Once one had been taken the Germans merely fell back to the next, and the operation to drive them back towards the Alps had to start all over again. Taking each point presented problems because so many of them could be defended by fire from mutually supporting locations. The strongest layer of defences was the Gustav Line, the centrepiece of which was the town of Cassino and the 1,500-foot mountain which lay immediately behind it, on top of which sat the Benedictine Monastery. Behind that prominence lay the 5,000-foot high Monte Cairo. This strongpoint commanded the eastern side of the entrance to the Liri river valley, up which Highway 6 ran to Rome. There were three main roads running up the 'leg' of Italy: Highway 5 followed the Adriatic coastline, the route on which the Eighth Army was advancing. Highway 7 ran from Naples along the Tyrrhenian coast, at times running along narrow plains dominated by steep mountains. In places, for example north of Gaeta, the coastal plain was so narrow as to make an advance here almost impossible, although farther north towards Rome the road entered the wider, flatter landscape which had once been known as the Pontine Marshes, poorly drained and a breeding ground for malarial mosquitoes. Between Highways 5 and 7 ran the third route northwards; Highway 6 struck inland from Naples and worked its way through mountain passes until it reached the town of Cassino, after which it followed the Liri Valley onwards, eventually coming to Rome.

Highway 6 was a magnet to Allied planners, for it offered a limited opportunity to use their strength in armour, albeit a restricted one because the valley was little more than seven miles across at its widest point. To the north of the valley the Apennines rose to over 9,000 feet, a difficult passage for an army at the best of times and which would become impossible in the winter which was fast approaching. Both the Allies and the Germans were well aware that the Gustav Line could not be turned from the north-east by the Eighth Army once the bad weather set in, and Montgomery had earlier come to the conclusion that to continue the drive along the Adriatic coastline was futile: until the weather improved little would be achieved but senseless loss of life, and British lives were a diminishing and precious commodity, a factor which was not always appreciated by Americans like Clark who felt that their ally was overcautious.

To the Liri Valley's south lay the Aurunci and Lepini Mountains, almost as formidable an obstacle as the Apennines, with Monte Maio overlooking the crossings of the Rivers Gari and Garigliano below. These rivers were part of the drainage system to the Tyrrhenian Sea which started north of Cassino as the Rapido river before running into the Gari and finally the Garigliano. In places the rivers were over forty yards wide and they flowed swiftly in the winter rain. The way onto Highway 6 and into the Liri Valley could only be made past Cassino or via a secondary road running up the Ausente river valley from Minturno, close to the sea, over the mountains near Ausonia, and then into the Liri Valley near S. Giorgio. This route would also be made very much more difficult in winter. Both possible ways forward involved making crossings of defended rivers.

The gap in the mountains through which Highway 6 ran made it the obvious route to Rome. While the Allies made plans to use it, the Germans identified it as a place where solid defences should be built and manned. Without the mountains to assist, it was here that a concentration of man-made fortifications should be established. The strength of Monte Cassino itself was enhanced by the ruins of a medieval castle which sat above the town and protected the approaches to the monastery. To these natural and historical defences the Germans had added their own skills in military engineering: the Rapido had been dammed and its river valley flooded north of Cassino; both banks had been liberally sown with mines and booby-traps; and artillery and machine-gun emplacements, interspersed with dug-in tank turrets and reinforced with steel and concrete, had been constructed in the three months since the Salerno landings. The town of Cassino itself had been transformed into a fortress with pill-boxes and tanks and guns concealed inside buildings, and on the hillsides behind it yet more emplacements had been dug and blasted out of the rock. Wire and minefields were everywhere, and any feature or vegetation which might provide an attacker with cover, and which might conceivably be removed, had long since disappeared. The Gustav Line was probably the strongest defensive position in Europe and Cassino was the centrepiece which would have to be broken if the most promising route to Rome was to be opened.

Although Alexander urged that the momentum of the advance be kept up, the realities of the weather and of stubborn German resistance dictated that things would slow down. Clark had expected that, by 20 December, X Corps would be firm on Monte Camino, La Difensa and Maggiore, and would be preparing for operations on the Garigliano. II (US) Corps would have captured Monte Sambucaro, and VI (US) Corps would have advanced towards the mountains north and northwest of Cassino. Before the Cassino defences could be broached, however, II Corps would have to capture Mounts Porchia and Trocchio, which overlook the Rapido.

Operation SHINGLE
The strength of the Gustav Line was such that the planners began to look for a way to bypass it rather than to engage in a frontal assault, but the only way to do so was up the coastline in a manoeuvre which the Americans called an 'end run'. The term came from the game of American football and describes the action whereby a player carries the ball around the end of the opposing team's defensive line. Use of such phrases probably assisted those in the US Army to quickly grasp the intention, but they were less helpful to those of their allies who were unfamiliar with the game – as was the British use of terms such as 'knocking the enemy for six' which probably puzzled those who did not play cricket.

The site selected for the end run was the small port of Anzio-Nettuno, some thirty miles south of Rome. It had been chosen by the Allied commanders when they met in Tunis on Christmas Day 1943 and the plan built on an earlier version which had been proposed in November. That first plan had suggested that a single division – 3rd (US) Division had been earmarked for the task – be landed to support an advance by the Eighth Army up the Adriatic coast on Highway 5, while the Fifth Army pushed up the Liri Valley. The landings were to have linked up with these two thrusts and were to have occurred once Fifth Army had reached a line running from Capistrello–Ferentino–Priverno, near Frosinone, about forty miles southeast of Rome. Their limited objective was to assist in the capture of the Alban Hills (also known as the Colli Laziali) which lay some twenty miles inland and about fifteen miles south of Rome, overlooking Highway 6 and the main German lines of communication to the south. The landing force was to have been reached by the Fifth Army no more than a week after coming ashore, which was considered to be a feasible objective as there would be only twenty-five miles or so to cover between Frosinone and the Alban Hills. The revised plan was a different matter to simply being on hand to assist in capturing the hills, however. It proposed that the landing force should be expanded to two divisions and some airborne and armoured forces, and that their intent should be to strike inland to the Alban Hills. Their presence there would block German supply routes south to the Gustav Line, where its defenders would be threatened with being cut off. The landings would not wait until the Gustav Line had been broken and the distance to be covered before the hills were reached by the force pushing up the Liri Valley had now grown to about sixty miles. The increased distance, when added to the task of breaking through the Gustav Line, cast a new light on the difficulties ahead. Given that it had taken the Allies over three months to progress from Salerno to Cassino, a distance of some eighty miles, the prospect of a swift meeting between the Fifth Army and the Anzio force seemed ambitious to say the least. Although the Allies may not have fully appreciated the strength of the German defences which faced them, the experience of fighting their way from the Volturno to Cassino should surely have left them with few illusions about the magnitude of the task ahead.

The task of planning Operation SHINGLE was given to General Clark and the Fifth Army staff, who were faced with the immediate problem of the limited numbers of landing craft that would be available for the operation. It will be remembered that preparations for OVERLORD had priority and amphibious shipping was being withdrawn from the Mediterranean for that purpose, but Churchill prevailed upon the Americans to retain a number of Landing Ships Tank (LSTs) in the theatre until 5 February 1944 for Operation SHINGLE, the Anzio landing. There were sufficient for only two divisions to make the initial landing, but it was hoped that this force would be enough to compel the Germans to take troops from the Gustav Line to deal with the fresh threat. Weakened defences in the south would be more easily breached, and it was considered possible that the enemy might even decide to withdraw from the line completely to deal with the threat to their rear. VI Corps and 3rd Division would have to be pulled back from the front for the Anzio operation and the newly arrived French Expeditionary Corps would take its place on the northern flank of the Fifth Army.

As a forerunner to the landings Clark ordered an attack on the Gustav Line with the intention of drawing German forces away from the Anzio area. This would allow the landing force to make a strong lodgement before the enemy could mount an effective counterattack with whatever forces they had left in the Rome area. If successful, the attack on the Gustav Line might even make a breakthrough and throw the road to Rome open for the Fifth Army.

The formations available to Clark were more numerous than he had under his command when fighting through the Winter Line. At the turn of the year Alexander had restructured the Fifth and Eighth Armies as fresh troops arrived in Italy and as the strategic situation changed. The 1st (British) Division arrived in early December, and was assigned to the Fifth Army, joining VI Corps. The 5th (British) Division was transferred to X (British) Corps, still with the Fifth, and on 13 December the French Expeditionary Corps (*Corps expéditionaire français* – CEF. It officially assumed this title in January) had relieved the 34th Division which had suffered 1,500 casualties. The 7th (British) Armoured Division was withdrawn to be sent to England. Alexander moved the 2nd New Zealand Division from the Eighth Army to Army Group Reserve, and Eighth Army received 5th Canadian Armoured, 4th Indian, and the Polish 3rd Carpathian Divisions. For Anzio, Alexander selected General Lucas and his VI (US) Corps Headquarters to command a force assembled especially for the landing. There were advantages in doing things in this fashion rather than trying to extricate a United States or British Corps from the line, which risked giving the game away, and there was not time to form a completely new corps for the operation. HQ VI Corps had experience of amphibious operations from Salerno, and the Corps' 3rd (US) Division had been chosen for the single-division landing which had been considered earlier. First (British) Division was also readily available and not yet committed elsewhere. The other divisions that had been part of VI Corps' order of battle, the 34th and 36th, went to II (US) Corps, with Combat Command B of 1st Armored Division. The Special Service Force left II Corps on 17 January.

In early January the Eighth Army front became static. It was not to move again until March and April when the Army started to take up positions to advance into the Liri Valley. The weather in January was appalling: a blizzard on New Year's Eve was followed by a thaw which brought snowfalls, rain, frost, and freezing conditions. With little happening here Alexander was able to send more forces to the Fifth Army, and on 30 January General Leese, commander of the Eighth Army, was ordered to despatch 4th Indian Division thence, and to be prepared to have 78th Division follow after 7 February.

The Gustav Line
The Fifth Army front ran from the mountains north of Cassino down to the Gulf of Gaeta. On its right were the French, filling the gap between Sant' Elia and the Eighth Army, then the II (US) Corps with 34th and 36th Infantry Divisions either side of Highway 6, supported by Combat Command B (two tank battalions-strong, plus supporting artillery, engineers and service troops) of the 1st (US) Armored Division. The stretch to the sea was occupied by X Corps, with the 46th, 56th and 5th Divisions placed right to left. The Fifth

Army front was manned by two French, two and a half American, and three British divisions. Facing them was General von Senger und Etterlin's *XIV Panzer Corps*.

The CEF was to open the attack on the Gustav Line on 12 January; II Corps was to secure Monte Trocchio three days later. On a date to be determined later, but estimated as D+8 (20 January), II Corps was to force the Rapido, establish a bridgehead and exploit with armour to the west and northwest up the Liri Valley. X Corps was to attack on D+5 (17 January) and force the Garigliano in the Minturno area, and exploit north towards San Giorgio. It was also, on 19 January, to establish a second bridgehead at Sant' Ambrogio, two miles south of the junction of the Rapido and Liri Rivers, and exploit westwards. This would cover the left flank of II Corps when it attacked across the Rapido. The timetable therefore ran as follows:

12 January   CEF drive in the enemy's left.

15 January   II Corps drive in the centre to reach the Gustav Line.

17 January   X Corps attack to draw in the *29th* and *90th Panzer Grenadier Divisions* which were within reach of Anzio.

20 January   II Corps attack across the Rapido.

22 January   VI Corps land at Anzio to threaten the enemy's rear.

On the north of the Fifth Army front General Juin's CEF mounted its advance and made slow but steady progress against stiff opposition; events followed what was becoming a pattern for the campaign: Allied forces would take a position with difficulty and usually with the support of a heavy artillery bombardment, whereupon the Germans would mount a series of counterattacks hoping to catch the Allies in a state of disorganization as they consolidated on the objective. Having expended much of their small-arms ammunition during an attack on 12 and 13 January Moroccan soldiers on one feature were reduced to throwing stones at the enemy, counterattacking in the snow. The Germans were forced to evacuate Sant' Elia on 15 January, and II Corps captured Monte Trocchio on the same day. The schedule could now continue with X Corps crossing the Garigliano on 17 January as the prelude to the planned II (US) Corps operation to open up the Liri Valley.

The 36th Division was given the task of making the assault crossing of the Rapido downstream from Cassino (actually, at this point the river has

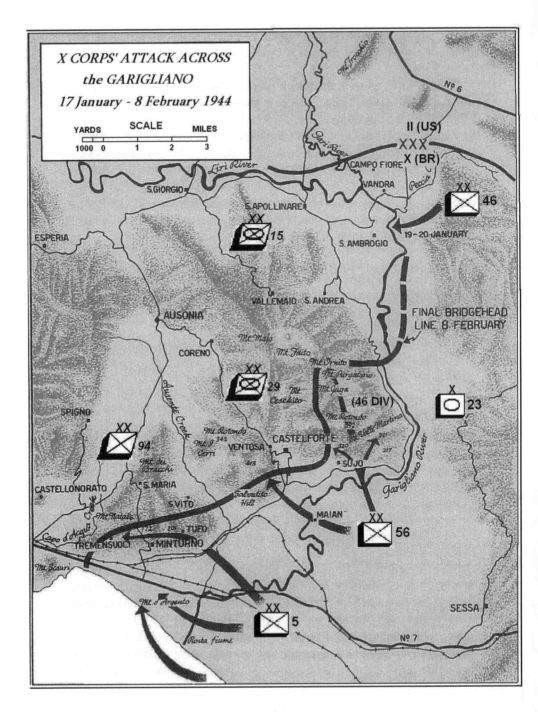

X CORPS' ATTACK ACROSS
the GARIGLIANO
17 January - 8 February 1944

become the Gari, but as American histories use the term Rapido this name is retained here for simplicity). The lie of the land, the weather, and the German defences combined to make the operation difficult in the extreme. The American command doctrine of discouraging discussion of orders did not make things any easier. To the division's left X (British) Corps was to cross the lower reaches of the Garigliano stretching down to the Gulf of Gaeta, with 5th (British) Division on the coast and 56th (British) Division attacking towards Castelforte and the high ground which lay above the Ausente river. The assault opened on 17 January, and by dawn on the following day the two British divisions had pushed ten battalions across the Garigliano; the 5th Division was positioned on either side of Castelforte when the Germans mounted their counterattack. The hard-pressed *94th Division* was reinforced by the arrival of the *29th* and *90th Panzer Grenadier Divisions*, with elements of the *Herman Göring Panzer Division,* ordered forward by Kesselring to block the British attempt to enter the Liri river plain by way of the Ausente valley. By 20 January the X Corps bridgehead had been expanded to a width of ten miles, but it had not reached its objectives and the advance had come to a halt. McCreery's promising advance in the Minturno area could not be exploited without the assistance of the 46th Division, which was committed to the separate attack on Sant' Ambroglio.

The 46th Division attack was hindered from the outset by having only enough boats for one brigade and most of those were lost or capsized in the fast-flowing river; the brigade's frontage for the crossing was so narrow that the Germans were able to concentrate their fire into a small area, and only one battalion managed to make a bridgehead on the far bank. It was withdrawn the next day to prevent needless loss of life, and McCreery refused to renew the attack. Although Clark agreed with the decision to pull the battalion back, the refusal to attack again served only to reinforce his poor opinion of the British.

The failure of the 46th Division's attack left the left flank of 36th (US) Division exposed. Major General Fred Walker, its commander, was less than enthusiastic about the task he had been given of forcing a defended river. In the First World War he had been on the receiving side when the German Army tried to cross the River Marne, and he was fully aware of the difficulties involved. Without the support of the British on his left he asked for a twenty-four hour delay in mounting his assault, but Clark had no room for manoeuvre – the Anzio landing was scheduled for 22 January and could not be changed, and the timetable for the Rapido and Garigliano attacks was locked into that date.

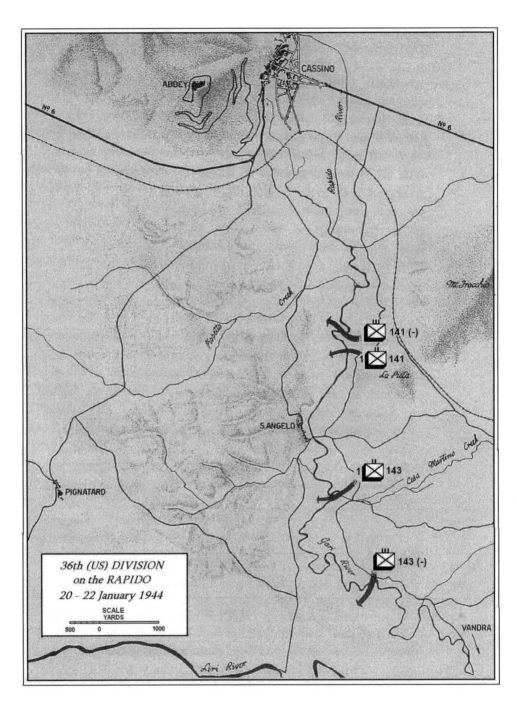

36th (US) DIVISION
on the RAPIDO
20 - 22 January 1944

SCALE
YARDS
500   0   1000

The 36th Division's plan for the assault involved two of its regimental combat teams (141st and 143rd; the third – 142nd RCT – was in reserve), which were to make the attempt north and south of the village of Sant' Angelo in Theodice. During the night of 20 January US engineers carried bridging equipment and assault boats forward towards the river across flooded ground. Obstructed by enemy minefields and subjected to artillery and machine-gun fire, they abandoned their loads short of their objective and left the infantry to complete the job. In heavy fog they did so, suffering casualties as they advanced, weighed down by the matériel. The river was swiftly running and the banks were two to three feet high, making the launch of boats difficult. Many were swept away, and by daybreak only two-and-a-half companies from one regimental combat team had made the crossing north of the village; only one of the four footbridges they had attempted to install remained standing. To the south, a single battalion crossed, but was then compelled to fall back to the eastern bank. Confusion reigned.

During the evening of 21 January the attack was renewed, despite Walker's objections. The II Corps commander, Keyes, was under pressure from Clark to try again in what was now a desperate attempt to make his plan succeed. Limited gains were made by both RCTs, yet once again they were forced back. The division suffered 1,681 casualties to no avail.

The fatal part of Clark's plan to break the Gustav Line, as identified by Graham and Bidwell,[3] was that in the original version of SHINGLE – the single division landing at Anzio which would assist Fifth Army's advance to Rome once the move up the Liri Valley had reached Frosinone – the breakthrough of the Gustav Line would be achieved where 36th Division was now to cross the Rapido. II Corps would progress up the Liri Valley and follow Highway 6 to Rome. Clark had set X Corps two objectives, which gave McCreery no reserves to exploit his success on the left of the line, but this was one area which the Germans could not easily reinforce from the Liri Valley. When the opportunity presented itself to take another way forward Clark was unable – or unwilling – to seize it. He stuck to his original plan, which had the 36th (US) Division making the assault to clear the entrance to the Liri Valley. His decision to do so has been ascribed, by not only Graham and Bidwell but also by Fred Walker, 36th Division's commander, to an inability to react quickly.[4] There is another possible reason for Clark insisting that 36th Division went ahead with his plan: already disillusioned with the British performance since Salerno, rightly or wrongly, Clark must have hoped for an American success. Tellingly, d'Este notes that Clark was to be found wherever there were American troops[5] but Clark's command included men from many other nationalities, and it was his job to lead them as an integrated body in a common endeavour. Favouring the American elements, however understandable this inclination might have been because of his familiarity with their operating procedures and a natural gravitation towards his own countrymen, did little for international teambuilding, nor for the success he sought. Clark went beyond his tendency to seek the company of his own kind; not only did he prefer the company of Americans, he let them know his low opinion of his allies.

Many historians have explained Clark's behaviour as being prompted by his ambition to succeed in the eyes of his countrymen, especially those who held high military and political appointments and might further his career. This undoubtedly played its part. There are other factors which might be considered: amongst these may have been an underlying sense of insecurity about his own abilities as a general. With only a token experience of battle before taking command of the Fifth Army, working for and with British officers who had been schooled in the First World War and who had faced the Germans since the outbreak of the Second must have been intimidating, and any attempts that they made to advise and encourage him came across as patronizing – perhaps they sometimes were. It was not only British advice that Clark resented: Admiral Hewitt's attempts to get him to employ a preparatory naval barrage on VI Corps' Salerno beaches fell on deaf ears. Clark had to be seen to be in charge, for good or bad, and in this he was very much the animal of the greatly expanded US Army, which discouraged discussion of orders and the use of initiative by subordinates because the training system could not adequately prepare them to act with more independence.

To position himself strongly for future promotion Clark had also to show that he was capable of creating an outstanding American feat of arms in a theatre that his superiors believed to be almost an irrelevance. Marshall and the Chiefs of Staff provided only such matériel and moral support for the campaign as they could get away with, but they certainly did not want to see an American army – or its general – disgrace themselves. Clark had to provide Washington with headlines of victory if he was to rise further up the ladder to the highest echelons. By far the preferred option was to do this in a manner that positioned his American forces in the spotlight – an American general winning a battle with allied troops was fine, but such a victory would look much better at home if it were United States soldiers that were earning the glory and the medals rather than the British, the French or whoever else was around. The fact that II (US) Corps found itself positioned to open the

Liri Valley may have been unplanned, but it was too fortuitous a situation to be wasted. Like it or not – and Fred Walker did not – the 36th Division was fated to make the attempt.

Operation SHINGLE

At 0200 hours on 22 January 1944 the first landing craft headed for the beaches around the neighbouring towns of Anzio and Nettuno. The Germans had expected the Allies to make an 'end run' at some stage, but not until later in the year. Consequently they had nothing more than three companies of engineers and one battalion of *71st Panzer Grenadier Regiment* manning the coastal defences from the mouth of the Tiber to the Mussolini Canal, a distance of thirty miles. The Allied landings ran into virtually no opposition – most of the casualties were caused by minefields – and by midday VI Corps had achieved its initial objectives, including capturing the port facilities.

German reaction was swift. Elements of *4th Parachute* and the *Hermann Göring Divisions* were moved south from the Rome area to block the roads running north from the Alban Hills. The beachhead was ringed with 88mm guns from the Rome anti-aircraft defences and further units were ordered to the area from France, Yugoslavia and Germany to reinforce those from *3rd Panzer Grenadier* and *71st Infantry Divisions* which were on their way within twenty-four hours. What had not happened was for the Germans to make substantial troop movements from the Gustav Line to counter the threat at Anzio.

Operation SHINGLE was yet another of the plans which Montgomery would have scorned as being put together by inexperienced staff officers who worked from maps without any real understanding of the ground. Pushed on by Churchill and Alexander, the Fifth Army planners produced a scheme which placed VI Corps some sixty miles behind enemy lines; with the Gustav Line unbroken it was unlikely to be reached by Allied forces quickly. Anzio offered Churchill a way to inject new life into the faltering Italian campaign and to set it back on the course he wanted it to follow. If successful it might yet persuade the Americans to do away with their plan to land Allied forces on the Mediterranean coast of France after OVERLORD. Operation ANVIL was intended to draw German forces away from Normandy and to open a second front in France, but it would have its affect on the Italian campaign because the Allied armies there would be providing the troops to carry it out. Such a move would almost certainly kill off Churchill's thoughts on moving into the Balkans. SHINGLE was driven by Churchill's vision of the way he saw the war being fought, and by his vision of the way the postwar world would be shaped. It was a longer-term view of the world than that held by his American allies, who at times appeared to see no further than the crushing of Nazi Germany. It was a perception which they had to revise once the war was over, when they had to face up to the reality of Soviet expansionism. For the time being, however, the decision to launch SHINGLE owed as much, if not more, to political as to military considerations. Politics also played a part in the composition of the force which was to make the landing. Military considerations would have suggested that the troops that landed at Anzio were best drawn from only one nation because of operational and logistic compatibility, and as Fifth Army was responsible these should be American. Churchill was emphatic that the British must participate in the capture of Rome, not least for purposes of national prestige. The wider effects of coalition warfare were coming into play again, and yet again they were to cause friction between the Allies at all levels from the strategic to local operations.

The execution of SHINGLE was beset by the underlying problem of lack of clarity about its objective. At different command levels different objectives emerged, and the further down the chain, the more limited they appeared. To Churchill, the intention was to 'hurl a wildcat on the shore' (a hope which was to become a disappointment and 'a stranded whale'), which would draw German reserves from the Gustav Line and quickly lead to the fall of Rome, a highly significant psychological and political prize. Admiral Sir John Cunningham (Commander-in-Chief, Mediterranean Fleet) thought of the operation as a lightning thrust by two or three divisions, while Alexander's Operations Instruction dated 12 January 1944 saw the objective as cutting the enemy's main lines of communication 'in the Colli Laziali area south-east of Rome, and to threaten the rear of the German 14 Corps'. Clark's Field Order listed the aims as: '(a) To seize and secure a beachhead in the vicinity of Anzio; (b) Advance on Colli Laziali.' Lucas, commander of VI Corps, had little enthusiasm for the operation. In late December, shortly after learning that his formation was to carry out the operation, he confided to his diary that 'these "Battles of the Little Big Horn" aren't much fun and a failure now would ruin Clark, probably kill me, and certainly prolong the war'. After being informed by Alexander that the date was set for 22 January and that there were no more troops available to him than had been already assigned, he wrote, 'I felt like a lamb being led to the slaughter … the whole affair has a strong odor of Gallipoli and apparently the same amateur was still on the coach's bench'. His orders to VI Corps read that they were to seize and secure the beachhead and then advance in the direction of Colli Lazialli, a far less ambitious aim than the wildcat in Churchill's mind, but probably a more realistic assessment of his prospects. Clark had deliberately left the second part of his orders – the 'advance in the direction of' – vague so that Lucas could make his own decision on whether to take the riskier option of striking inland as Alexander wanted, or to adopt the more cautious line of protecting his rear by ensuring that the beachhead was not overextended.[6]

At the back of the minds of both Clark and Lucas was the Salerno landing, only four months earlier. A repeat of such a close-run thing was not to be countenanced. And Lucas was not alone among senior officers who had studied the Great War and the failed Gallipoli expedition, and who saw uncomfortable parallels, particularly with the Suvla landings. There, in an attempt to break the deadlock at Helles, where British, ANZAC and French troops could not progress against the Turkish defences, a landing had been made farther up the Gallipoli peninsula. As was to occur at Anzio, the force commander chose to establish a firm beachhead before pushing inland, an action which allowed the Turks to seal off the landing area before the British could achieve their objectives. If Lucas had taken the lessons of Suvla to heart, he might have been more aggressive; but he might also be remembered for throwing away VI Corps on an unsupported and futile expedition deep into enemy-held territory.

It was apparent to many of those involved that Anzio was too far away from the front which it was supposed to be influencing. Such concerns failed to swing the argument against the operation; the pressure from Churchill, at a time when Eisenhower was leaving his post as Supreme Allied Commander Mediterranean and Wilson was not yet firmly in the job, was too much to resist. Alexander certainly fell in line, and Brooke and Montgomery's criticisms of his abilities as a top-level commander gain weight as a result. His decisions – or sometimes his failure to intervene to influence the questionable decisions of others – led to errors which cost lives and endangered the success of the campaign, and Brooke was firm in his view that Alexander lacked 'grip' of his generals and permitted them too much leeway.

There were occasions when Alexander's ostensibly laid-back style was inappropriate. Overseeing the Salerno planning he should have foreseen the difficulties of landing the American and British forces so far apart that the Germans were able to pose a serious threat of driving a wedge between them before dealing with them in a piecemeal fashion. Patton had seen the danger, but neither Alexander nor Clark recognized it – or if they did, they failed to remedy the situation by changing the plan. Secondly, again in the context of

Salerno, Alexander should have anticipated that the Eighth Army was poorly positioned to make a swift advance to the beachhead. He, of all people, was aware of Montgomery's arguments for ensuring that the Anglo-American landings in Sicily were close enough to be mutually supporting. And with SHINGLE, the same danger emerged: VI Corps and the remainder of Fifth Army were separated by miles of hostile terrain and by a determined and well-entrenched enemy. Battles are not won, however, by being timid. According to Alexander, SHINGLE was a bluff to scare the Germans into pulling back.[7]

Cassino

With X Corps halted on the Garigliano and 36th (US) Division's attempt to break through into the Liri Valley defeated, Clark's next move was to try to outflank Cassino from the north. His plan for doing so was once again to place American troops at what he considered to be the key positions to win the battle. If in Sicily Alexander and Montgomery had seen the US Seventh Army as being little more than a flank guard for the British, then, as far as Clark was concerned, in Italy forces from other nations would play only a supporting role to his Americans. Clark's plan to break through the Gustav Line was to interfere with General Juin's operations farther to the north of the town, where the French planned to drive into the Abruzzi Mountains to the town of Atina, from whence a valley ran down to the Liri plain well behind the German defences. Such a manoeuvre would unhinge the Gustav Line and render it impotent to halt the Allied advance. Atina itself was an important German communications and artillery centre, and its facilities were linked to observation posts on Monte Cifalco which looked right down the Rapido valley and over Allied movements around Cassino town and Monte Trocchio. In essence Juin's intent was to outflank the Cassino-centred position in a wide-sweeping arc which would also remove the troublesome observation positions on Cifalco. It was not to be, however. If Clark even listened to Juin's arguments for the French plan, he dismissed them in favour of a scheme which placed the Americans in the limelight, just as he had done only days earlier when he failed to exploit X Corps' advance across the Garigliano.

Juin and General Monsabert, commander of the 3rd Algerian Division, which was given the task of carrying out the French part of Clark's plan, were unimpressed. Clark wanted them to move on Terelle and Piedimonte to cover the flank of the 34th (US) Division, which would cross the Rapido and move into the mountains a mile or so north of Cassino. The intention was for the

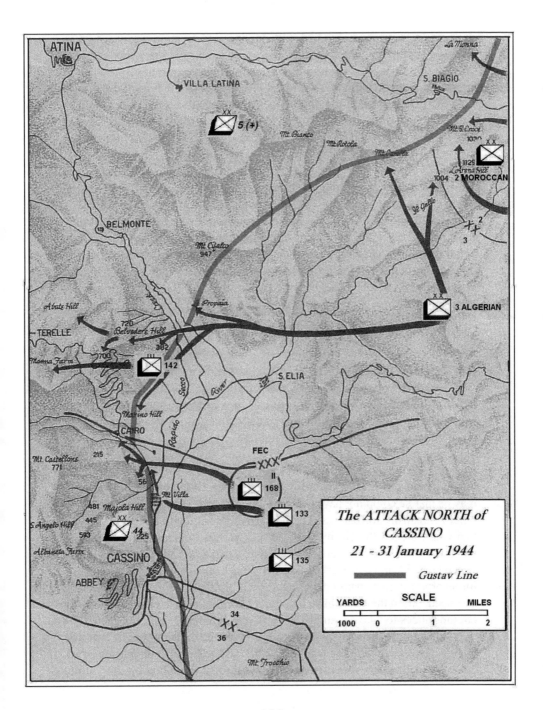

ATINA

VILLA LATINA

5 (+)

Mt. Bianco

Mt. Rotola

La Monna

S. BIAGIO

Mt. S. Croce
1020

1129
Arena Hill
1004   2 MOROCCAN

Il Gallo

3 ALGERIAN

Mt. Cifalco
947

BELMONTE

419

Propaia

Abate Hill

720
Belvedere Hill

TERELLE

382

Monna Farm

700

142

S. ELIA

Secco   River

Marino Hill

CAIRO

Mt. Castellone
771

215

Rapido

56

Mt. Villa

481   Majola Hill

445

S. Angelo Hill

593

225

44

Albaneta Farm

CASSINO

ABBEY

FEC

XXX

II

168

133

135

34

XX

36

Mt. Trocchio

**The ATTACK NORTH of
CASSINO
21 - 31 January 1944**

Gustav Line

YARDS   SCALE   MILES

1000   0   1   2

Americans to swing behind Monte Cassino and to push on into the Liri Valley, an operation which they opened on 24 January. It was a much smaller version of Juin's plan, on a tighter arc, and it was exposed to the view of enemy gunners on Cifalco. Despite their reservations the French fell in line; they felt that they had little alternative. It was a matter of honour, and they believed that they had a duty to carry out Clark's orders despite their belief that their attack would be carried out in full view of the enemy on Cifalco and the artillery fire that would inevitably be brought down on them.

On 25 January the French attack opened. Two battalions of the 4th Tunisian Infantry forded the waist-deep Secco river and pushed their way up a steep gully in the mountainside, which gave them some cover from Cifalco. They faced an ascent of 2,500 feet on an incline that was more of a climb than a walk, carrying all of their equipment and supplies with them. Once again the North Africans – and their opponents – were at times reduced to throwing rocks when their ammunition ran out. After four days of intense fighting the French had broken into, but not through, the German positions after heroic efforts. Two-thirds of the Tunisians were dead or wounded, and supplying the survivors was virtually impossible: an eighty-strong mule train which attempted to reach them one night came under enemy fire and only two of the mules arrived. With no reserves available, on 29 January Juin was forced to report to Clark that the French could do no more. Belvedere and Abata had been won, but the French now focused on holding the ground they had won rather than advancing farther. On 4 February the 4th Moroccan Mountain Division arrived. It came under command six days later but was not immediately committed to the front line.

Whether or not Juin's plan to outflank the Cassino defences would have worked will never be known, of course. With the limited forces at his disposal, and considering the difficulties the CEF had in taking Belvedere, it may be that he could not have achieved his objective without assistance from other Fifth Army formations. The point made by Graham and Bidwell[8] was that Clark lacked the ability to discern what was operationally sound and what was not. His plans were assembled on a map and followed a set of rules which he had learned at Staff College. His mechanical approach did not allow for incorporating or adapting the suggestions of others, no matter how worthy of consideration they may have been, and he was unable to adapt to changing circumstances to take advantage of fresh opportunities.

Clark's plan to attack Cassino head-on with one division was flawed. His attempts to by-pass the town to the south and north had been unsuccessful, the enemy defences were especially forbidding at this point on the Gustav

Line, and the Germans were able to concentrate their forces here now that the earlier Fifth Army attacks had ground to a standstill and because of the inactivity on the Eighth Army front. The 34th Division was far from being fresh. It had been heavily involved in the fighting during the previous months and there had been little or no opportunity for it to recover; morale was low.[9] Nevertheless it was fed into the next phase of the struggle to open the entrance to the Liri Valley – the division was about all that Clark had, and with VI Corps ashore at Anzio it was essential that pressure be maintained on the Gustav Line.

The 34th Division's attack opened on 24 January, across the flooded Rapido valley and then through minefields, wire and defensive positions at the base of the ridge which ran northwards from the Monastery to Belvedere. By midnight on the following day a small bridgehead had been established across the river and one company had pushed its way south along the foot of the hillside to the outskirts of Cassino before being forced back. In the face of waterlogged ground and enemy preparations progress was slow, and it was to take until 29 January before enough track was laid through the mud to permit tanks to cross in strength. On the last day of January the Americans captured Caira village, complete with the headquarters of *131st Grenadier Regiment*. But to counter their attacks the Germans were able to bring reinforcements into the Cassino stretch of front from elsewhere on the Gustav Line: a regiment from the *71st Infantry Regiment* was moved into the town itself, and on 1 February the headquarters and two battalions of *90th Panzer Grenadier Division* were in the mountains above it, having been transferred from their earlier positions opposite X Corps. A day later a battalion from *1st Parachute Division* arrived from the Adriatic. More were to follow.

Between the 34th Division and the French, the 142nd Regimental Combat Team from 36th (US) Division – which had been in reserve and had not participated in the attempts to force the Rapido – was to move into the mountains and force its way through to the Liri. The terrain and the enemy proved too much for the task. With the weather deteriorating daily the troops attempted to fight their way across mountain slopes in which it was impossible to dig trenches – unless one had the time and the explosives to construct them; the Germans had had both of these in abundance while they waited for the Allies to fight their way thus far. Despite these factors the Americans captured a number of features by 3 February, and from 8 to 11 of that month they made their final attempts to capture the town and the Monastery. Advances were made towards Albaneta Farm, lying in the valley west of the Monastery on the far side of what was to become known as

Snakeshead Ridge, which dominates the crestline above the Rapido valley. Point 593, which overlooks the Monastery from the mountains to its west, changed hands three times in as many days. The Germans held on to it, and by the 12th the Americans had been fought to a standstill in the freezing rain, sleet and snow. Some companies were reduced to fewer than thirty men, and some of the eighteen battalions involved had lost eighty percent of their effective strength. On 6 February the New Zealand Corps took over the area south of Highway 6, in readiness to advance into the Liri valley as soon as 34th Division had cleared the way. The Corps, under the command of Lieutenant General Sir Bernard Freyberg VC, consisted of the 2nd New Zealand and the 4th Indian Divisions. Clark anticipated difficulties in dealing with these fresh arrivals to the Fifth Army: 'these are dominion troops who are very jealous of their prerogatives. The British have found them difficult to handle. They have always been given special considerations which we would not give to our own troops.'[10] Furthermore, these reinforcements were 'British' not American. Clark really did not want them, and told Alexander so.[11] Nevertheless, the New Zealand Corps was placed under his command, like it or not. Clark made a final attempt to break the line with II (US) Corps, and it was only when it became blindingly apparent that the Americans were not going to succeed that the New Zealand Corps began to play its part. Instead of using the reinforcements together with II Corps to give added strength to his operations, Clark used them separately and allowed his Americans to be destroyed piecemeal.

The strength of Clark's American formations was depleting rapidly. After the attempt to cross the Rapido on 20/22 January, 36th Division was under strength by more than 3,000 infantrymen. It would continue to hold Monte Castellone until the New Zealanders passed through, but for the present it was a spent force. Elements of the 34th Division would occupy positions on the north of Cassino town, but their numbers were also critical (for example, the 100th Battalion – the Nisei – was reduced to seven officers and seventy-eight men). Morale was also dangerously low. Sent by Alexander to gauge the situation, his American deputy General Lemnitzer reported that the 34th was so dispirited as to be almost mutinous.[12]

Having consolidated the Belvedere bridgehead and unable to advance farther, the French assumed a defensive position. At the end of February only one American battalion was in line on the southern (i.e. Gustav Line) front. The rest of II Corps was now withdrawn into reserve while it was brought back to strength, and VI Corps was at Anzio. The Fifth Army front was lightly held by the CEF with a combat team from 1st Italian Motorized Group up to

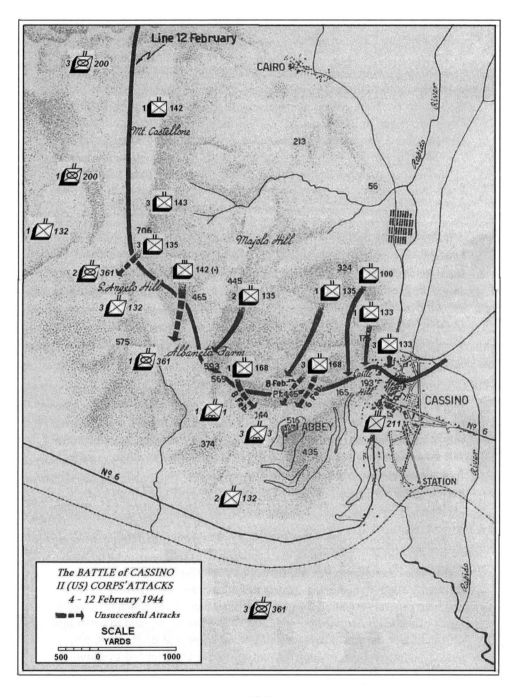

Line 12 February

CAIRO

3 200

1 142

Mt. Castellone

213

1 200

3 143

56

1 132

706

3 135

Majola Hill

2 361

S.Angelo Hill

142 (-)

465

445

2 135

324

1 135

100

3 132

575

Albaneta Farm

593

1 361

569

1 168

3 168

Castle Hill

1 133

3 133

193

165

1 1

8 Feb.
Pt.445

6 Feb.

211

CASSINO

No. 6

3 3

544

516

374

ABBEY

435

STATION

2 132

The BATTLE of CASSINO
II (US) CORPS' ATTACKS
4 - 12 February 1944

Unsuccessful Attacks

SCALE
YARDS

500   0   1000

3 361

the Eighth Army boundary in the north; the New Zealand Corps was in the centre opposite Cassino; and X Corps held the rest of the line to the sea in the south. On 8 February 78th (British) Division was placed under command of the New Zealand Corps, but deep snow on the Eighth Army front delayed its arrival in the Corps area until 17 February. More reinforcements were on the way to the Fifth Army, but were not ready for combat: the 88th (US) Division arrived in Italy in early February, and the first element of the 85th Division, the 339th Infantry Regiment, disembarked on 15 March.

The failure of the Fifth Army to take the Cassino strongpoint began to cause concern at higher levels. On 7 February General Wilson had received a less than encouraging report on the limited gains that had been achieved, and two days previously General Marshall had sent a telegram to London expressing the concern felt by the US Chiefs of Staff that the battle was deteriorating into attrition: there were heavy losses for little advantage. Unhappy with the tardy progress of a campaign that they had little enthusiasm for, the Chiefs raised the point that instead of an aggressively-mounted heavy assault on the Gustav Line there had, instead, been a series of limited attacks by comparatively small formations. This message caused some unease in London, where Churchill and Brooke feared that American support for the campaign might erode to the extent that they would let it stagnate and withhold further supplies of men and matériel.[13]

With the American attacks in the mountains above Cassino having been considered as being close to success, it was decided to repeat them with the Indian Division while the New Zealanders assaulted Cassino town, this time by advancing along the line of the railway which ran from the town's southeast rather than by the route the 34th Division had taken from the north. The railway embankment offered a route along which tanks might be brought forward without having to cross the flooded Rapido valley. The railway was in full view of the enemy, however, and had to be cleared of mines and other obstacles, while culverts and bridges would have to be repaired before tanks could cross into the town.

Neither General Tuker, GOC 4th Indian Division, nor Juin could agree with the argument for repeating the attacks on the strongly-defended Cassino sector. The carefully-prepared fortifications and forbidding natural features, manned by determined troops, made it the least welcoming route to Rome, and both generals favoured a wider-sweeping manoeuvre which involved as much of the Fifth Army as possible to deceive the enemy and to catch him off-guard, not the squandering of individual corps and divisions in penny-packet attempts. Both of their formations were experienced in mountain warfare and could see the potential of operating in such terrain. Juin had expressed his views to Clark, but again his recommendations fell on deaf ears. Clark appeared incapable of thinking on a grander scale, and Juin's proposal to make the ground the CEF held on Belvedere the Fifth Army's main axis of attack was ignored. Not Alexander, nor Clark, nor yet Freyberg, could see past – nor around – Monte Cassino. Tuker was to come to believe that Freyberg should not have been given command of a corps; his understanding of tactics and of mountain warfare was simply not up to the job.[14] In more recent times Freyberg might have been regarded as an example of the 'Peter Principle', wherein every employee in a hierarchical organization is promoted to the level of his incompetence.

Freyberg's appointment as Corps Commander highlights the political nuances that permeated coalition warfare, and – in particular – the relationships between nations within the British Commonwealth. He had distinguished himself during the Great War, serving both at Gallipoli and on the Western Front where he had been wounded four times and had been awarded the Victoria Cross. He was lionized both in New Zealand and in Great Britain, and when New Zealand sent an expeditionary force, one division strong, to the Middle East in 1940 Freyberg was appointed its commander. The division had fought in Egypt, Crete, and North Africa before coming to Italy. Popular with his men, Freyberg was nevertheless not intellectually up to the important position he held, and his staff officers often found his orders confusing.[15] As commander of the New Zealand Expeditionary Force Freyberg was more than just another divisional commander: he was directly answerable to his government for the wellbeing of the nation's troops. He held the authority to determine where and how they were committed to battle, an authority that went far beyond the formal military rank that he held and allowed him to bypass military superiors of other nations, Alexander and Clark included. The high casualty rate suffered by the division by May 1943 (18,500 from a total of 43,500 men) had prompted the New Zealand government to debate whether or not to bring it home; the fact that it stayed was at least partly because of Freyberg's arguments to keep it in the Mediterranean.

Whether or not Freyberg was the best choice as Corps Commander, political considerations probably played their part in determining his appointment. Churchill had made an emotional appeal to the New Zealand Government for its forces to remain alongside those of the rest of the Commonwealth at the time that the subject was being debated, and now the New Zealand Corps was nothing if not a force of Commonwealth countries.

As such, it illustrates – albeit on a smaller scale – the complexities of coalition warfare experienced by the Fifth Army and the Army Group as wholes. Among the nationalities that contributed units to the Corps were Great Britain, New Zealand, India, Nepal, Cyprus, and Bechuanaland. In support were also those elements of the American Army that had not been withdrawn into reserve, primarily artillery and armoured units. The War Graves Cemetery in Cassino displays headstones from throughout the Commonwealth.

The operations planned for the Indian Division in the mountains exposed more difficulties of working with allied armies. During the handover from the Americans to the Indian Brigade it had become apparent that senior American commanders had not been anywhere near the troops on the heights and were under the false impression that Point 593 was in their hands. The feature's position overlooking the rear of the Monastery was key to its defence; situated at the southern end of Snakeshead Ridge, which was the only viable approach to it, the Point had to be captured before the Monastery could be attacked from that direction. The Americans, despite valiant efforts, had failed to take it, but the Indians were not made aware of this fact.

The next phase of the battles for Cassino opened with one of the most controversial events of the Italian campaign, the bombing of the historic Benedictine Monastery. The feeling that everything could be seen from the Monastery was uppermost in the minds of many of the Allied troops in the valley below. It was a realistic expectation, for the building dominated the skyline of Monte Cassino, but singling it out as the only place from which the defenders were observing preparations for the continuance of the battle was irrational, for the mountain slopes offered a multiplicity of sites from which the Germans were able to overlook the valley. Indeed, both General Juin and General von Senger und Etterlin, the commander of *XIV Panzer Corps*,[16] regarded Monte Cifalco, in the mountains to the east of the town, as being more valuable to the defenders as an observation point because it looked right down the Rapido valley, Cassino town and across Monte Trocchio. From the perspective of its use as a defensive position, the Monastery was undoubtedly a formidable building – if it was really necessary to attack it. General Tuker had researched the Monastery's construction from books which he had obtained in second-hand shops in Naples. He considered it to be a strongpoint in the German defences, as did most of the men in the New Zealand Corps, and argued that it had to be reduced before being attacked. Whether it posed a realistic threat or not, the fact that Allied soldiers believed it to be one was enough for him to press for the building to be bombed, despite the fact that the Germans had declared that they had ordered their forces to stay away from the Monastery.

The centuries-old Monastery was a site of great religious and historical importance, a fact which had to be catered for when planning operations in its vicinity. The Allies had imposed limits on the way the Italian campaign was to be fought: before the invasion of Sicily the Combined Chiefs of Staff had given directions to Eisenhower that 'the position of the church and of all religious institutions shall be respected and all efforts made to preserve the local archives, historical and classical monuments and objects of art'.[17] It was an order which was to add another complication to the manner in which warfare was conducted in the Mediterranean theatre.

Whether or not the Germans were making use of the Monastery became a matter of dispute. Some Allied observers reported sighting enemy troops in the building, and among these were Generals Eaker and Devers, the commander of the Mediterranean Air Force and Wilson's deputy respectively. They had flown low over the Monastery and claimed to have seen German soldiers and radio aerials there. Clark gave Freyberg written permission to bring artillery fire onto the Monastery if the New Zealander decided that it was a militarily necessity. On receiving Tuker's request for the Monastery to be neutralized, Freyberg sent a message to Fifth Army Headquarters asking for it to be bombed. What followed became an exercise in buck-passing on national lines, at the time and since, as to who took the responsibility for the destruction of the historic building. As Clark was visiting Anzio and temporarily out of contact when Freyberg's request arrived, the Fifth Army Chief of Staff, General Gruenther, referred the decision to Lieutenant General Sir John Harding, Alexander's Chief of Staff. In doing so, he stated that he believed Clark would not support the bombing on the grounds of military necessity; however, because of the international and religious implications he would like Alexander's opinion on the matter. Later Gruenther also made contact with Clark, whose response was to state that while he did not agree with bombing the Monastery, he found it difficult to deny Freyberg's request because he – Clark – would be blamed if the attack were then to fail. The II (US) Corps GOC, Keyes, also felt that the bombing was unnecessary, but Alexander decided to support Freyberg.

The decision was heavily influenced by Freyberg's position as both the commander of the New Zealand Expeditionary Force and his government's representative. As such, Clark felt that he could not treat him in the same manner as he would an American officer of the same rank, who would not have been given the permission he sought. Alexander may have had the same reasons for agreeing with Freyberg; he did not record why he made the decision to bomb the Monastery other than to note that it was 'an integral part of the German defensive system, mainly from the superb observation it afforded.'[18] It was a decision in which Clark's reservations were overruled; he was not alone in his belief, for – apart from Keyes – both Generals Juin and Monsabert disagreed with the destruction of the Monastery.[19] If strictly military considerations did not provide justification for what many regarded as pure mindless vandalism, then what did? Ellis[20] records the feelings of hatred that many Allied soldiers felt for what they saw as the all-seeing, dominating, evil edifice that sat on the mountain glaring down at them, and the joy they experienced when they witnessed it disappear in clouds of smoke and dust as the bombers passed overhead. Alexander believed that it was his duty to provide his troops with whatever moral and physical support they needed to carry out their jobs, and in this it is possible to once again detect the Commonwealth inclination to try to reduce casualties to the barest possible minimum. Both Alexander and Freyberg had to conserve manpower, and Brooke's diary note of 31 March 1944 after the later bombing of Cassino town reflects this reality: 'Freyberg has been fighting with a casualty conscious mind. He has been sparing the NZ infantry and hoping to accomplish results by heavy bombers and infantry, without using too much infantry. As a result he has failed.' As an afternote he was to write: 'The New Zealanders had suffered their full share of casualties for such a small country. It had recently been frequently impressed on Freyberg by the NZ Government that it was most desirable to avoid unnecessary heavy casualties in future. The war was evidently drawing near its close … and making him loath to risk heavy losses. Unfortunately it is hard in war to make omelettes without breaking eggs, and it is often in trying to do so that we break most eggs!'[21]

The act of bombing the Monastery was, however, to provide another bone of contention between the Allies, particularly for Clark, who avoided witnessing the event and was at pains to record his opposition. He was keen to disassociate himself from an action which was bound to attract adverse opinion, and keen to emphasize that he could not refuse Freyberg's request because of the political implications of coalition warfare.

Issues of propaganda, religion and heritage aside, the bombing of the Monastery did little to improve the attackers' chances of success. Seven Indian Brigade was to make the attack along Snakeshead Ridge to take advantage of the bombardment, which was due to be delivered on 15 February, a date determined by anticipated events at Anzio. Allied intelligence expected the Germans to make a determined effort to remove the VI Corps' beachhead sometime after the 16th, and Allied airpower had to be on call to deal with that threat. This gave a bare minimum of time for the New Zealand Corps to position itself for its attacks, and the Indian brigade moved into place on the night of 14/15 February. Despite expectations from the American briefings it was to find that Point 593 was still in enemy hands. As it was necessary to capture this position as a prelude to attacking the Monastery, and as this preliminary attack could not be carried out in daylight, the decision was taken to postpone it until twelve hours after the bombing. The attack on Point 593 would be difficult: the approaches to it ran along Snakeshead Ridge, the narrowness of which limited the number of troops who could make the assault, and the American experience was not encouraging. The attack on the Monastery itself would take place twenty-four hours later, despite the time that this would give the Germans to find their feet again after the buildings had – hopefully – been destroyed. Understandably, the 4th Indian Division was unimpressed with the staff work which had failed to identify which features were in Allied hands.

Nor were matters any better in the valley where the 2nd New Zealand Division was to attack down the railway embankment into the town. This route, bounded on either side by floodwater, limited the frontage to two companies, which would not be enough to deliver a decisive blow.

Neither attack succeeded. On Snakeshead Ridge an attack by a single company of the 1st Battalion, The Royal Sussex Regiment, unsupported by artillery because of the closeness of the two sides and without mortars because the ammunition had been lost, failed with the loss of almost half the men committed. A second attempt by the whole battalion during the following night was also beaten back with heavy casualties. This battalion was one of those from the British Army that served with Indian Army brigades, there being one British to two Indian or Gurkha battalions in each brigade.

On the night of 17/18 February a third effort was made with three battalions, this time against Point 593 and the Monastery itself: the 4/6th Rajputana Rifles and the 1/2nd Gurkha Rifles from 7 Brigade, and 1/9th Gurkha Rifles from 5 Indian Brigade.[22] As on the previous occasions, the attack was unsuccessful, although German reports later stated that a small party from 1/2nd Gurkhas had managed to get as far as the Monastery before being killed. And as on the previous occasions, casualties were heavy.

This last assault on the Cassino Ridge had been timed to coincide with the New Zealand advance along the railway embankment. The unit selected to carry out the task was the 28th (Maori) Battalion, which had been raised at the suggestion of Sir Apirana Ngata, a prominent Maori politician, supported by two Maori Members of Parliament. The battalion attracted recruits from the Maori community where military service was seen as an opportunity to demonstrate loyalty to the Empire and to enhance their skills as warriors. Initially New Zealanders of European descent filled the officer and NCO posts, although Maoris were appointed when they became qualified and the first Maori commanding officer was appointed in May 1942, a much swifter process than had happened in battalions of the Indian Army. The battalion's four rifle companies were organized on tribal and recruiting area lines. As with the French North African units, the lack of technical experience among the recruits posed difficulties in finding sufficient men to become drivers, signallers and clerks, a problem that had to be addressed by training from basics.

During the night of 17/18 February two companies of the battalion advanced down the railway line, accompanied by sappers whose task was to remove mines and to construct bridges over the Rapido so that tanks might be brought forward to support the infantry. Supported by a continuous mortar barrage the Maoris captured one of their objectives, the railway station, but were unable to reach the second, a group of mounds south of the engine shed. Support was not forthcoming, however, because the mine-clearing operation had been hindered by the metal of the disused railway track which interfered with the detectors. Unable to complete the second of the two bridges and now under enemy fire, the tanks could not advance and the infantry had to fend for themselves. A day-long smokescreen was laid on to conceal the Maoris from observation, but it proved to be a double-edged weapon when the Germans took advantage of its cover to bring their own tanks and infantry forward to drive the New Zealand troops out. Once again casualties had been heavy, with 128 men being killed or wounded out of the 200 who had commenced the operation. This time the only gain was a single bridge over the Rapido.[23]

The day that the battle drew to a close, 18 February, was also the climax of the fighting at Anzio.

Freyberg's next attempt to take Cassino again had elements of II (US) Corps' plan in it. 34th (US) Division had tried to break through to Highway 6 by working its way southwards along the foot of the Cassino mountains and fighting its way through the town. The New Zealanders would take much the same route, following roads which led down the Rapido valley and met in Cassino. The town was to be subjected to a heavy aerial bombardment to smother the resistance of the enemy who were ensconced in what were already ruins, in preparation for the infantry and armour that would make the final attack.

A second objective was the castle which stood above the town on the road leading up to the Monastery. Once this had been captured by New Zealand troops 5 Indian Brigade units would take control of it and would use the castle as the jumping-off point to take Hangman's Hill, a feature just below the Monastery ruins. From Hangman's Hill an attack would be mounted on the building itself.

As a distraction to this last phase a diversionary attack would be made in the mountains. Whereas II Corps had tried to take Albaneta Farm which lay below and to the west of Point 593 with infantry, Freyberg proposed doing so with a force of tanks. These were to move south from Caira village along a track which ran through the valley on the western side of Snakeshead Ridge. With considerable skill and without letting the enemy know what they were doing, sappers had expanded the track to permit armour access to Albaneta; the route was christened Cavendish Road.

Before anything could happen, however, the weather – which had been abysmal – had to break to allow the bombers to fly their mission. Once again Freyberg was trying to conserve men's lives by expending explosives. Although preparations for the operation had been completed by 24 February, it was not until 15 March that the opportunity arose to carry it out. Three rainless days were required for flying and to allow the ground to dry out sufficiently for tanks, but waiting for this window in the weather took three weeks, during which time the New Zealand Corps existed in their drenched shell-scrapes, sangars and trenches. While the Allied troops suffered and soaked, the Germans took advantage of the lull in the fighting to place Monte Cassino and the town in the hands of the *1st Parachute Division.*[24] Under control of the determined paratroops the town was turned into an even stronger defensive position, with tanks, self-propelled guns and pillboxes built into the rubble. Two hotels at the base of the heights leading up to the Monastery were transformed into particularly tough strongpoints, and mines were strewn around in abundance: nearly a million were cleared after the battles.

On 15 March 455 aircraft delivered over 1,100 tons of bombs over a three-and-a-half-hour period, not all of them on the town. Surrounding villages and Allied troops – and General Leese's caravan at Eighth Army HQ – were also hit. Nevertheless no building was left standing in Cassino, and half of the German defenders were wiped out. The survivors of *2nd Battalion, 3rd Parachute Regiment*, prepared to continue the fight despite their losses. The bombing was followed by an intensive artillery barrage delivered by 890 guns; 195,969 shells were delivered until 2000 hours that evening, when the infantry commenced their attack from the north supported by tanks.[25] The effect of the bombardment now became all too clear: the cratered route through the rubble of the town's buildings was virtually impassable to armour. Attempts to improve the entry roads into and through the town fell prey to German snipers, machine-gun and mortar fire, and the advance slowed to a crawl. Highway 6, running through the town, was reached at dusk, but now the heavens opened again and torrential rain began to fall. As the craters filled with water and visibility was reduced to a matter of feet, the infantry had to proceed by hanging onto the belts of the men in front as they felt their way forward. Three battalions moved into the northern end of town.

Above the ruins the castle was captured by a detached company which was relieved by 1/4th Essex Regiment (another of the British units serving with the Indian Division) and 1/6th Rajputana Rifles moved through to take the next objective on the way to Hangman's Hill, which was in turn occupied by troops of 1/9th Gurkhas. It was a night of confusion, but one in which the British Commonwealth approach to coalition warfare worked. Despite operational difficulties, some of which (such as the renewal of the rain after its brief interlude) could not have been entirely foreseen, the units involved worked well together. They failed, however, to clear the town. Much of the reason for this lay with the capabilities and doctrine of the enemy; the paratroops took a perverse pride in surviving the bombardment and implemented the practice of counterattacking at the earliest opportunity, before the New Zealand troops could establish themselves in the town.

During the next days progress was slow. On Hangman's Hill the Gurkhas were joined by two companies of Rajputs, but were cut off and had to rely on air-dropped supplies – most of which fell into German hands. In the town the station was captured but the hotels remained in enemy hands.

A major effort was planned for 19 March. The Maori Battalion would attack the Continental Hotel and the Gurkhas and the Essex would attack the Monastery from Hangman's Hill once the latter battalion had moved up to the start point. To draw attention away from this operation the tank attack was to be made up the Cavendish Road to the rear of the Monastery defences. The plan was thrown into disarray when the Germans launched an attack on the castle as two companies of the Essex were leaving it en route for Hangman's. Only seventy men arrived at their destination, thirty of whom were wounded. Unable to provide reinforcements to support the attack on the Monastery from this direction, it was called off.

The tank attack up the Cavendish Road went ahead, however, although it is difficult to see what it hoped to achieve as its purpose – to distract attention from Hangman's – was now redundant. Forty Sherman and Stuart tanks from 20 New Zealand Armoured Brigade, 7 Indian Infantry Brigade and 760th (US) Tank Battalion proceeded along the road without infantry support, without which they got no closer than 1,000 yards of the Monastery. Having lost six tanks and with a further sixteen damaged, they withdrew. Once again, it was an example of coalition troops working well together to carry out a flawed plan which achieved little more than to raise the casualty figures.

With failed attacks in and above the town, and on Cavendish Road, the operation was called off on 23 March. General Wilson's suggestion that a final push might achieve the desired result was met by Freyberg's retort, 'Passchendaele', and Alexander agreed. The Third Battle of Cassino was over at a cost to the 2nd New Zealand Division of 1,600 casualties and more than 3,000 to the 4th Indian Division, which – like the American divisions from II (US) Corps – effectively ceased to be a fighting formation until such time as it could be brought back to strength. It was relieved by the 78th Division and on 26 March XIII (British) Corps from the Eighth Army took command of the sector and the New Zealand Corps was dissolved. Cassino had ceased to be a Fifth Army concern.

While the continued assaults on Cassino kept up the pressure on that sector of the Gustav Line and ensured that German formations were tied down there, and hence on a smaller scale represented a miniature version of the whole raison d'etre for the Italian campaign, hammering at Cassino itself was already being seen by HQ 15th Army Group as being the wrong way to break the German defences. On 22 February Alexander had restated the objective of the Italian Campaign: 'to force the enemy to commit the maximum number of divisions in Italy at the time OVERLORD is launched.'[26] He had already decided that an Army Group offensive was the only way to break the German line. Although it was necessary to continue to pound away at Cassino so that there would not be a lull in the fighting, the solution lay in regrouping the Allied forces to ensure that full strength could be brought to bear at the critical point. Military thinking held that a superiority of three-to-one was necessary to ensure a successful attack, but the Allies did not have this sort of number of formations or men in Italy. It was, however, possible to assemble this superiority at the chosen attack position provided that the intention was hidden from the enemy. Alexander's

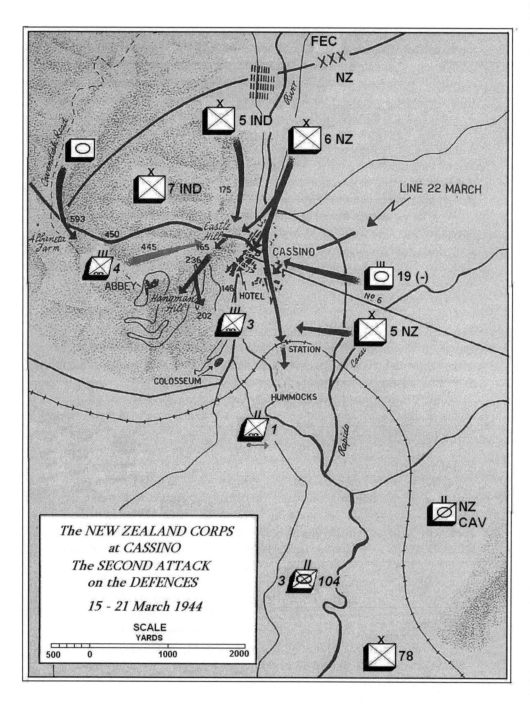

The NEW ZEALAND CORPS
at CASSINO
The SECOND ATTACK
on the DEFENCES

15 - 21 March 1944

SCALE
YARDS

500   0   1000   2000

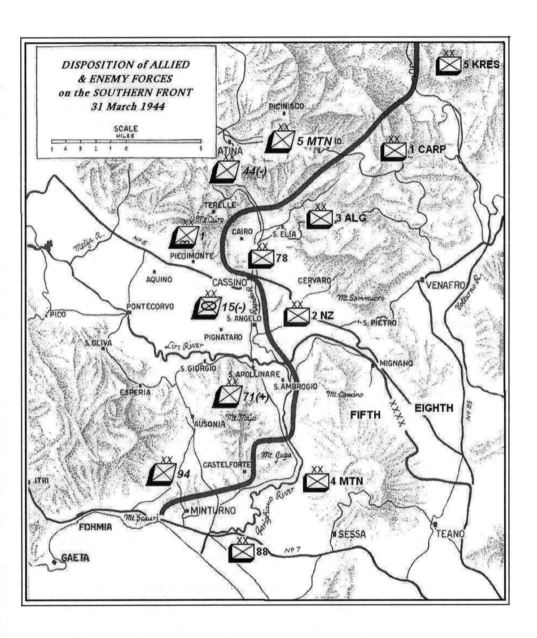

DISPOSITION of ALLIED
& ENEMY FORCES
on the SOUTHERN FRONT
31 March 1944

SCALE
MILES

re-grouping, based on thorough planning by his Chief of Staff, Lieutenant General Harding, was designed to do just that. The Army Group operation that Juin had sought was now emerging.

Before the fresh offensive could begin the re-grouping had to be completed under conditions of great secrecy – and the weather had to have improved sufficiently to harden the ground and to give some degree of certainty that dry conditions would continue uninterrupted. The operation was therefore timetabled for the month of May, time enough for these conditions to have been met while still early enough to precede OVERLORD. In X (British) Corps, 4th Division would relieve 46th Division, and the 88th (US) Division would take over the quiet coastal sector from 5th (British) Division, which would go to Anzio in early March; 34th (US) Division would also go to Anzio, at a later date.[27] Alexander's intention was to have II (US) Corps and the French replace X Corps in the south for the drive planned for May, when the weather should have improved and the ground dried out. The inter-army boundary would move southwards so that the Eighth Army, with the X and XIII (British) Corps, II Polish Corps and I Canadian Corps under command, could attack up the Liri Valley. The French were relieved by the Poles by 26 March, and on 29 March command of the sector south of the Liri river passed to II (US) Corps and the French Expeditionary Corps.

There had been some gains from the Cassino battles. A bridgehead had been established at Cassino and the ground taken by X (British) Corps in January would be of great value to the Fifth Army in the operations that were being planned for the future. On 2 April Alexander was optimistic that the campaign was achieving its objectives, for twenty-three German divisions were held down in Italy, four of them just around Anzio. Furthermore, the threat which Italian-based Allied forces posed to the Balkans ensured that more enemy formations were forced to remain there.

Anzio

Anzio was to be at the centre of two controversies in which coalition operations were to come under scrutiny. The first was the overall concept of SHINGLE, which divided the Fifth Army and placed the smaller part of it in a location that was too far away from the front which it was intended to influence – and made VI Corps vulnerable to defeat because it was too far away from the support it needed. The second controversy was the difference of opinion between Alexander and Clark about the use of VI Corps once the stalemate had been broken and the Germans retreated from the Gustav Line. As the battles for Cassino were being fought through the months of February and March, VI (US) Corps struggled to retain its beachhead at Anzio. The landings had been carried out against minimum resistance and – unexpectedly – had achieved complete surprise. Third (US) Division came ashore south of Nettuno and reached its objectives, where it waited for a counterattack that failed to materialize. The port of Anzio was captured by the Rangers, and Nettuno by the 509th Parachute Battalion. First (British) Division landed north of Anzio, and despite delays caused by minefields and difficulties caused by shallow water off the beach was two miles inland just after noon. To forestall a counterattack, commandos established a roadblock on the Albano road north of Anzio.

Having understood that he had a degree of discretion on interpreting his orders, Lucas elected to establish as firm a base as possible before moving towards the Alban Hills. Not the least of his concerns was that the Germans should be able to supply and reinforce their troops quicker by land than he could his own by sea, especially with the constraints on shipping. While the option of building up his base gave him a degree of security, it also gave the Germans time to throw a defensive line around the Allied forces. By the time he was prepared to advance once the 45th (US) Infantry and Combat Command A of the 1st (US) Armored Division were ashore, Lucas faced blocking lines on the roads running inland and every moment saw the Germans being reinforced. Kesselring had been swift to identify a lack of aggressiveness and his decision – despite advice from von Vietinghoff, the *Tenth Army* commander, to withdraw forces from the Gustav Line – was to bring troops from elsewhere. Within twenty-four hours German reinforcements were on their way from Yugoslavia, France and Germany – but not from the Gustav Line. Kesselring had gambled that Lucas would not act in a hurry, and he had won. By the time VI Corps was ready to make preparatory moves towards the Alban Hills on 25 January, Kesselring had enough forces assembled to give him the confidence to order *Headquarters Fourteenth Army*, which he had brought from north Italy, to plan a counterattack to throw the invaders back into the sea. By bringing General von Mackensen from Verona, Kesselring ensured that each of the two fronts on which he was now fighting – Anzio and the Gustav Line – had an army headquarters concentrating on it, that of the *Tenth Army* on the Gustav Line, and the *Fourteenth* at Anzio. Each of these headquarters also had two subordinate corps headquarters to command the formations available to them. In the case of Anzio von Mackensen soon had elements of eight divisions, with another five on their way. Headquarters Fifth Army had the problem of dealing with both fronts, and at Anzio its divisions were outnumbered. If

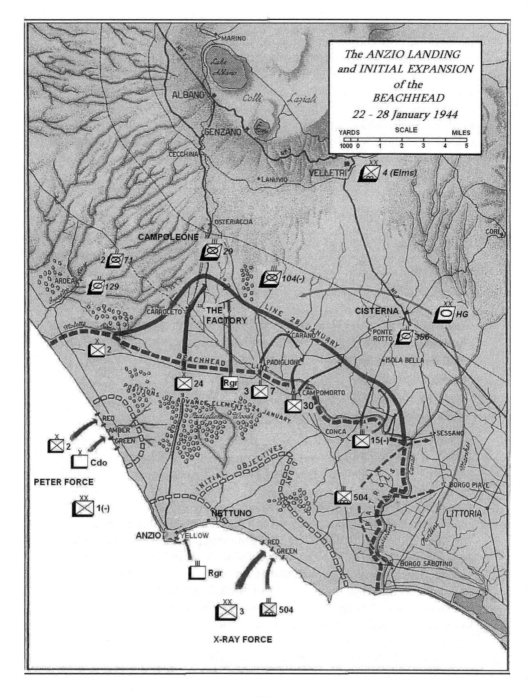

The *ANZIO LANDING*
and *INITIAL EXPANSION*
of the
BEACHHEAD
22 - 28 January 1944

Lucas had seriously considered a dash to the hills, the opportunity had now passed. The question of where the responsibility lay for this failure (if it was such) to achieve Alexander's intention is debatable. Clark had advised Lucas not to stick his neck out and had phrased his orders to allow Lucas to make up his own mind; neither officer had much enthusiasm for the venture as envisaged by Churchill and Alexander, but whether or not they had the right to avoid the attempt is arguable.

On 27 January Alexander talked to Clark about his unhappiness at the speed of Lucas' operations, a sentiment which Clark was beginning to share.[28] They were not alone in their concern: in London Churchill and Brooke discussed their doubts about Lucas' handling of the operation, doubts which they were to forward to Alexander thus increasing the pressure on him.[29] Clark visited the beachhead the next day and urged Lucas to be more aggressive: the town of Cisterna should be captured as a strongpoint in a defensive line around the landing area. It was beginning to become apparent that there were two main routes out of the beachhead, through Cisterna and through the town of Aprilia (known as the Factory because of its appearance). The SHINGLE planners had drawn the wrong conclusions from aerial reconnaissance photographs of the area and what had appeared to be hedgerows on the western side of the beachhead were to prove to be deep gullies caused by water erosion; these were impassable to tanks. To the east drainage ditches posed a similar problem, and in the wet winter weather the best routes for armoured vehicles were on the roads through the two aforementioned towns. They were also the best routes for the Germans to take into the beachhead, and holding them was key to those planning to attack, be they Allied or German. On 28 January Kesselring ordered his counterattack, which was delayed until 1 February and the arrival of more troops; at this stage the Germans had about 70,000 men ready, with more to follow.

Lucas' advance was planned for 30 January. Highway 7 was to be cut at Cisterna by 3rd (US) Division and three Ranger battalions, while 1st (British) Division pushed up the road through the Factory towards the Alban Hills. Combat Command A was to swing wide to the left of the British movement and come in on the hills from the west – but, as has been noted, their way was blocked by the gullies. Unknown to Lucas, German forces were concentrating in strength near Cisterna for their own attack; two Ranger battalions advanced right into them and suffered the usual consequences of lightly-equipped troops engaging those having armour. Of the 767 Americans involved, only six returned to their own lines; the remainder were dead or captive.

On the British front, despite having to fight its way through German blocking positions with heavy losses, the 1st Division advance got nearly as far as the Campoleone railway before coming to a halt; but the division was stretched out in a narrow salient jutting into enemy territory.

The situation at Anzio impelled Clark to suggest a possible way to take the pressure off VI Corps. He approached Alexander on 1 February with a proposal to make another end run, this time at Civitavecchia to the north of Anzio.[30] His idea was to put two divisions ashore at a date no later than mid-February, an idea that was clearly open to question because of the lack of shipping that already hindered the SHINGLE operation. Clark had complained about this restriction, so what made him think that it could possibly be made good for another scheme, and what troops were going to be available to carry it out, can only be imagined – but the plan has to contribute to the evidence that Clark's grasp of strategy was somewhat limited.

The failure of the attacks and the growing evidence of German strength moved Alexander to order extra units into the beachhead. The First Special Service Force and elements of 56th (British) Division, supported by extra anti-aircraft and other artillery units, swelled VI Corps to about 100,000 men. By now, however, even this number was outnumbered by the Germans who were still receiving reinforcements, and von Mackensen was preparing his next counterattacks. The first was directed at the British salient stretching to Campoleone, with the intention of cutting it off and recapturing the Factory. Having succeeded there, the Germans were to push down the road to Anzio. The second attack would advance south of Cisterna towards Nettuno and Anzio.

On 3 February the attack on the salient opened; after heavy fighting Lucas ordered the forward elements of the 1st (British) Division to retire to a less exposed line which might be more easily defended. The British lost over 1,400 killed, wounded and missing during a period of intense fighting as the enemy threw their weight against them. The Germans were expected to try to capture the Factory and the nearby town of Carroceto, less than half a mile to its south-west, to gain control of the northern end of their proposed route to Anzio itself. Possession of the road network at these points was essential to their intentions of pushing armoured forces southwards because of the state of the sodden countryside – and the river gullies – at this time. By now 1st (British) Division was under-strength and the troops had had little rest since they had come ashore.

A final defence position based on the initial beachhead line was identified, to which VI Corps would retreat if necessary, and German pressure was soon to make that prospect a very real possibility. As German numbers rose, Alexander sent the remainders of 45th (US) and 56th (British) Divisions, and 1st (US) Armored Division, less the Combat Command that was at Cassino. More reinforcements were planned: on 25 February, 18 Infantry Brigade, from the British 1st Armoured Division in North Africa, began to disembark.

On 7 February the Germans attacked again. They made a preliminary move to clear the Factory area to secure a firm base, with the intention of achieving this part of their plan overnight. Dogged resistance by 1st Division and counterattacks by the 45th (US) Division held them for five days, and the defenders fell back to an intermediate defensive position astride the Albano-Anzio road on 12 February. It was apparent that this road was the enemy's main axis of attack, and to meet it the battered 1st Division (now at less than fifty per cent of its strength) was relieved by 56th (British) and 45th (US) Divisions.

Behind the front lines all was not well for Anglo-American relationships in VI Corps. The GOC 1st Division, Major General W. R. C. Penney, had experienced considerable frustration in his dealings with Lucas, who was reluctant to leave his headquarters based in the cellars of Nettuno to see for himself what was happening in the battle line. Penney (a Royal Signals officer who was considered by Clark, in his usual dismissive tone towards British officers, to be 'a divisional commander who was a good telephone operator')[31] and Lucas failed to establish a good working relationship, the latter seemingly disinterested in the problems the British faced in the salient.

The critical stage in the battle for Anzio opened on 16 February when the Germans launched yet another attack, codenamed FISCHFANG, on the same axis. The intent was to drive a wedge into the beachhead but it also failed to achieve its objective, despite five days of intense fighting. The climax came on 18 February as the Germans were held on a defensive line based on a flyover crossing the Albano-Anzio road, after which the attacks dried up. Casualties were heavy on both sides, 5,389 Germans killed, wounded and missing; 3,496 on the Allied side.[32] For the rest of the month of February a series of smaller actions were fought, but nothing on the scale of what had gone before.

After the German counter-offensive Lucas was relieved of command of VI Corps, which passed to Lucian Truscott, the commander of 3rd (US) Division. Lucas had anticipated the move when Truscott had been appointed Deputy Corps Commander on 17 February, ostensibly to support him – but Clark was already preparing for Lucas' exit. The reason for Lucas going was hedged about: Clark told him that Alexander thought that Lucas was defeated and that Devers had said that he was tired.[33] Lucas was the victim of the circumstances in which he had been placed by Churchill's determination that SHINGLE went ahead; he had been given an impossible task, and even Penney thought that Lucas had little alternative but to concentrate on establishing his base before venturing off into the hinterland. Marshall agreed, pointing out that with the limited forces he had, for every mile Lucas advanced inland he extended his front by about seven miles and made it more vulnerable – as indeed happened with 1st Division.[34] Be that as it may, Lucas became the scapegoat for what must be considered to be an ill-advised operation.

Truscott's approach to command was radically different to his predecessor's. Within twenty-four hours of taking over he had visited every unit in the beachhead and discussed its problems. It became common practice for British officers to join Truscott for drinks in his quarters (which unlike Lucas' arrangements, were above ground) for informal discussions during which serious business was carried out in a relaxed manner. Truscott also went out of his way to cultivate a good relationship with his British deputy commander, Major General Vivian Evelegh.[35] With previous experience of working with the British Truscott was far better placed to command them than were either Clark or Lucas who did not understand their ally. On 8 February Lucas had complained to his diary that he wished that he had an American division on his left flank rather than the British, whom he rarely visited and whose difficulties he could not understand.[36]

As at Cassino, Anzio became a stalemate. The beachhead assumed a First World War atmosphere, with life (or, all too often, death) inflicted by artillery fire on trench-bound soldiers who huddled in the rain-imposed misery. Churchill was, of course, frustrated by the failure of his scheme to break the deadlock of the campaign. There was little he could do about it, but as the weeks passed while the combatants waited for the arrival of drier weather, both here and on the Gustav Line, VI Corps' strength was steadily increased as men and matériel were shipped in, rising to six divisions: the British 1st and 56th, and the American 3rd, 34th, 36th and 45th. There were also the 1st (US) Armored Division and the First Special Service Force. Harding's plans for May involved not only the forces waiting on the Gustav Line, but also those at Anzio. These would play their part once the breakthrough of the Gustav Line had been achieved.

The codeword for the May offensive was Operation DIADEM. As outlined earlier, it was to involve both the Fifth and the Eighth Armies in a co-ordinated attack on the Gustav Line, unlike the piecemeal offensives that had been employed earlier. The Liri Valley was again to feature as the route by which Allied armour would concentrate to drive on towards Rome, but this time the Allied assault would take place along the whole front from north of Cassino down to the sea. Once the line had been broken and the German *Tenth Army* was in the process of withdrawing, the Anzio force would break out from the beachhead and push about fifteen miles inland to Valmontone, which sat on Highway 6. Possession of this point would give Truscott control of the road and rail links between Rome and Cassino – and would place an obstacle in the German line of retreat.

Clark was unimpressed with DIADEM. Obsessed with Rome, he saw the plan as a British ploy to rob the Americans (and perhaps more importantly himself) of the glory of capturing the Eternal City. Against the objections of Truscott, he ordered that alternative plans be prepared. VI Corps was to be ready to take any one of four courses of action; two of these avoided Valmontone altogether and thrust towards Rome. Briefed on these alternatives by Truscott, Alexander made it clear to the American that the Valmontone option, Plan BUFFALO, was the one that he wanted carried out to achieve his wider aim of trapping the enemy forces as they fell back from the Gustav Line. The fact that he had discussed this directly with Truscott led Clark to maintain that Alexander had interfered with the chain of command, notwithstanding the fact that he himself had circumvented Alexander's orders by having the alternative plans prepared, which could be considered disloyal, at least. The issue raises the question of how much freedom of action a subordinate could, or should, be permitted. Had Alexander and Clark been of the same nationality and serving in the same army, the answer would be clear; that they were of different nationalities working in a coalition made it less straightforward. Alexander saw DIADEM and BUFFALO as two plans which were closely linked, but it was becoming apparent that Clark had intentions of thwarting the latter operation. The American had known of Alexander's intentions for some two months, but had adopted the technique of regarding any order with which he did not agree as being no more than a 'suggestion' which he was at liberty to ignore. In this he may well have been encouraged by Alexander's style, which contrasted strongly with Clark's. As Graham and Bidwell point out,[37] 'Where Alexander would discuss endlessly and never give orders, Clark gave orders and refused to discuss them.' Clark was also following the precedent that Patton and Montgomery had established in Sicily, of ignoring Alexander when they saw fit.

DIADEM was launched on 11 May. In the Fifth Army sector at the southern end of the line II (US) Corps initially made little progress, but Juin's French Expeditionary Corps made an impressive start by capturing all of its opening objectives within four hours. Juin pushed the 1st French Motorized Division through and to its right to roll up the enemy towards the Liri Valley. By 21 May the CEF had reached Pontecorvo, surpassing the expectations of many officers in the Allied high command who had hitherto regarded the French formations as being of doubtful ability.

II (US) Corps made its advance to the south of the CEF, and by the morning of 25 May it was in contact with troops from VI Corps which had been sent to meet it. After 123 days the siege of Anzio officially came to an end near the town of Borgo Grappa. Clark claimed to have heard the news by radio when he was in his jeep, whereupon he rushed to the scene. The truth is more characteristic of his manipulation of the media to boost his career: in reality he was in his Fifth Army Command Post waiting for the expected news, surrounded by twenty-three war correspondents and photographers, who descended on Borgo Grappa en masse. It was not long before Clark's face would appear on the front pages – yet again – and it would be far from the last time that this would happen.

The breakout from the Anzio beachhead started on 23 May, with five United States' divisions and the FSSF attacking towards Cisterna while the two British ones, 1st and 5th, covered Truscott's left flank. Alexander had asked Truscott to avoid committing the British to combat, if possible, not least because 1st Division was a spent force. Two days later Truscott's troops had succeeded in capturing Cisterna as an initial step in advancing to Valmontone in accordance with Operation BUFFALO, and it was at this time that Clark made his decision on whether or not to adhere to Alexander's concept of operations. The alternatives facing him were, firstly, to implement BUFFALO by having the five American divisions involved continue onwards to cut Highway 6. Secondly, he could order the complete force to turn to the north-west and aim for Rome. The third possibility was to divide the force and try to achieve both objectives. Clark maintained that BUFFALO was based on questionable reasoning; he doubted that possession of Valmontone would, in itself, be sufficient to block the *Tenth Army's* retreat because there were additional routes it could take, for example through the mountains to Highway 5. He also felt that Rome should be Fifth Army's prize, not least because the American formations under his command had suffered heavier casualties than had the British troops under his command, or the Eighth Army.[38] The fact that he had consistently employed American troops in what

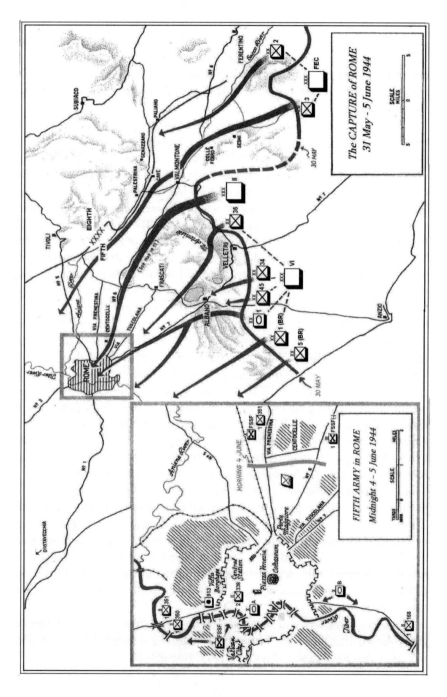

The CAPTURE of ROME
31 May - 5 June 1944

FIFTH ARMY in ROME
Midnight 4 - 5 June 1944

he saw as the key engagements, and had comparatively little regard for the casualty statistics that resulted from his tactics – for example II Corps on the Rapido and at Cassino – did not appear to enter into the argument. Nor did the fact that the British formation commanders fought a more casualty-conscious battle, which might be part of the reason for the lower figures, matter to him.

Clark took the third option and ordered Truscott to divide his command. His stated belief was that a single division supported by the FSSF and an armoured task force would be enough to carry out the Valmontone part of the plan – and this would at least pay lip-service to Alexander's intent. He did not expect enemy resistance to call for a larger force. Four divisions, the 34th, 45th, 36th and the 1st Armored, would change direction and go north-west against the Alban Hills. Clark's Operations Officer, Brigadier General Brann, was left with the task of passing the necessary orders to Truscott. The VI Corps commander protested.[39] He had no evidence that the enemy had weakened his forces on the western side of the Anzio beachhead, and this was not the time to change direction to attack areas where the Germans were still strong. Moreover, to change the Corps' axis of advance at this stage was hardly straightforward; apart from other matters, the supply lines, communications systems and command posts had all been designed for the move on Valmontone, not the new objective. With congested roads and limited space in which to manoeuvre, the task was complicated. The new direction also took VI Corps to a strong sector of the German defence positions surrounding the beachhead, and to part of the Caesar Line, which ran from the mouth of the Tiber through Cisterna and then across Italy, which Kesselring had ordered to be built in anticipation of the May attack. It was to take VI Corps ten days to reach Rome, and nor was the enemy's rear cut. It might have been quicker to have got there via Valmontone, after all.

Clark had made the strike against Valmontone a secondary operation, and in doing so he altered Alexander's concept of operations in the rear of the *Tenth Army*. The force he employed was sufficient only to establish a defensive position to interfere with the enemy withdrawal, whereas the five divisions (plus the FSSF) that should have been engaged could have taken a much more active role. Alexander was informed of the change of plan by Clark's Chief of Staff, Gruenther, only after the decision was irrevocable. It was a fait accompli.

Argument on Clark's decision was to continue, fuelled by the evidence that emerged after the event. The early accounts, for example Clark's version in *Calculated Risk*[40] and Sidney Mathews' (the official historian) version in

Command Decisions[41], which was published in 1960, relied on Clark's account, which may be summed up as being self-serving. Subsequent interpretations such as d'Este's *Fatal Decision*[42] are far more critical and were able to draw on previously unpublished material such as Clark's diaries. Truscott himself was unsympathetic towards Clark's decision, saying that to be the first in Rome was poor compensation for not achieving the strategic objective of Anzio.[43]

Clark, then, got to Rome first. His address to the crowds and to the press from the steps of city hall focused on the 'great day for the Fifth Army' to the embarrassment of Juin, Keyes, Crittenberger and Truscott – and to the war correspondent Eric Sevareid, who noted that there was no mention of it being 'a great day for the world, for the Allies, for all the suffering people who had desperately looked toward the time of peace ...'[44] Nor was there any mention of the Eighth Army, whose efforts in breaking the Gustav line had made the liberation of Rome possible.

Notes

1. D'Este, *Fatal Decision: Anzio and the Battle for Rome*
2. Ibid
3. Graham & Bidwell, *Tug of War*
4. Walker, *General Walker's Story of the Rapido Crossing*
5. Graham & Bidwell, op cit.
6. Blumenson, *General Lucas at Anzio*
7. D'Este, op cit.
8. Graham & Bidwell, op cit.
9. Ellis, *Cassino: The Hollow Victory*
10. Clark diaries, quoted in Blumenson, *Salerno to Cassino*
11. Ellis, op cit.
12. Blumenson, *Salerno to Cassino*
13. Danchev & Todman (Eds), *War Diaries 1939–1945, Field Marshal Lord Alanbrooke*
14. Ellis, op cit.
15. Hapgood & Richardson, *Monte Cassino*
16. Von Senger und Etterlin, *Neither Fear nor Hope*
17. CCS to Eisenhower, 10 June 1943, quoted in Blumenson, *Salerno to Cassino*
18. Alexander, *Alexander's Despatch*
19. Ellis, op cit.
20. Ibid
21. Danchev & Todman (Eds), op cit.
22. Hingston, *The Tiger Triumphs*

23. Cody, *28 Maori Battalion*
24. Phillips, *Italy Vol 1: The Sangro to Cassino*
25. Starr, *Fifth Army History*
26. Alexander, op cit.
27. Ibid
28. Blumenson, *General Lucas at Anzio*
29. Danchev & Todman (Eds), op cit.
30. D'Este, op cit.
31. Clark interviews, cited in d'Este, op cit.
32. D'Este, *World War II in the Mediterranean*
33. Ibid
34. Quoted in d'Este, *Fatal Decision: Anzio and the Battle for Rome*
35. D'Este, *Fatal Decision: Anzio and the Battle for Rome*
36. Quoted in d'Este, *Fatal Decision: Anzio and the Battle for Rome*
37. Graham & Bidwell, op cit.
38. Mathews, *General Clark's Decision to Drive on Rome*
39. Truscott, *Command Missions*
40. Clark, *Calculated Risk*
41. Mathews, op cit.
42. D'Este, op cit.
43. Truscott, op cit.
44. Quoted in D'Este, *Fatal Decision*

CHAPTER 10

The Road to the Alps

The solitary day of triumph that the Allied armies had after Rome fell was too short to compensate them for the months of bloodshed and effort that had passed since they arrived in Italy. On 6 June the OVERLORD landings forced their achievements onto the inner pages and by-lines of the world's press, and three days after the entry to the Eternal City General Wilson informed London that he was now ready to mount Operation ANVIL and to start the invasion of southern France.

A week after Rome fell Alexander was ordered to withdraw VI Corps Headquarters and the 3rd, 36th and 45th (US) Infantry Divisions from the line. They, along with the First Special Service Force, would take part in ANVIL. The French Expeditionary Corps would withdraw from the Italian fighting by early July. Their departure was particularly disappointing to Alexander, for he had hoped to use them when he attacked into the Apennines. The 4th Moroccan Mountain Division was the only formation specifically trained for mountain warfare in the Army Group. Alexander saw ANVIL as having a very negative effect on the Italian campaign: robbing him of so many troops slowed the pursuit of a beaten enemy and gave the Germans time to gather themselves together.[1] Once again the retreating Germans, as in Sicily and then after the breakthrough of the Gustav Line, and Clark's failure to halt them at Valmontone, were permitted to withdraw in some semblance of good order and to conserve much of their strength for the next round. Kesselring still had enough troops ready to hand on which to base his continued resistance to the Allied advance.

The familiar pattern of the Germans fighting delaying actions on a series of defensive lines while continuing to strengthen a deeper belt of fortifications to the rear, was repeated. While work progressed on the Gothic Line to the north, the Allied advance was held on the Trasimene Line, which ran from south of Ancona to near Grosseto, on the east and west coasts of Italy respectively. Behind this line the next hurdle was the Arno Line, both of which were intended to slow the Army Group while the Gothic Line was

215

built up to a ten-mile deep work. This, like the Gustav Line earlier, was constructed along stretches of natural stongpoints in the Apennine Mountains, reinforced with wire, mines, anti-tank ditches and artillery and machine-gun positions.

The loss of the Allied formations to ANVIL notwithstanding, the Italian campaign had to continue; the intention of tying down German forces to keep them from being employed in North West Europe against the Allied landings was as important as ever, and Churchill still held hopes of using Italy as a springboard from which to move into central Europe to forestall the Russians.

Alexander's plans for pursuing the enemy north of Rome placed the Fifth Army on the west coast and the Eighth Army astride the River Tiber. The Fifth Army was to capture the port of Civitavecchia which was needed to supply the armies, while the Eighth was to take the area of Terni and Rieti to forestall any German intentions of establishing a defensive front right across the peninsula. With 34th Division on the coast and 36th inland, supported by 1st Armored Division, VI Corps entered Civitavecchia on 7 June.

The Fifth Army was directed towards Pisa and the Eighth towards Florence, with instructions to advance as swiftly as possible to keep the enemy off-balance. Clark and Leese were ordered to maintain general contact with each other but not to wait on each other's advance; they were authorized 'to take extreme risks ... before the enemy can reorganize or be reinforced'.[2] For ten days the momentum was maintained, but by 20 June the advance slowed as the Germans began their well-rehearsed drill of blowing bridges and destroying roads. The first delaying position ran from the Ombrone river to Chiusi and then east of Lake Trasimene; the pursuit was over and hard fighting was about to recommence.

Facing the Allies was the *Fourteenth Army*, which consisted of three corps: *XIV Panzer*, *LXXVI Panzer*, and *LI Mountain*. A fourth formation, *Gruppe Hauck*, was also operational on the Adriatic flank, and there were additional forces, a panzer, a *Luftwaffe*, an infantry and a *Turkomen infantry* division in reserve. The *Turkomen* division was manned by former Russian prisoners of war but with German officers and NCOs, and could not be regarded as reliable. It and the *Luftwaffe Division* would be sent to reinforce the *Fourteenth Army*. After the departure of the Allied forces for the south of France, Alexander was left with eighteen divisions to combat the German strength of fourteen, plus at least four more in reserve. In many respects the situation was assuming a replay of the impasse on the Gustav Line.

Although Churchill had hoped for a cancellation, the Anglo-American debate about ANVIL was now resolved. In Normandy storms had destroyed the Mulberry Harbour off Omaha Beach and damaged the British one at Arromanches. Eisenhower had to contemplate the possibility that the OVERLORD forces would be contained on the beachheads because of the supply difficulties and the expectation of autumn weather. He was strongly in favour of any action which would divert German formations from North West Europe and he believed that ANVIL was the best way to achieve this. The British believed that sending forces from Italy would weaken the effort there to no good effect, and would close the door on the option of expanding operations into the Balkans. A move into the Balkans would deny the Germans access to oil and would deny the Soviets control of the region, which would give the Western Allies an advantageous negotiating position in postwar negotiations. Churchill, supported by Smuts, held out for ANVIL to be abandoned; Marshall argued otherwise, and Roosevelt ended the debate by reminding everyone that it had long been agreed that OVERLORD should take priority over Mediterranean operations. His trump card, moreover, was to point out that he was to face an election at home, which he could not survive if the Normandy invasion should stall. He could not possibly explain away allowing OVERLORD to fail while sending forces into the Balkans. Once again domestic issues influenced international affairs.

The Italian campaign would continue, but with reduced resources: by 1 August the strength of the Fifth Army was little more than fifty percent of what it had been on 4 June. On 1 June it totalled 248,989 men, by 1 July it stood at 205,992, and on 1 August it had fallen to 153,323.[3] Nine full infantry divisions and the equivalent of a tenth were transferred out. Third Division was assigned to garrison duties in Rome; 1st and 5th British Divisions left, to go to V (British) Corps and to the Middle East respectively; and 36th and 45th (US) Divisions went to Seventh Army for ANVIL. The FSSF and 509th Parachute Infantry Battalion went with them. The *1e Division de March d'Infanterie*, and the *3e Division d'Infanterie Algerienne* followed, and the *4e Division de Montagne Morocaine* and the *2e Division d'Infanterie Marocaine*, with the tabors and all of the CEF Corps troops, also left. Additionally, VI Corps and the CEF Headquarters and several service units were lost, including hospitals, ordnance, signals and quartermaster companies, and engineers. Artillery, tank, reconnaissance and other units went with them.

The Army Group was now forced to halt and to fill the gap left by the departure of these forces. The possibility had gone of maintaining pressure on the retreating Germans and reaching northern Italy swiftly, and Alexander now had to plan for a slower autumn and winter campaign.

The frustrations of working with the Americans were evidently beginning to tell on Alexander and his Chief of Staff, so much so that they began to give thought to ways of working without them. While visiting Army Group Headquarters in August Brooke was informed that Harding had produced a very important paper for the CIGS to consider. Harding's proposal was that all of the American forces in Italy be transferred to North West Europe, and that all British forces be sent to Italy. The Americans would then be wholly responsible for one theatre, the British for the other, and each nation would be fighting the campaign which it saw as being the most important. The British would be thus able to concentrate on Churchill's thoughts on pushing through the Alps to capture Vienna. As Brooke pointed out – and it is difficult to understand why neither Harding nor Alexander had foreseen these problems – with the limited amount of shipping available, moving such large numbers of troops would take months. Secondly, on political grounds, it would not be advisable to leave the task of finally defeating Germany to the Americans while Britain took an insignificant role on the sidelines; and thirdly, at the present rate of advance in Italy, by the time the Allies reached the Alps winter would have set in and only one pass would be open – and well-defended.[4]

The proposal was obviously prompted by the irritation that Churchill, Alexander and Harding were experiencing with the American attitude to the Italian campaign. It was also indicative of Alexander's inability– at least in Brooke's eyes – to think for himself. He absented himself from the discussions Brooke had with Harding on his paper 'as if he feared getting out of his depth'.[5]

To the CIGS, Alexander was a 'small calibre man' who had been supported by Montgomery and McCreery in North Africa. Now in Italy he was relying on Leese and Harding, neither of whom was of the same quality.

Fifth Army would be reduced to five divisions, and would initially receive only the 91st Infantry Division to fill the gaps. The first of its regiments went into action on 11 June, the remainder being attached to IV Corps a month later. The 92nd Infantry Division was destined to join the Army, but only the 370th RCT arrived in time to see action in late August. Brazil, the first South American nation to send troops into the war, despatched its Expeditionary Force to Italy, but only one combat team had arrived by 15 August and it needed preparation before it could be employed in the line. To compensate for its lack of infantry Fifth Army formed two provisional regiments from anti-aircraft troops, which together with the 91st Cavalry Reconnaissance Squadron and the 2nd Armored Group comprised the newly-named Task Force 45, which amounted to division strength. From the month of August

1944 onwards, the Fifth Army order of battle was to change even more rapidly than it had done during its previous time in Italy, as fresh formations were placed under its command from the Eighth Army or were transferred in from overseas. Once again the fact that Washington regarded the campaign as increasingly irrelevant was having its effect on American support, and some of the formations that joined the ranks of the Fifth Army did so because they were superfluous to the requirements of North West Europe or ANVIL – renamed DRAGOON. With its Army's expansion the United States was becoming even more powerful, not just in comparison to the enemy, but also with respect to the British.

In both the United Kingdom and in the Commonwealth countries manpower was becoming an ever-increasing concern. Not only was the pool of available men decreasing, the numbers under arms were being steadily eroded by both casualty figures and by a growing number of desertions. The infantry was particularly affected by both of these factors: casualties were higher in the infantry than in other branches of the army, and desertion rates rose noticeably after Rome fell. This was partly because of the prolonged periods the infantry had spent in action during the months of the battles for the Gustav Line and Anzio, when they had been pushed to the limits of their endurance. With no readily-available sources of reinforcement there had been little alternative to keeping units in the line for long periods. There were other reasons for the rising numbers of deserters, including – for the British, although not for the Americans (one was executed in France) – the fact that the death penalty for this offence no longer existed. The prospect of spending time behind bars for desertion was preferable to the discomfort, danger and possible death of continuing to serve on the front line. It was possible to disappear into the cities of Naples or Rome, or into the villages and countryside of Italy, and the fact that the end of the war appeared to be nearing drove many men to improve the odds of surviving the conflict by going absent from their units.[6] This factor was not unique to the Italian Front: the US Provost-Marshal estimated that more than 18,000 American deserters were on the run in the European Theatre of Operations on 1 January 1945.[7] Even the threat of a firing-squad did not deter these men from avoiding their duties.

The morale of the Fifth Army in the post-D Day period was of concern in Washington. On Christmas Day 1944 General Marshall wrote to the Assistant Secretary of State for Public and Cultural Relations, Archibald MacLeish, requesting him to include positive mention of the Italian campaign in the President's annual State of the Union Message to Congress. Marshall's action was prompted by a report that he had received from General McNarney, Deputy Supreme Commander in the Mediterranean, that Fifth Army morale 'is suffering for lack of appropriate treatment of importance of Italian campaign. Inactive period in Italy during great activity in France, spectacular forays of B-29s and political implications of the Balkan situation is not only detracting from but obscuring all importance of the Italian campaign in the press in the United States, *which is reflected in mail received by troops at the front.*' (Marshall's emphasis)[8]

While the Allies were decreasing their strength in Italy, the Germans were doing the reverse: eight divisions were on their way. From Holland and Denmark the *19th* and *20th Luftwaffe Field Divisions*, from the Balkans *16th SS Panzer Grenadier* and *42nd Jäger Divisions*, and *34th Infantry Division* from Russia. Three more divisions which were forming in Germany were sent to Italy where they assumed the titles of formations which had been destroyed in the Battle for Rome. In addition *504 Heavy Tank Battalion*, equipped with Tigers, was sent from the GHQ reserve in France. The Germans evidently believed that Italy was worth defending, regardless of the relative lack of importance the Americans were giving it. Kesselring was also moving reinforcements south from the formations that were already in Italy, for example the *162nd Division* was sent from Leghorn to the *Fourteenth Army*, an arrival it marked with a charge of Cossack cavalry – which Alexander recorded as being ineffective against the Fifth Army.

With no change in his objective, to tie down Kesselring's forces and keep them away from North West Europe, Alexander believed that he had to mount a full-scale offensive using both of his armies. Harding identified two possible routes by which the Allies might advance, with Eighth Army along the Adriatic or by pushing Fifth Army through the mountain passes between Florence and Bologna, the actual choice of which was to be kept from the enemy by a deception plan which made it appear that either was practicable. Harding's selection for the main effort was through the passes because he regarded the series of ridges and valleys along the Adriatic as being too difficult. They were too similar to the terrain which had caused the Eighth Army so many difficulties during the previous winter. The prospect of attacking through the passes appealed to Clark – it would give the Fifth Army the lion's share of the action, and him the lion's share of the glory.

General Kirkman, commander of XIII (British) Corps, saw things differently. The natural mountain obstacles would seriously hinder the movement of an army reliant on mechanized weapons and transport; for that

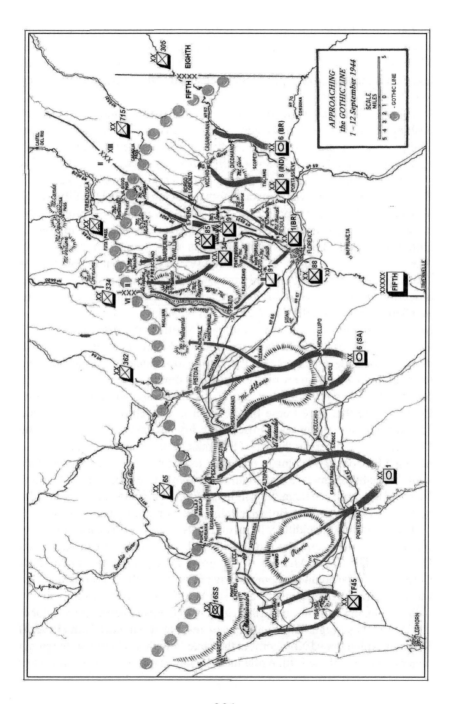

reason, the Adriatic side was to be preferred; the Eighth Army's strength could be best employed there. He argued his case persuasively with Leese, who in turn took it to Alexander, who reversed his earlier decision. Clark was less than impressed with a plan which relegated Fifth Army to a supporting role.

By now Clark had come to the view that the British strategic concept of pushing through the Po valley and then into Austria via the Ljubjana Gap held promise, and he was determined that he would take the leading role in achieving this goal.[9] In his view the British were not up to the task and it should be assigned to the Americans – under his command, naturally. Hanging over his head was also the fear that, having depleted the Fifth Army of American formations and seeing no further advantage in continuing the Italian campaign, Washington might transfer the remainder of it to France. Hitherto Clark had gained prominence as the commander of the only American army in combat – at least until OVERLORD – but to send his last United States troops to southern France would relegate him to comparative obscurity; the world's focus on Normandy was already diminishing his status.

Clark manoeuvred the discussion about which army would take the lead role in the Italian advance around to consideration of what was to happen about the Fifth Army's right flank and who was to have control of the British division alongside it. His price for giving way to Alexander's decision to give the Eighth Army the main role in the forthcoming operation was to gain command, not merely of the adjacent British division, but of the entire XIII Corps. While this gave Leese the freedom to concentrate on his Adriatic advance without concerning himself with his left flank, it also denied the Eighth Army commander the use of Kirkman's corps as a reserve. For Clark, having XIII Corps gave him an increased length of front and better balance with the Eighth Army as the strength of the two armies became more equal. He could now take a meaningful part in the forthcoming operations, hopefully now being able to capture Bologna before the worst of winter arrived.

Clark now had an additional four divisions, the 1st British and 8th Indian Infantry Divisions, and the 6th British and 6th South African Armoured Divisions. The South Africans would go to IV Corps. Additionally, XIII Corps had 1 Canadian Armoured Brigade with its three regiments: 11th Canadian Armoured Regiment was in support of 1st Division, 14th Regiment with 8th Indian Division, and 12th Regiment in Corps Reserve. On 3 October the last of these regiments came out of reserve to support 78th (British) Division, which joined XIII Corps at the same time. XIII Corps was to remain under command of the Fifth Army until 18 January 1945. It was not always a happy affiliation, particularly – as so often in this coalition – for the senior officers who had to co-ordinate the actions of their respective formations.

Clark's most promising route for the advance to Bologna was along highways which ran through the mountain passes. The passes would not be easy to force, particularly without mountain troops, but Clark maintained his confidence in his American formations. His plan was to contain the enemy on his left with IV (US) Corps to prevent the Germans from transferring reinforcements to his centre, where II (US) Corps was to make the main thrust. On his right, XIII Corps would keep up with the main attack and broaden his front. Clark, as he had done earlier in the campaign, was prepared to put his Americans in the key positions and to have them take whatever casualties it took to achieve the job. And, again as before, this attitude towards casualties could not be supported by the British commanders who served under him, and Kirkman was no different from the others. The two generals did not see eye-to-eye. Kirkman was unable to understand why Clark was not prepared to let the Eighth Army play the main part in the forthcoming operations, which were of course intended to achieve what he saw as a common goal. He did not see it as a competition between commanders and armies that were in pursuit of a common goal. Clark saw it differently. Nor was Kirkman enthusiastic about Clark's intention to mount a full-scale offensive in which XIII Corps would incur unnecessary casualties which he could ill-afford. Relationships were not improved when neither Clark nor Gruenther visited Kirkman to keep him informed as to the Army commander's concept of future operations. Once again, the procedures and practices of the British and American armies were sufficiently different, if not to actually cause open friction, then to fail to ease the way. Kirkman was used to dealing with officers such as Alexander who preferred to consult and listen, as contrasted to Clark who gave orders and refused to discuss them. It was like trying to mix oil with water.

As the advance progressed over the coming days and weeks the American casualty rate rose to a level which swamped the US reinforcement organization in Italy. Clark was forced to call a halt on 27 October, deeply frustrated. He had been defeated by the weather, determined enemy resistance, and by tactics which had reduced his manpower to a level which made it impossible to continue. According to Clark the fault – as ever – lay elsewhere. Kirkman was accused (in front of several American officers including Gruenther, the two US Corps commanders and a number of staff officers) of a lack of drive, an argument Clark supported by reference to the casualty figures for American (13,082) and Commonwealth (7,087) troops respectively.[10] The fact that XIII Corps had not suffered as heavily, despite the fact that some of their formations had been very badly mauled, was apparently evidence that they were not pulling their weight. To harangue a senior officer from an allied nation in front of subordinate officers in this fashion was inexcusable, and was hardly calculated to improve coalition relationships. Having had Dawley, Lucas, McCreery and Freyberg to blame for past failures, Clark was now seeking to find yet another scapegoat.

Clark's humour was not improved by a letter from Devers, who told him he was driving his men too hard. But the fault, of course, he saw as lying firmly with the British, who wanted the Eighth Army to take the credit for the campaign. He did not have long to sulk, however: his ego was given a boost on 24 November when a signal arrived from Churchill with the news of a reorganization of the Allied commanders in the Mediterranean. Field Marshal Sir John Dill, the British Representative of the Combined Chiefs of Staff in Washington (and a man who had contributed a great deal to ensuring that the coalition worked as well as it had done) had died and was to be succeeded by Maitland Wilson. He, in turn, was to be replaced by Alexander as Commander in the Mediterranean theatre – and Clark was to assume the appointment of Commander 15th Army Group.

There were other changes. Leese departed from Eighth Army for Burma, and was replaced by McCreery, an appointment which Clark would not have welcomed. For the Fifth Army, Truscott returned from France, an appointment which many of the British would have welcomed. Kirkman returned to the United Kingdom and a home command, his appointment as commander XIII Corps going to Harding. Clark took Gruenther with him to 15th Army Group.

On 16 December 1944 General Clark left the Fifth Army Headquarters at Futa Pass to take command of the Army Group. The *Fifth Army History* marked the change of command with the following words:

> From 5 January 1943, when he activated Fifth Army in North Africa as the first American army to be organized in the field outside the continental United States, until 16 December 1944, General Clark had guided the destinies of Fifth Army through many months of hard campaigning. Like the Gothic Line fighting of the past fall, it had been a campaign marked by brilliant victories and bitter disappointments. Fifth Army could take pride in being the first American army to invade Hitler's Fortress Europe; the first Allied Army to capture a European capital; and until 6 June 1944 the only American army opposing the German Wehrmacht.[11]

As with the *History*'s introduction, written by Clark on 27 October 1944, the entry failed to draw attention to the international nature of the Army, nor of Seventh Army's participation in the Sicilian campaign.

The Fifth Army was now destined to spend the winter in the mountains, waiting for the spring weather to bring better conditions for a renewed offensive. On its right flank the Eighth Army was able to continue moving northwards until mid-December, when it also came to a halt.

As the war in Italy entered its final phase a number of formations were added to, or passed through, the Fifth Army's order of battle. Three of these, the 6th South African Armoured Division, the Brazilian Expeditionary Force, and the 92nd (Negro) Division, exemplified different aspects of coalition forces and are worth considering separately from the chronological account of the campaign.

The 6th (South African) Armoured Division

On 17 August the 6th (South African) Armoured Division was transferred to the Fifth Army, the latest in a series of international formations to find themselves as part of Clark's order of battle.

The division included soldiers from several Commonwealth countries, which gave them at least some degree of shared background and military ethos. In broad terms the command structure, training, doctrine and operational procedures were familiar to all of the division's units, as were the weapons and matériel. To that extent the division had a degree of uniformity and cohesion, although in other respects there were concerns which could have proved difficult, particularly with regard to South African racial policies. There was also a significant anti-war faction in South Africa which was of relevance to recruiting policies and which limited the deployment of the division.

South African units had been involved with the Fifth Army since before its arrival in Italy. On 14 August 1943 46 Survey Company, South African Engineers, was assigned to Fifth Army to assist in the preparations for AVALANCHE, and 83 Engineer Base Stores Depot SAEC had been occupied in packing tons of equipment for the invasion for weeks before it happened. The Survey Company landed at Salerno on 8 September, its immediate task being to revise the available maps. On 27 November it was ordered to carry out a survey network of control points which would tie in the Fifth Army artillery units to the south Italy map grid. The main South African contribution to the Fifth Army was to arrive later, in the shape of 6th South African Armoured Division. Its pedigree was – like that of many formations

– a chequered one which reflected the constraints under which the South African government operated, some of which were self-imposed for domestic reasons, others by the wider conditions faced by all of the United Nations, such as scarcity of equipment.

Service in the armed forces of the Union of South Africa was voluntary. Prevailing attitudes regarding racial equality limited the potential pool of volunteers for combat arms to whites, and those of other racial groups could only serve in non-combatant support roles, with Cape Coloured and Indian personnel as drivers and pioneers in the Cape Corps, and Africans in pioneer and labour units of the Native Military Corps. Restrictions were also placed on the ranks which could be attained by non-whites: warrant officer in the Cape Corps and sergeant in the NMC; Coloured troops were paid half the rates that whites earned, and Africans two-thirds of the Coloured rate.[12] Apart from guard duties and self-defence, firearms were not given to these soldiers – they would not be employed to kill Europeans. This policy reduced the available numbers of men for the fighting arms aged between twenty and forty to some 320,000; at the outbreak of war the standing army was only 3,353-strong, with another 14,631 in the Active Citizen Force. With no expectation that the army would serve outside southern Africa these men were trained and equipped accordingly. With a sizeable minority of South Africans opposed to involvement in the war (it will be recalled that the initial response of Prime Minister Hertzog was to declare the country neutral, leading to his overthrow by Smuts) conscription was never a viable choice. The shortage of personnel was to hinder the nation's attempts to maintain two effective divisions for deployment in North Africa. The numbers of men raised were sufficient for only the 1st and 2nd SA Infantry Divisions, each of 24,108 men, with a third division – based in South Africa – having a strength of only 6,000 from which to provide reinforcements for the other two. As early as April 1941 a possible solution to this manning problem had been suggested whereby one of the infantry divisions would be converted to armour. This reduced the manpower requirement, because an armoured division comprised only two (one armoured, one infantry) brigades rather than the three brigades which made up an infantry division; the establishment of an armoured division was only 14,195 officers and men. This proposal was taken a stage further in May 1942 when Field Marshal Smuts announced that both infantry divisions would convert. The following month an estimated 10,772 South Africans from two entire infantry brigades and most of the 2nd Division's supporting units were taken prisoner at Tobruk.[13] This blow finalized the argument, which was given further impetus by the way in which the North African campaign was developing, with an emphasis on armoured warfare.

There was another factor which played its part in constraining the numbers of men available for service in the armed forces, again caused by the hesitancy of the government to press too strongly for a wholehearted commitment to a war which many at home did not support. Until the early part of 1940 the South African Army saw little prospect of action and anticipated little more than a home defence role. In March of that year, however, the British Government requested reinforcements – initially a South African infantry brigade – to be sent to Kenya to defend the country against any Italian incursions. This deployment was not covered by the oath of service taken by the volunteers, and they were now invited to take a fresh one which committed them to service anywhere in Africa. This move provided sufficient willing personnel to meet the initial needs of operations in East Africa and took the Army to the conclusion of the North African campaign, but as the fighting there drew to a close at the beginning of 1943 the South African government found it necessary to introduce a new general service oath, voluntary acceptance of which committed their servicemen to worldwide operations. To some soldiers it appeared that the goalposts were shifting yet again: the uptake was not encouraging, and the outcome divided the forces between those who were prepared to continue the battle against the Axis to its conclusion, and those who elected to stick to the 'Africa Service Personnel' terms of engagement – and who became known disparagingly as 'asps' by those who signed the new oath and who wore an orange flash on their epaulettes to indicate their status. Nevertheless, the hope remained that two armoured divisions could be raised, even though both could not be fielded. One, the 1st SA Armoured Division, could not be established at full strength and remained in South Africa; the other, the 6th SA Armoured Division, was formed from units that had previously served with the 2nd SA Infantry Division. To raise the manpower required in the face of shortages caused by losses during the fighting thus far, by the reluctance of men to serve outside Africa, and by some veterans who were unwilling to serve again, shortfalls in the infantry were resolved by merging some regiments. These retained the titles of both of the original units which had been united, for example 'The Imperial Light Horse/Kimberley Regiment', which became – confusingly to the outsider – 'ILH/KimR' in its abbreviated form. The Divisional Commander was Major General W. H. Evered Poole.

While the British welcomed units for which they had a requirement in Italy, such as those from the South African Engineer Corps, they were initially reluctant to take the armoured division; the need was for more infantry. In March 1944 the Division was ordered to prepare to move to Palestine, an order which was countermanded nine days later. The Division's potential could not be ignored and it was destined for Italy. Sixth SA Armoured Division disembarked in Taranto on 20 and 21 April 1944 but it was to be strengthened for the forthcoming battles. Experience had shown that the composition of armoured divisions with one armoured and one infantry brigades (in this case 11 Armoured and 12 Motorised South African Brigades) was too light in infantry, especially in the context of the Italian terrain which did not lend itself to armoured warfare as it had been fought in the desert. To rectify this weakness 24 Guards Infantry Brigade, one of the independent formations serving with the Eighth Army, was attached to the Division. The Guards Brigade was to serve with the South Africans until it was removed to bring the British 56th Infantry Division up to strength in February 1945.

The Division's first taste of action was when 12 Motorised Brigade with artillery and support units was detached and placed under command of 2nd New Zealand Division, then part of Eighth Army's X (British) Corps in the Cassino area. Relieving 11 Canadian Infantry Brigade the South Africans held the line there until the Gustav Line was broken, after which they rejoined the Division which was in the Eighth Army reserve, attached to I Canadian Corps. Passing through Rome on 6 June, with the GOC and his GSO 2 (Ops) taking it in turns to listen to reports from the British Broadcasting Corporation on the progress of OVERLORD on the radio in their command tank, the Division moved into the spearhead position of the Eighth Army advance. This it led up the western bank of the Tiber, fighting actions south of Celleno against elements of the *365th Infantry Division* before taking the town of Orvieto. By 17 June its first attempt to enter Chiusi had been halted by the *Herman Göring Division*, but the town was captured six days later. During this operation A Company of First City/Cape Town Highlanders, which had led the attack, was surrounded by the enemy and its survivors forced to surrender – the event referred to earlier in this narrative, which caused Field Marshal Smuts to divert his aircraft from its flight from London to South Africa so that he might discuss the military and political implications of another surrender to follow that of 2nd SA Infantry Division in Tobruk.

As the advance continued towards Florence XIII Corps had 4th Infantry Division as its centre, with the British 6th Armoured and 6th SA Armoured Divisions on its right and left respectively. The South Africans moved forward in two columns until they ran into the Georg Line, a delaying position manned by the *LXXVI Panzer Corps*. It was only when the 2nd New

Zealand and the British 6th Armoured Divisions succeeded in taking the high ground that the Germans were forced to withdraw, allowing the South Africans to resume their progress. By 4 August the outskirts of Florence were entered, a patrol from ILH/KimR being the first to arrive. In a Special Order of the Day Major General Poole highlighted the fact that the Division had covered 601 miles since leaving Taranto, that the artillery had fired 201,500 rounds, that its engineers had constructed sixty-five bridges, and that 3,752 miles of telephone cable had been laid. The Division was then withdrawn into Eighth Army reserve for rest. On 17 August the Division was ordered to be transferred to the US IV Corps to partially fill the gaps left by the transfer of American divisions which were bound for Operation ANVIL/DRAGOON.

Now part of the United States Fifth Army, 6th SA Armoured Division, which had a British brigade under command and which was further augmented by the addition of 4/13th Frontier Force Rifles (an Indian Army unit trained in mountain warfare manned by Hindus, Muslims and Sikhs with predominantly British officers, notwithstanding the South Africans' aversion to employing non-whites in a combat role) and 74th British Light Anti-Aircraft Regiment Royal Artillery with the attachment of the mortar platoon from ILH/KimR, organized as an infantry battalion, found itself to be the epitome of coalition warfare at the operational level. The 166th (Newfoundland) Field Regiment Royal Artillery also joined the Division, which added yet another nationality to its complement. The regiment was part of the British Army, recruited in Newfoundland, which was a Dominion directly governed from the United Kingdom and did not become a Canadian province until 1949. The international flavour went deeper than unit level, for many of the nursing sisters who served in 108th South African Mobile Hospital came from Canada, 300 having been recruited under an agreement between the two governments involved, to cover the shortfall in required numbers.[14] The Division now comprised three armoured regiments, nine infantry battalions, and three field and one medium artillery regiments as well as supporting troops. It was not long before the ramifications of such an amalgamation of different nationalities, cultures, and of different command styles became apparent.

Having served operationally in the Eighth Army since June 1941, General Poole and his staff had now to adapt to the methods and policies of the American Army, a task which was far from straightforward, particularly when in the middle of fighting a war. Poole's preference was for commanding well forward from a Tactical HQ which was no more than a jeep containing his G2 and two radio sets manned by an operator, the jeep being accompanied by a motorcycle driven by his Provost Corporal bodyguard armed with a tommy-gun. The GOC and the G2 shared the driving. When the situation demanded, Poole would mount the motorcycle for greater speed and mobility, and through this practice he was able to maintain frequent face-to-face discussions with his brigade commanders, making swift decisions on the spot. The presence of the GOC well forward, with his pennant flying on the 'two-star' jeep, also had a beneficial effect on the morale of the troops.[15]

To continue the Allied advance northwards from Florence the River Arno had first to be crossed, a task which was achieved when patrols from the First City/Cape Town Highlanders found workable crossing points near Le Piagge for 12 Motorised Brigade. As the enemy withdrew to take up fresh defensive positions on the Gothic Line the Division crossed the river on Bailey bridges which the SAEC erected on the remnants of the demolished bridges. With only light resistance being encountered, General Poole planned a swift pursuit but this intent was countermanded by orders from above; General Clark feared that the South Africans' advance would alert the Germans and compromise his main attack north of Florence. Poole was ordered to halt and to hold the Albano Massif.

While the *Fifth Army History* stated that it was particularly important that the element of surprise was not endangered by any move by the South Africans, the latter felt strongly that such an approach indicated a lack of initiative and a rigidity which permitted the Germans more time to improve their defences. With winter approaching there was even more reason to inject a sense of urgency and to take full advantage of any opportunity to put the enemy on the wrong foot. Nevertheless, the 6th SA Armoured Division was required to sit on its hands and let the opportunity pass.

A second instance of Fifth Army's lack of understanding the *modus operandi* of the different nationalities under command, and of the possible implications of decisions taken with inadequate knowledge of local conditions or of the consequences which might occur from poorly thought-out plans, came a few days later. On 14 September an order arrived from IV (US) Corps for a brigade from the Division to attack and capture Femina Morta, one of the Gothic Line's strongest features. Following its fall, the brigade was to move on and take a second position, Monte Bersano, and then to exploit forward some 6,000 metres beyond it. The 24 Guards Brigade, with First City/Cape Town Highlanders under command, was given the task, and although the Divisional staff knew that it would carry it out to its best ability, experience told them that the Brigade would probably be lost in the attempt. While General Poole's professionalism led him to accept the order and to prepare to carry it out, his GSO1, Colonel Maggs, was perhaps more understanding of the political consequences of writing off an élite British brigade in a South African division which was part of an American army in an impossible operation.

Fortunately Maggs was not only on good terms with the IV Corps Chief of Staff, Brigadier General Ladue, but was quickly able to contact him by telephone. Having expressed his concerns, he requested that a light aircraft be sent to fly him to Corps Headquarters. Without telling Poole, he set off to a stretch of road on which the aircraft could land, and was taken to meet Ladue and General Crittenberger, the Corps Commander. Maggs presented his case strongly: as the South African military historian, Neil Orpen,[16] put it, what the governments of the United States, Great Britain and South Africa might make of an American corps ordering a South African division to send a British Guards Brigade to destruction would be 'pretty colourful'. Maggs' view of matters was accepted: Crittenberger and Ladue promised to do what they could to have the orders rescinded, and later that evening news arrived at Divisional Headquarters to the effect that the operation had been cancelled. The incident was a clear demonstration of the difficulties encountered by commanders of multinational forces; the Guards Brigade – not to mention international relations – was fortunate that Maggs exercised his initiative and acted as he did. A similar formation in an army that was composed only of troops from a single nationality would have not had the same reasons to object and nor would the objections have received such a sympathetic reaction, as was seen earlier in the campaign when the 36th (US) Division was ordered to cross the Rapido.

Major General Poole summed up five stages of 6th SA Armoured Division's Italian operations in his Operations Report which was released in June 1945. The first phase was the pursuit of the enemy when the Germans withdrew from Cassino, and the second covered the setpiece assaults on strong natural positions held by the enemy at Monte Catarelto, Stanco, and Point 826. In November 1944 the third phase opened as the weather deteriorated. Deep snow halted movement, and Divisional Headquarters was to remain in Castiglione dei Pepoli, which it had reached on 26 September, until mid-April the next year. It was, again, a period of frustration as Bologna and open tank country lay only about twenty miles ahead. With tanks and guns dug into the snow and mule trains having to be used to supply troops in the line, operations slowed until warmer weather improved matters, but hostilities continued as the tanks were employed to give fire support from static positions, supplementing the artillery. Re-organization continued regardless of the weather: on 15 January the Division was placed under command of II (US) Corps, having previously been Fifth Army troops.

Phase four of Poole's report opened at the beginning of April when the Division began to take up positions for an attack on the defences of Monte Sole, Monte Caprara and Monte Abelle. The newly-formed 13 SA Motorised Brigade, with 11 SA Armoured Brigade made the assault after a period of intensive planning. The attack went in following heavy air attacks, followed by an artillery barrage, at 2230 hours on 15 April; at 0100 hours the leading troops were on the summit of Monte Sole. Their platoon commander, Second Lieutenant Mollett, was awarded an immediate DSO, but the event was not one of unalloyed celebration, for his Commanding Officer was killed in the hour of victory.

The taking of the mountain stronghold opened the way for the breakthrough to Bologna, which fell on 21 April, and the pursuit of the enemy, who were becoming increasingly disorganized, across the Lombardy plains – phase five of Poole's report. At the end of April the Division reverted to Fifth Army command and was ordered to the Milan area, 200 miles away, to support IV (US) Corps, which was facing two German divisions, *34th Infantry* and *5th Mountain*. On 2 May the Germans in Italy surrendered. General Poole refused to enter Milan until the bodies of Mussolini and his mistress had been removed from the service station where they had been hanging after being shot.[17]

The Brazilian Expeditionary Force

Brazil had fought in the First World War as an ally of the United States, Great Britain and France, primarily contributing naval units, although military observers were placed with the French Army. After the war the Brazilian government recognized that it was necessary to establish a capable army for defensive purposes; at the time the national army was smaller and less well equipped than some of the states' police forces. In 1919 an agreement was established for a French Military Mission to assist in modernizing the Brazilian Army and bringing it up to European standards. The Mission's work ended on the outbreak of war between France and Germany in 1939.

Notwithstanding the work of the French Mission, the Brazilian Army's main role was one of internal security and during the previous century it had dealt with rebellions organized by secessionist movements. The lessons which the First World War threw up were largely irrelevant to the Brazilian scenario and were not implemented; indeed, the internal security role was brought to the fore again during the 1920s when there was a number of insurrections against the central government, some of them involving young army officers. Loyalist troops were successful in putting these movements down.

The army's involvement in politics did not cease, and in 1930 it deposed the President and installed Getúlio Vargas in his place. A right-winger, Vargas did away with the constitution and the National Assembly and introduced a series of emergency measures with which to rule the country. In 1937 he outlawed opposition parties, including the Communists, modelling his dictatorship on European Fascism. His admiration for the Axis powers, together with the fact that Germany was fast becoming one of Brazil's most important trading partners, led the United States to become concerned about the country's political alliances; however, when the Axis invited Brazil to join them in 1937 Vargas declined and announced a non-alignment posture. The pro-German party, *Ação Integralista Brasileira*, followed the Communists into the political wilderness when it was banned in 1938, retaliating by being behind an assassination attempt on Vargas. Brazil declared its neutrality on 2 September 1939.[18]

Pan-American unity had been emphasized during the Buenos Aires and Lima Conferences in 1936 and 1938 respectively, and at the latter meeting all of the American republics agreed to assist each other against invasion. The United States continued to build relationships with Brazil, donating financial support for industrial modernization in return for an agreement on rubber production. Brazil's strategic location jutting out into the Atlantic towards Africa and dominating shipping lanes, the strategically important air route between Natal and Dakar, and as a key potential ally in denying the Axis access to South America, together with its wealth of raw materials made the country important to the United States. As he did with Great Britain, President Roosevelt pursued a policy of discreet discussions with the Brazilian government which laid the ground for an alliance in the event of war, and in January 1942 cooperation between the two countries further increased when Brazil broke off diplomatic relations with Germany and American air bases were established in the north of Brazil. Hitler's response was to expand the area of operations of his U-boats in attempting to enforce a blockade against American countries and Europe, an act which was to result in the sinking of Brazilian shipping and the deaths of over 1,600 passengers and crew members during the first eight months of 1942. This led to a swing of opinion in Brazil and, with growing anti-German feelings and demonstrations in cities such as Rio de Janeiro, Brazil declared war on Germany and Italy on 22 August that year, despite the apparent contradiction of having a fascist-style dictatorship at home.

By now the US-Brazilian relationship had shifted. Whereas earlier in the war America had courted Brazil avidly for the reasons outlined above, by late 1942 the reverse situation was emerging. Brazil was no longer in the front line; in fact, with the war moving eastwards across the Atlantic and the Axis powers being strongly contested in North Africa, the country was finding itself in the rear areas. To benefit from the war and in the hope that it would emerge as the leading South American nation once it was over, Brazil needed to do more than provide raw material, transit bases and diplomatic support. At a secret meeting with President Vargas in Natal on 28 January 1943 Roosevelt encouraged the Brazilian government to commit troops to the conflict. This step would, he maintained, entitle Brazil to a larger role in the postwar restructuring of the world. The argument, together with the prospect of modernizing the country's armed forces for the future, was convincing. From the United States' perspective, an alliance with the largest Latin-American country would enhance its status as the leading power in this hemisphere.

Military reactions to the proposal to send Brazilian troops were mixed. Some Brazilian officers supported the idea, others were less enthusiastic about sending their defence forces overseas when Argentina posed a potential threat to the south of the country. Some American officers felt that the provision of bases in Brazil was all that the United States needed from the country; but in May 1943 the Joint Chiefs of Staff approved the idea.[19]

At the time of Brazilian entry to the war its armed forces were outdated. Equipment and training was far below the standards required to participate in combat against the Axis powers, and an immediate concern was to provide shore defences for the country. Consequently, it took over eighteen months for the nation to train and prepare an expeditionary force of one division with support troops. The process was not an easy one, and was bedevilled by fears that pro-German elements in the south of the country might foment civil unrest or even encourage an invasion by Argentina, Brazil's challenger as the supreme South American power.

Major General Mascarenhas de Morais commanded the Brazilian Expeditionary Force throughout its time in Italy. He recorded several difficulties in preparing the Brazilian Expeditionary Force (BEF) for service with American forces, amongst which was the fact that the Brazilian Army had been trained by the French Military Mission which had versed it in the organization, regulations and doctrine of the French Army – all of which were rendered redundant in 1940 anyway. The Brazilians were now tasked with repeating the learning process, but now in line with US Army practices and using American equipment. The BEF was to depart for Italy only with personal equipment such as clothing. All other matériel, including weapons and vehicles, was to be provided by the Americans in theatre. Final training was to be given in Italy – and was unexpectedly intensive – although there was an exchange of Brazilian and American officers before the BEF arrived there to facilitate the process. A popular Brazilian saying at the time, 'It is easier for a snake to smoke than it is for Brazil to go to war', led to the BEF adopting an insignia depicting a cobra smoking a pipe.

The 1st Brazilian Infantry Division was organized on American lines with three regimental combat teams, the first of which (the 6th RCT) entered the war on 6 September 1944. It was deployed to the Serchio valley, west of Lucca, where it fought until 30 October, Clark having considered that this part of the Fifth Army front would give them a comparatively gentle introduction to combat. From early November the division was engaged in the Reno valley under command of IV (US) Corps; it spent 239 uninterrupted days in action, in the Apennines and then the Po valley where it received the surrender of 13,000 men from the *148th Infantry* and *90th Panzergrenadier Divisions* and Italians from the *Italian Fascist Army*. Brazilian ground forces in Italy numbered 25,334. [20]

The Fifth Army took the Force's arrival in its stride, putting its customary gloss on the matter:

> After many months' experience in commanding British, French, and Italian troops the Army encountered no special difficulty in incorporating the Brazilian troops other than that imposed by the scarcity of personnel capable of speaking Portuguese.[21]

The British, French and Italians may have questioned this sentiment – the South Africans were certainly aware that Fifth Army decision-making procedures were less than sensitive to considerations of international relationships. Nor were the Brazilians so sanguine of the relationships with their commanding formation. The language difficulty certainly presented problems, not just the expected ones that would occur between commanders of different nationalities' units, but lower down the chain of command. Brazilian soldiers found it easier to converse with the Italian population than with American soldiers because of the similarities between Portuguese and Italian, a factor which led to American complaints about Brazilian soldiers breaking the regulations which banned fraternization. In turn this led to accusations about lack of Brazilian discipline.

There were other, possibly more mundane, difficulties in assimilating the Brazilians into the Fifth Army. The point made by Clark regarding different rations being required by different nationalities[22] was applicable to the BEF as well as to the other nationalities involved in the campaign. US rations were not liked by the Brazilians, particularly those who had come from poorer backgrounds, and efforts had to be made to provide them with a diet they were more used to, including black beans, rice, and more fresh meat and Brazilian coffee.[23]

The comparatively short time allowed to the BEF to prepare for deployment presented problems of individual equipment. The footwear and clothing worn by Brazilian soldiers was unsuitable for the Italian winter, and Brazilian industry was ill-prepared to provide appropriate substitutes – once again, supplies had to be found from within American resources. Shoe repair was a particular problem, finally resolved when some fifty Italian civilians were employed to carry out the task using the Brazilian methodology. Why Brazilians could not have been supplied with American footwear is unclear; much of the rest of their clothing and equipment came from that source.

The Expeditionary Force's combat role was mostly carried out at platoon level (its chief of staff noted that 'at no time did the FEB engage in strategic level operations'.[24] With only one division it could hardly have been otherwise. The Brazilian presence brought more to the propaganda battle than to the military struggle – the nation entered the war for political ends, and benefited accordingly.

The 92nd (Negro) Division
On 30 July 1944 the 370th Regimental Combat Team arrived in Naples from the United States, having trans-shipped in Oran. The newcomers comprised the 370th Infantry Regiment, the 598th Artillery Battalion and detachments (including the headquarters companies) from each of the specialist units of the 92nd Infantry Division. Their arrival was greeted with excitement by the African-American troops (then called Negro or Colored troops) already serving in Italy. Apart from the 99th Fighter Squadron and the 332nd Fighter Group which had been operating in the country since October 1943 and February 1944 respectively, all Negroes were in service units such as the Quartermaster Corps. The 370th RCT was the first US Army Negro formation specifically trained for ground combat to serve in Italy. Its presence there followed years of political pressure from the Negro civil rights movement in the United States and a slow progression towards equality which would not be achieved until well after the war ended.

Some 909,000 African Americans were enlisted into the US Army during the Second World War. Of these, the great majority served in support and service arms, about half a million being sent overseas. With pressing manpower problems the American government had been persuaded to deploy Black soldiers for combat duties overseas for the first time since the First World War. The main difficulty in doing so earlier, as expressed by the Chief of Military History of the US Army in 1956, was that their civilian backgrounds did not prepare them as well as whites to become soldiers or leaders. Another obstacle – perhaps the overwhelming one – was contemporary attitudes, which militated against integration.

Negro expectations were based on their history of fighting in the Civil War, the Spanish-American War and the First World War. In the last of these conflicts two infantry divisions, the 92nd and 93rd, had been sent to France, as had various service units for quartermaster, stevedore and pioneer duties. Of the two infantry divisions, the 92nd spent only two days in an 'active' (as compared to 'quiet') sector, the active part being to participate in the assault on the second Hindenburg Line on 10 and 11 November 1918. The war ended on the second date. The 93rd Division's component regiments were split up and used as part of French divisions, where they fought in Champagne, the Vosges, and in the Oise-Aisne offensive from the early summer of 1918 to the end of the war. Both divisions had Negro junior officers, but the majority of the remaining officers, including the commanders, were white. The attention paid to the divisions both during and immediately after the war played no small part in raising Negro expectations in later years, although Black views of the value of their contribution to the war effort generally varied considerably from those of the US Army and of the white officers who served with the two formations. Reports in the press, particularly the publications that catered to the Black readership, featured stories of Negro heroism and praised their devotion to duty and the high standards they achieved. Reports from whites who had served with these two divisions were far less enthusiastic, some arguing that Black soldiers did not, and could not, perform well in combat. These views had an influence on the debate that was to come about the role of Negroes in the Second World War, for in that conflict many American senior officers had been the field and junior officers of the Great War, and many of the leading Negro spokesmen of later years had been officers and soldiers of the two divisions which served in France. Historically, Negroes had helped secure civil rights through enlisting during the American War of Independence, the Civil War, and the Spanish-American War, although they still had some way to go to achieve full equality with white Americans. Serving in the Second World War was seen by many activists as furthering their cause, but it had to be as more than noncombatants. To be seen to be carrying out only support functions would merely underline the role that many of them felt they had been restricted to in American society as a whole.

Rumours had circulated about the divisions that had gone to France in 1918 – denied by the authorities, who described them as German propaganda – that Negro soldiers were subject to discrimination and bad treatment. The stories maintained that the 92nd Division had been established by Secretary of State for War Newton Baker and approved by President Woodrow Wilson over the objections of the Army General Staff, which had then worked to ensure its failure. This rumour was given a degree of credence by the fact that the senior Negro Regular Army officer of the time, Lieutenant Colonel Charles Young, had not been given a command appointment. Whether this was because of his state of health (he had been diagnosed with high blood pressure during a regular medical examination and downgraded, although his supporters refused to accept the finding) or because of institutional resistance to Black officers was almost irrelevant – those who wished to interpret the matter as discrimination were bound to do so and to make political capital out of the affair. Young was to gain the status of a martyr in the post-war period, as Negroes became convinced that had he been commanding the 92nd then the division would have gained a better reputation, a reputation that had suffered because of the prejudice of white officers who had served in the formation. Certainly, the division's commander, Major General Charles Ballou, had antagonized his men by attitudes which left an unhappy legacy in the eyes of the wider Negro population. This popular perception of the situation could be summarized as follows: when the opportunity presented itself, Negro officers and men performed well; when they failed to do so, it was the fault of prejudiced white leaders who themselves did not perform their jobs properly; and, thirdly, Negroes of all ranks were not given sufficient credit for doing their jobs well. To give them appropriate recognition would be to open the door to Negroes gaining full civil rights, and therefore credit was deliberately withheld.

Part of the underlying problem on which the contrasting views of the 92nd's performance were based was that some forty percent of the division's enlisted men were illiterate. Blacks claimed that this was because it was deliberate Army policy to enlist the lowest standards, probably to discredit the unit. Another factor – as claimed by Black activists – was that the white officers were Southerners who brought with them the prejudices and attitudes of their home states. Negroes who were awarded commissions earned them not because they had officer qualities, but because they came close to their white superiors' ideas of how Blacks should behave. One was reputedly commissioned because he sang plantation songs.[25] The list of criticisms by and about Negroes went on.

Through the interwar period Negroes became more convinced that the US Army would restrict them to pioneer and labour units, and that it would resist granting commissions to Blacks. Combat roles and service under their own officers became important issues for racial equality. Negro ambitions were not assisted by testimonies from commanders of the 92nd and 93rd Divisions for a postwar study into the future shape of the US Army. The evidence from these officers was almost – but not entirely – uniformly damning of the performance of Negro troops, and particularly of Negro officers. The evidence against Negroes being employed in combat units was overwhelming, and the prevailing opinion was that they should be restricted to labour duties; even here, the period of training should be twice as long as carried out by white soldiers. And it was essential that leaders should be white, an assertion supported by the evidence of commanders of Negro engineer units who had found that efficiency rose when they replaced junior Negro officers with whites. Some respondents recommended that Negro units be assimilated within white formations as a move towards improving their efficiency, but the overriding testimony from the majority of 92nd and 93rd Division officers predominated, and the Army General Staff concluded that Negro combat soldiers during the Great War had failed to reach the standards of the United States Army.

In the following years the employment of Negroes was considered in the context of mobilization for war. The problem lay in deciding how best to employ a sizeable proportion of the general population which, it was believed, had neither the experience of military administration and leadership nor the opportunity to acquire it. To a certain extent this mirrored their position in civilian life, where comparatively few had managerial, technical or leadership jobs, experience of which could be transferred to military positions. Where Negroes and whites worked together in civilian jobs, the former were generally in subordinate positions, many as unskilled workers.

The 1940 Mobilization Plan placed Negroes mainly in the infantry, the engineers, and the Quartermaster Corps, largely because of the objections of chiefs of arms and services who were against the posting of Negro troops to their particular branches of the Army. These objections were partly a legacy of the First World War opinions, but also because of stereotypes based on popular views of racial differences, some of which came from 'scientific' studies of the time (the same studies contributed to Nazi dogma on racial purity).

The War Department found itself in a situation not of its own making. In many respects it was powerless to make and implement policies about racial equality and opportunity which should properly have been addressed at governmental levels. As the Army was about to embark on the biggest expansion programme in its history, the War Department's stance was that Negroes would be mobilized in proportion to their representation in the nation's manpower of military age, but that they would, preferably, be called up early so that they might receive extra training to raise them to an acceptable standard. Secondly, they would be employed in whatever arm or service for which they were qualified, and combat assignments would be made in the same ratios as for whites. They would serve in units with all-Negro enlisted personnel, but these units did not have to be employed separately. Officers for these units could be Negro or white, but there were to be fifty percent more officers in Negro units than in similar types of white units. Negro officers were to be trained to the same standards, and preferably in the same military schools, as whites, but were to serve only in Negro units and command only Negro troops. There was to be no difference in the training, quartering, and other facilities between white and Negro troops.

Unaware of the mobilization plans Black organizations continued to press the War Department for equality. They received little more than bland assurances which failed to reassure them; war plans were not about to be released for general debate. Consequently, campaigns were opened to pursue the demand for parity, supported by a variety of organizations and publications. The subject became more heated as the possibility was recognized that the debate would fuel subversion. Articles which suggested that the subject of democracy at home should be addressed before fighting for it overseas were published, and the Communist Party gave financial support to the National Negro Congress, which passed a resolution that its members would refuse to fight in the event that war should break out with the Soviet Union. The questions of British colonialism, of the oppression of Blacks worldwide, and of the identification of the Japanese as being the natural leaders of dark-skinned races, were all brought into the argument to prove that Negroes were oppressed. These indications of unrest were seen by some as presaging internal revolution, a threat which could not be ignored, but which it was impossible to counter with disclosure of mobilization plans.

During the summer of 1940, as the threat from Japan became clearer, a number of new Negro units was added to the Army's establishment, effectively doubling the Negro strength. On 1 August that year new white units were opened for enlistment; the Negro units' enlistment followed on the 15th, having been delayed while accommodation was completed. As the newspapers reported, enlistment of Blacks began to break records: in Chicago, for example, over 100 men were enrolled in a day. Not only were Negroes keen to enlist, they were determined to do so on equal grounds. Representatives of Negro pressure groups asked the House Committee on Military Affairs for safeguards that would lead to fuller service, in contradiction to the majority of bodies which gave testimony asking for exemption, for example on the grounds of pacifism.

On the same day that the Selective Service Act was approved (16 September 1940) the War Department released a press release explaining that 36,000 of the first 400,000 men to be called up would be Negroes; it listed the units in which they would serve, and noted that consideration was being given to the creation of additional combat organizations. Three weeks later a second release gave details of the decisions which the War Department had already taken in 1937, but had not publicized, on the proportional representation of Negroes in the armed forces, on Negro officers and their assignments, that Negroes would serve in all branches of the services – including being trained as pilots – and that they were being given equal opportunity for employment. The release also stated that Negro and white personnel would not be intermingled in the same regimental organizations.

The decision to form Negro combat units presented more difficulties than those outlined above. Regardless of whether Negroes served in combat or support arms, the colour of their skin was the dominant problem. The American government had to be sensitive to the opinions of the allies on whose soil they deployed Negro units, and these varied. In the United Kingdom Negro soldiers were readily accepted, and British servicemen and civilians alike resented the attempts by Americans to introduce their own discriminatory attitudes. Restaurant and public house owners failed to see why Negroes should be refused entry because white Americans practised a colour bar at home; the British position on the matter was that Negroes' money was as good as anyone else's, that their company was welcome, and that racial segregation was out of place when one was fighting a war to preserve democracy. Various solutions were proposed to resolve the problem, including limiting the numbers of Negroes sent to the United Kingdom or billeting Negroes and whites in separate towns, which was hardly an answer to the protest that Americans should not expect to impose their own ideas on racial differences on a host nation.[26]

In the Commonwealth the situation was different. Australia, for example, had a 'whites only' immigration policy which did not allow the entry of Blacks, and therefore only limited numbers of American Negroes were deployed there. Other colonies were reluctant to accept well-paid Negroes whose presence might upset the status quo between the ruling classes and those ruled, and Bermuda made a case to Washington to prevent any Negro troops being sent to the island.

Host nation considerations aside, the US theatre commanders had to agree to accept Negro units. For combat formations – with the question-mark of their capabilities still hanging over their heads – the question was serious: no commander wanted large bodies of unproven troops in the firing line. Theatre commanders could, and did, refuse to accept units (the 9th Cavalry was rejected after it had been moved to a staging area before being sent overseas; it had to return to a training camp). The concept of proportional representation had to be re-assessed, and in the summer of 1943 the possibility of de-activating Negro combat units and redeploying their manpower to non-technical service units was under consideration. Negro service units were more easily employed and the use of soldiers here would salvage manpower which might otherwise sit idle, and manpower could not be wasted. After three years of trying to achieve a balance between Negro combat and service troops, the planners gave up the struggle and henceforth the majority of Negroes joining the army went into the service branches.

This situation did not pass unnoticed by the Negro press or by those urging the formation of Negro combat units as a route towards full equality of the races. The problem was not only a question of convincing theatre commanders and host nations that they ought to accept Negro troops; it affected the Army's training and deployment policies. With the press involved, it also became a question of public policy. In short, the topic of Black combat units was a hot potato in the United States. It was to continue to be so throughout and after the war, and opinions about the performance of the 92nd Division in Italy fed the debate.

At Christmas 1944 the 92nd Division, assigned to IV (US) Corps, found itself defending a wide – probably too wide – sector of the front line while the Allied armies waited for the winter to pass before renewing their advance northwards. The defence was based on holding key points which dominated the terrain and by constant patrolling of the intervening gaps, a practice which the 92nd failed to carry out effectively. The division's steadiness was doubted by its own commander, a fact of which Truscott was aware. Clark agreed with their opinion, and two regiments from 85th (US) Division and the 8th Indian Division were placed under IV Corps command to back up the 92nd should it come under attack, a possibility which was considered to be very real.

Although the Allies had accepted that there was to be a lull in the fighting because of the weather, the enemy did not. Opposing the 92nd was the *LI Mountain Corps* which was prepared to take a more proactive role. Having identified the 92nd's sector as vulnerable because of the weakness in the defence, the shakiness of the troops (whom they considered inferior to other American divisions in their training and combat efficiency, and to be lacking in tenacity) and the general inactivity of the Fifth Army, the Germans mounted an attack with a *Kampfgruppe* made up of two mountain and two line battalions supported by artillery. Achieving complete surprise the Germans punched a line through the Americans on 26 December, causing the majority of them to flee. In the context of coalition warfare it is of interest to note that the German attack on the 92nd had been planned as an operation (codenamed *WINTERGEWITTER*) by that other coalition, the German-Italian partnership. Mussolini's Italian Social Republic's *Monte Rosa Division* – whose ability was doubted by the Germans – was to have participated in what would have been a significant Axis operation. German reservations ensured that the proposed Italian part in the operation did not survive the planning stage.[27]

The gap in the American line was plugged by two brigades from the 8th Indian Division which the Eighth Army had provided to IV Corps as a reserve force. The already uncertain reputation of Negro soldiers had been given a further blow, and in February it deteriorated when it failed in a local offensive which had been designed to straighten the line.

The morale of the division was of great concern to the Allied commanders.

> General Marshall, in Italy with General Clark at the time of the February attack, made … a dicker—a wager with Clark: that he could take those three regiments of the 92d Division and form one regiment out of them, take the one regiment made up of AAA troops who had already been converted to infantry and I would bring back the Japanese regiment, the 442d from Southern France. He was to put the Negroes in front and the Japs in reserve behind them. The Germans would think the Negro regiment was a weak spot, and then would hit the Japs. The Japanese regiment was spectacular …[28]

This re-organization was, in fact, what happened. The division was restructured along the lines described by Marshall, and it is indicative of his opinion of Negro troops that he thought that their best use was to employ them to draw the enemy into a trap in which the Nisei would crush them. The question to be considered is why the 92nd performed poorly, and the answer probably lies in their heritage.

Lincoln's Emancipation Statement had been made only seventy-eight years before Pearl Harbor. Those Negros who served in the Second World War included a large number who were the grandsons of slaves, and discrimination in terms of educational and occupational opportunities was to extend well beyond the Second World War. Illiteracy rates were better than those of the Great War, but were still high: some thirteen per cent of riflemen fell into this category, and the practice of sending the better educated and qualified recruits to technical arms contributed to the low overall standard of the infantry. Graham and Bidwell[29] make the point that the division was the American equivalent of a 'colonial' formation, manned by Black soldiers and NCOs and a few Black officers, but with all of the command and staff appointments held by whites. However, in British and French colonial units racial pride was actively encouraged and the white officers were among the best in their respective armies. This was not the case in America: Marshall was to note, 'We had, as I say, an almost unsoluble question, because we couldn't do away with feelings and reactions and customs in the Deep South.'[30] A survey conducted by the Research Branch of the Special Service Division, completed in March 1943, echoed this view. The overwhelming feeling among Negro soldiers was that they preferred Negro to white lieutenants, and they preferred Northern lieutenants to Southern lieutenants.

Leadership, or the lack of it, was a serious problem which had been identified earlier than the episodes described above. A recommendation had been made that the commanding officer of one of the division's units should be relieved because of a series of leadership failures, but instead he remained to command a task force in one of the 92nd Division's disasters.[31] Underlying this general weakness in leadership was the fact that many of the white officers were uncomfortable with their jobs. According to a study carried out at Washington's behest white officers in the 92nd Division 'generally disliked their assignments, had no confidence in their men and believed that the "experiment" of using Negroes in combat would fail'. One staff officer believed that 'the Negro generally could not overcome or escape his background of no property ownership, irresponsibility, and subservience. The

244

Negro is panicky and his environment has not conditioned him to accept responsibilities.'[32]

With attitudes like these among their officers, it is little wonder that Negro soldiers underperformed. Even disregarding questions about their efficiency, the future of the 92nd was going to be limited, however. In February 1945 the lack of appropriate reinforcements for this division, for the Brazilians, and for the new Italian Legnagno Group meant that Fifth Army planners determined that these three formations could only be considered for defensive roles.

1945

The great offensive planned for the beginning of 1945 was to start at the beginning of April when the snows had cleared. Truscott's Fifth Army benefited from an influx of reinforcements; some 7,000 arrived over the numbers required to bring his divisions up to strength. He attached these men to the units that they would join as casualty replacements after future fighting. The Fifth Army also received a new division, the 10th (Mountain), a welcome addition. A specialist formation, it attracted young fit men familiar with skiing and other mountain activities such as rock-climbing.

The requirement for a fresh offensive might well have been questioned. The Combined Chiefs of Staff saw no strategic value in developing matters, but Alexander held firm to the objective he had been set much earlier, that of pinning down as many German formations as possible. The best way to achieve this, he argued, was to eliminate *Army Group C*.

The prospect of being in at the kill suited Clark. Hitherto he had found it necessary to place himself in the limelight by manoeuvring himself into the right position – in capturing Rome, for example – by judicious manipulation of Alexander's orders. Now he was in command of both armies and could legitimately plan to have American forces take the prize. Although the United States formations were still outnumbered by the British and Commonwealth ones, he was still firmly of the opinion that the Americans were the only ones up to the task – or at least of ensuring that his reputation would be further enhanced at home. It was not an attitude best suited to the commander of an international force. In an attempt to show Marshall that he had a 'hodge-podge outfit' whose units 'can't be switched around' Clark had formed an honour guard made up of representatives from every nationality to meet his superior when he visited Italy on his way home from the Yalta Conference. The response from Marshall was not what he had anticipated, for the Chief of Staff saw the

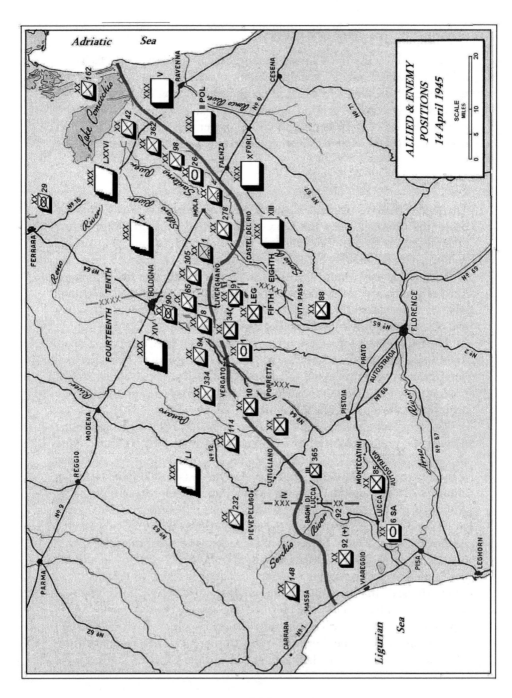

246

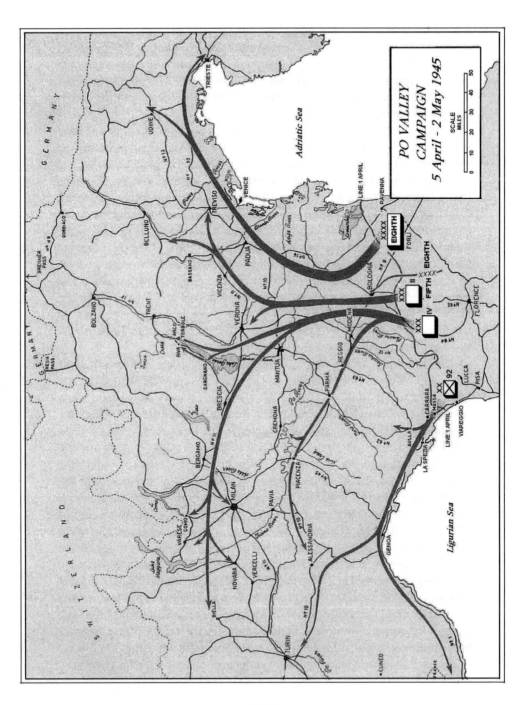

assembled troops as representing 'the most perfect example of team work among many nations united in a common cause'. Clark, of course, promptly agreed publically and was to push this point in his autobiography – although not in his private diaries which came to light later.[33] The opposing views of Marshall and Clark were a fair summary of the debate about the merits of coalition forces.

Clark's intention for the offensive, as with his previous plans, was to have the British play a supporting role to the Americans. And again as before, he identified a city as the goal; this time it was Bologna. His plan, however, had to be put into practice by Truscott and McCreery, and their views and actions (like Clark's interpretation of Alexander's views, although for very different reasons) would affect the outcome. Both the Fifth and the Eighth Army commanders envisaged swinging their commands around Bologna, to the west and east respectively, before meeting to the north of the city. Despite Clark's reservations about the British, it was they who broke through the lines of rivers barring their route northwards. The Eighth Army assault had commenced on 9 April, two days before Truscott's move; Clark had believed that this would draw the enemy reserves away from the Fifth Army, but poor weather delayed that army's move for another two days, until 14 April. By this time McCreery had broken the enemy's line.

The final days of the war in Italy saw all coalition members but the Canadians involved (they had been transferred to North West Europe in early March to take part in the last battles for Germany). American, British, South African, New Zealand, Indian and Italian forces all participated in the fighting around Bologna. The city itself was entered by the Poles shortly before seven o'clock on 21 April, about two hours before the 34th (US) Division arrived. The exploitation of the victory saw Fifth Army's II Corps (including the South Africans) strike north towards Verona, IV Corps (including the Brazilians) westwards towards Como and Parma; Eighth Army's XIII and V Corps went northeast towards Padua and Venice. On the Mediterranean coast 92nd (US) Division advanced on Genoa, which surrendered to Italian partisans the day before the Americans reached the city. Twenty miles farther north they met French forces from the Sixth US Army Group which were advancing eastwards. On 2 May the New Zealanders entered Trieste, and met Yugoslavian troops advancing westwards. That evening news of the surrender of *Army Group C* was made official, although many had heard it broadcast by the BBC earlier. For those Allied troops in Trieste it made little difference because the Germans still holding out in the area were not part of the *Group*; in any case, they were beginning to experience problems with the Yugoslavs.

It was an early indication of the Cold War, one that Churchill had hoped would have taken place farther to the east.

Behind the scenes negotiations had been underway between the Allies and SS General Wolff for the unconditional surrender of all German and pro-Axis forces in Italy. The agreement was signed at Caserta on 29 April, and the ceasefire came into effect on 2 May. The war in Italy was over.

Notes

1. Alexander, *Alexander's Despatch*
2. Ibid
3. Starr, *Fifth Army History. Part VII, the Gothic Line*
4. Danchev & Todman, *War Diaries 1939–1945, Field Marshal Lord Alanbrooke*
5. Ibid
6. Peaty, *The Desertion Crisis in Italy, 1944*
7. Hastings, *Armageddon*
8. Marshall, *Marshall Papers #4-622*, The George C Marshall Foundation
9. Graham & Bidwell, *Tug of War: The Battle for Italy 1943–-45*
10. Ibid
11. Starr, op cit.
12. Mohlamme, *Soldiers Without Reward: Africans in South Africa's Wars*
13. Agar-Hamilton & Turner, *Crisis in the Desert: May– July 1942*
14. Girard, *Canadian Nurses in the South African Military Nursing Service*
15. Theunissen, *Major General W. H. Evered Poole*
16. Orpen, Neil, *Victory in Italy*
17. Ibid
18. McCann, *Brazil and World War II: The Forgotten Ally*
19. Penteado, *The Brazilian Participation in World War II*
20. De Freitas, *Logistical Support of a Brazilian Expeditionary Force by American Supply Installations*
21. Starr, op cit.
22. Clark, Interview in 'Tough Old Gut', *World at War*
23. De Freitas, op cit.
24. Quoted in McCann, op cit.
25. Lee, *The Employment of Negro Troops*
26. Ibid
27. Jackson, *The Mediterranean and Middle East* Vol VI, Part III
28. Interview with Gen Marshall, 25 Jul 49, quoted in Lee, op cit.
29. Graham & Bidwell, op cit.
30. Marshall, *Marshall interview #17, 20 Feb 1957,* The George C Marshall Foundation
31. Lee, op cit.
32. Ibid
33. Graham & Bidwell, op cit

CHAPTER 11

Endnote

This book has been written not as a chronological account of the Fifth Army's participation in the Italian campaign, but as an examination of how a coalition force functioned when it was engaged in operations that some of its members regarded as secondary, if not completely irrelevant, to their main objective of defeating Hitler's Germany. As my research progressed, the sheer scale and variety of difficulties that the political and military leaders faced in assembling and then employing such a force became, if not necessarily clearer, then ever more daunting. What started out as a project to find answers to some of the questions that have arisen when discussing the campaign grew into something much greater as its complexities became more apparent. One is left with admiration for those who managed to overcome this mass of problems to produce an organization that was capable of operating against a very professional enemy in inhospitable country and often in appalling weather. In the words of Boswell:

> I told him I had been that morning at a meeting of the people called Quakers, where I had heard a woman preach. *Johnson:* 'Sir, a woman's preaching is like a dog's walking on his hind legs. It is not done well; but you are surprised to find it done at all.'
>
> Boswell: *Life*

As this volume has illustrated, there were times when the Fifth Army did not perform well, but nevertheless it did manage to fight its way up the leg of Italy and to do pretty much most of what was asked of it. Once one starts digging into the Army's background and composition – of its mongrel nature – it indeed appears surprising that it managed to operate at all. The magnitude of the task of bringing together peoples of some two dozen nations, each of which had its own interests to further (both at governmental and individual levels), with a bedlam of different languages, which had their own cultures, customs, religions, diets and a host of other variables, was immense. Add to these difficulties those of variances in education, of technical ability and

251

knowledge, of training (or lack of it) in the military profession, and the scale of the problem begins to become more apparent, even if the solution becomes less so. The logistics of the campaign were a nightmare in their own right. At times the rivalries between nations and individuals became so intense that they threatened the ability of the formation to perform effectively, and the dislike and distrust that some of those who served in the Fifth felt for their supposed allies almost surpassed that which they felt for the common enemy.

To what extent a modern coalition would work in the same way as the United Nations did during the Second World War is debatable. The reality at that time was that the world was engaged in a Total War in which the entire effort of the belligerents – the sum of their military, economic and other resources – was devoted to but one aim: the defeat of the enemy. National mobilization of manpower and industry in pursuit of this objective outweighed consideration of other factors: guns came before butter. In such an environment differences of opinion between allies became comparatively unimportant and played second place to winning the war. However, there were times and places where the war effort was not given wholehearted support by those involved. Italy after the fall of Rome was one such place (indeed as far as Washington was concerned this was the case from the very beginning of the campaign) as many of the participants began to question why they were risking their lives in a theatre of operations which they saw as being increasingly irrelevant to the objective of defeating Germany. And as the war drew to a close and Germany's fall became inevitable, many questioned why they should hazard their lives for a done deal. When coalitions are engaged in something less than Total War, as in Bosnia, Kosovo, Iraq and Afghanistan, it might be argued that dedication to the cause becomes less apparent and the coalition becomes less effective.

A number of thoughts about coalition warfare have been triggered while writing this book. Firstly, it will have been apparent that two strong personalities have dominated the story, those of Churchill and Clark. Churchill's role in ensuring that the Italian campaign was launched and then sustained is undeniable, and without his doggedness it might never have happened, for good or evil. His ability to see farther than the end of the Second World War and to at least attempt to set the stage for the postwar years played a decisive role in the way the campaign was fought, but he faced an uphill struggle with the Americans and ultimately he failed to get his way.

At the operational level, and having to make the Fifth Army coalition work, there was Clark. The task facing him was gigantic, and his personal ambition and his skills as a general (which were boundless and comparatively

252

limited, respectively) did not always help him. Part of the problem was not so much his strength of character as Alexander's lack of it. How much this was a factor of coalition warfare is uncertain, but it is an interesting point worthy of some consideration. Clark's decision not to follow Alexander's plan for the breakout from Anzio would have earned him at least a stiff reprimand had the two generals been of the same nationality, but Clark managed to pull off a coup which endeared him to his President and to the American people when he captured Rome, and his adept use of the press to glorify his achievement made his position virtually unassailable. It would have been difficult, if not impossible, for Alexander to demand that Clark be replaced after he had given Roosevelt the present of the Eternal City. One has a degree of sympathy for Alexander, having to command an officer who represented the greatest power in the alliance, as one has for Clark in commanding Freyberg. Both subordinates had channels of communication to higher authorities which leapfrogged the chain of command and undermined the authority of their superiors in theatre. Perhaps the lesson to take from this is that building personal relationships is among the most important of the factors in ensuring that a coalition is successful; Clark's inability to form good working relationships did not help him, and a comparison with Truscott's style is instructive.

On recent evidence coalitions still face many of the difficulties that they did in 1939–1945; perhaps even more so, because they have not been involved in Total War and therefore have not been subject to the same pressures to make things work. Freyberg had the authority to choose his battles, and so do coalition members today. The power to play the 'red card' to opt out can, and has been, invoked several times. As an example of this one has only to look at the occasion in Kosovo when General Sir Mike Jackson, as Commander of NATO's Rapid Reaction Corps, was ordered by General Wesley Clark, the Supreme Allied Commander, to block the runway at Pristina Airport to prevent its use by the Russians. This Jackson refused to do on the grounds that the action would provoke an international confrontation, and when the issue was referred to London the British government informed Washington that it agreed with him and would not support the move.[1] Strength of character still has its part to play.

Further examples of disunity amongst allies may be found in Afghanistan, where Coalition and NATO operations across southern Afghanistan have been bedevilled by 'national caveats and differing objectives'.[2] Much of the difficulty in this particular conflict has been caused by the lack of strategic direction, or agreement, about what NATO and Britain are trying to achieve.

253

There has not only been a lack of military resources but a complex number of plans, produced by virtually each and every participating nation and their different agencies, all trying to achieve something different.[3] There is an air of similarity to the Italian campaign in this.

If nothing else, I hope that this book has shed some light on the complexities of coalition warfare, at least as it was practised by the Fifth Army in Italy in the years 1943 to 1945.

Notes

1. Jackson, *Soldier. The Autobiography*
2. Ripley, *16 Air Assault Brigade*
3. Gall, *War Against the Taliban*

Coalition Warfare:
The Nationalities that Fought
for the Allied Cause in Italy

The 15th Army Group went through several changes in title during the Italian campaign. Its name was changed to Allied Forces in Italy on 11 January 1944, and a week later to Allied Central Mediterranean Force. On 9 March 1944 it became Allied Armies in Italy[1] before becoming 15th Army Group on 11 December 1944.[2] To simplify matters this title has been used throughout this book.

In his *Memoirs* Alexander counted the following nations as comprising the Allied forces in the Italian campaign:

Twenty-six nations contributed contingents to my command in Italy. Since we are unlikely to see such an array again take the field under one command – and for the benefit of the sceptical! – I will list them. The major partners, of course, were British and American; the others – Canadian, New Zealand, South African, Newfoundland, Indian, Singhalese, Basuto, Swazi, Bechuana, Seychellois, Mauritian, Rodriguez Islanders, Caribbean, Cypriot, French, Polish, Nepalese, Belgian, Greek, Brazilian, Syro-Lebanese, Jewish, Yugoslav, Italian.[3]

To the above may be added those that Alexander lumped together as 'French': the Algerians, Moroccans, and Tunisians. There were those whose country has since split away from the flag that they fought under during the war: Pakistanis and Bangladeshis. And there were those from other nations which served in the Mediterranean theatre in the navies and air forces, but not in the armies under Alexander's command: the Royal Netherlands Navy and the Royal Australian Air Force.

Not included in the list are those from other nations which did not have formed bodies of troops under their own flags in Italy, for example the men of many nationalities who served in the Foreign Legion (and the two Red Army soldiers who are buried in the Commonwealth War Graves Commission Cemetery in Cassino, whose presence is possibly because they were unfortunate enough to have been in the wrong place while on a liaison visit to their allies in Italy). I have, however, included Nepal, whose Gurkhas fought under the British flag rather than that of their own country.

The following nations contributed forces to the Fifth Army at some stage of the campaign:

- Algeria
- Bangladesh (part of India until 1947, then East Pakistan until 1971)
- Basutoland (now Lesotho)
- Bechuanaland (now Botswana)
- Brazil
- Canada (While the majority of Canadians served with I Canadian Corps under Eighth Army command, 1 Canadian Armoured Brigade, as part of XIII (Br) Corps, came under Fifth Army command in the latter half of 1944. Units such as a section from 1 Canadian Tunnelling Company were on the Fifth Army establishment, and Canadian nurses served with 6th South African Armoured Division which was part of Fifth Army for some of the campaign. In addition, the 1st Canadian Special Service Battalion was part of the First Special Service Force.)
- Cyprus (Cyprus Regiment included RASC Motor Transport, Mule Pack Transport, and Pioneer Companies)
- France
- India
- Italy
- Lebanon
- Morocco
- Nepal
- Newfoundland (separate Dominion, although voluntarily relinquished self-government to the British Crown in 1934. Became a Canadian province in 1949)
- New Zealand
- Pakistan (part of India until 1947)
- Rhodesia (now Zimbabwe. There were Rhodesian sub-units in 6th South African Armoured Division regiments, for example B Squadron of Prince Alfred's Guard (PAG) and C Squadron of the Special Service Battalion (SSB). 17 Rhodesian Field Battery formed part of 1/6th Field Regiment

and the Rhodesian 4 Anti-Tank Battery was re-designated as 1/22 Anti-Tank Battery in the Divisional Troops.)
• Senegal
• South Africa
• Swaziland
• Syria
• Tunisia
• United Kingdom
• United States

Forces from the following nations also fought for the Allies in Italy, although I have not been able to confirm that they were part of the Fifth Army order of battle at any stage:

• Australia (450, 454, 458 Squadrons, RAAF)
• Belgium (4 Troop, No. 10 [Inter-Allied] Commando)
• Caribbean (The Caribbean Regiment included men from the British West Indies and Bermuda. It was employed as lines of communication troops and did not see front-line action.)
• Greece
• Palestine
• Mauritius
• Netherlands (naval forces)
• Poland

On some occasions Americans formed less than half of the manpower of the Fifth Army, for example, on the day of the Salerno landing more British troops disembarked on the beaches than did those from the United States. Strictly speaking, from the perspective of composition the Fifth Army was American in name only; however, it was under American command.

Notes

1. Jackson, *The Mediterranean and Middle East Vol VI, Parts II & III*
2. Malony et al, *The Mediterranean and the Middle East Vol V*
3. Alexander, *The Alexander Memoirs 1940–1945*

Bibliography

Agar-Hamilton, J.A.I. & Turner, L.F.C., *Crisis in the Desert: May– July 1942* (Oxford University Press, Cape Town, 1952)

Alexander of Tunis, Field Marshal the Earl, *The Alexander Memoirs 1940–1945* (Pen & Sword, Barnsley, 2010)

, *Alexander's Despatch: The Allied Armies in Italy from 3rd September, 1943, to 12th December 1944* (Supplement to the *London Gazette* of Tuesday 6 June 1950)

Anderson, Charles R., *Tunisia* (Center for Military History, US Army Washington, 2003)

Anon, *From the Volturno to the Winter Line 6 October–15 November 1943* (Center for Military History US Army. Washington, 1945)

Atkinson, Rick, *An Army at Dawn: The War in North Africa 1942–1943* (Henry Holt, New York, 2002)

, *The Day of Battle: The War in Sicily and Italy 1943–1944* (Little, Brown, London, 2007)

Barkawi, Tarak, *Culture and Combat in the Colonies: The Indian Army in the Second World War* (Journal of Contemporary History, 2006)

Bent, R. A. R., *Ten Thousand Men of Africa: The Story of the Bechuanaland Pioneers and Gunners 1941–1946* (HMSO, London, 1952)

Bimberg, Edward L., *Augustin-Leon Guillaume's Goums in a Modern War* (MHQ: The Quarterly Journal of Military History, Winter 2007)

Black, Jeremy, *Rethinking Military History* (Routledge, London, 2004)

, *The Politics of World War Two* (Social Affairs Unit, 2009)

Blackwell, Ian, *Anzio* (Pen & Sword, Barnsley, 2006)

, *Battle for Sicily, Stepping Stone to Victory* (Pen & Sword, Barnsley, 2008)

, *Cassino* (Pen & Sword, Barnsley, 2005)

Blumenson, Martin, *A Deaf Ear to Clausewitz: Allied Operational Objectives in WW2* (Parameters 23, Summer 1993)

, *General Lucas at Anzio* (in *Command Decisions*, Center for Military History, US Army Washington, 1960)

, *Salerno to Cassino. US Army in World War II* (Center for Military History, US Army Washington, 1993)

, *Mark Clark* (Jonathan Cape, London, 1985)

Brooks, Thomas R., *The War North of Rome* (Da Capo Press, Cambridge, Mass., 1996)

Calkins,, Derreck T.,*A Military Force on a Political Mission: the Brazilian Expeditionary Force in World War II* (MA Dissertation Georgia Southern University, 2011)

Canadian Department of National Defence, *Report No 5: The 1st Canadian Special Service Battalion* (February 1946)

, *Report No 18: The Campaign in Southern Italy (September–December 1943); Information from German Military Documents regarding Allied Operations in General and Canadian Operations in Particular* (November 1947)

, *Report No 24: The Italian Campaign (From the Fall of Rome to the Evacuation of Florence); Information from German Military Documents regarding Allied*

BIBLIOGRAPHY

Operations in General and Canadian Operations in Particular (March 1949)
, *Operations in Italy Reports No 175* (1 Canadian Armoured Brigade in Italy Part III: May 44–Feb 45)

Carver, Field Marshal Lord, *The Imperial War Museum Book of the War in Italy 1943–1945* (Sidgwick & Jackson, London, 2001)

Clark, Mark W., *Calculated Risk* (Harper & Bros. New York, 1950)
, Interview in *Tough Old Gut* (World at War, Thames Television, 1974)

Cody, J.F., *28 Maori Battalion* (Historical Publications Branch, Wellington, 1956)

Cole, David, *Rough road to Rome, a foot-soldier in Sicily and Italy 1943–44* (William Kimber & Co., London, 1983)

Colville, Sir John, *The Fringes of Power: 10 Downing Street Diaries 1939–1955* (Weidenfeld & Nicolson, 2004)

Combat Studies Institute, *CSI Battlebook 14-A, Monte La Difensa* (1984)

Cook, Corporal Jud, *GIs from Brazil* (*Yank* newspaper article, September 1944)

D'Este, Carlo, *Fatal Decision: Anzio and the Battle for Rome* (Harper Collins, 2008)
, *World War II in the Mediterranean, 1942–1945* (Workman Publishing, 1990)
, *Patton – A Genius for War* (Harper Collins, London, 1995)

Danchev, Alex & Todman, Daniel (Eds), *War Diaries 1939–1945, Field Marshal Lord Alanbrooke* (Phoenix, London, 2002)

De Freitas, Major Tácito L.R., *Logistical Support of a Brazilian Expeditionary Force by American Supply Installations* (US Army Command & General Staff College Thesis. Fort Leavenworth ,1949)

De Oliveira, Frank Márcio, *Attaché Extraordinaire* (National Defense Intelligence College, Washington, 2009)

Doherty, Richard, *Eighth Army in Italy 1943–45, The Long Hard Slog* (Pen & Sword, Barnsley, 2007)

Dziuban, Colonel Stanley W., *Military Relations Between the United States and Canada 1939–1945* (US Army in World War II Special Studies, Center for Military History, Washington, 1959)

Eisenhower, Dwight D., *Crusade in Europe* (Doubleday, New York, 1948)

Ellis, John, *Cassino: The Hollow Victory* (André Deutsch, London, 1994)

Fisher, Ernest J., *Cassino to the Alps* (US Army in World War II. Center for Military History, US Army, Washington, 1993)

Forsythe, Colonel John D., *Fifth Army History Parts I-V, 1943–1944* (L'Impronta Press, Florence, 1944)

Foster, Stuart, *The British Empire and Commonwealth in World War II: Selection and Omission in English History Textbooks* (International Journal of Historical Learning, Teaching and Research, 2005)

Fraser, Allen M., *History of the Participation by Newfoundland in World War II* (Memorial University of Newfoundland Libraries, 2010)

French, David, *Raising Churchill's Army: The British Army and the War against Germany 1919–1945* (Oxford University Press, 2000)

Gall, Sandy, *War Against the Taliban: Why it all went wrong in Afghanistan* (Bloomsbury, London, 2012)

Girard, Charlotte S. M., *Canadian Nurses in the South African Military Nursing Service: Some Reminiscences Forty Years Later* (South African Military History Journal Vol 6 No 1, June 1983)

Graham, Dominick & Bidwell, Shelford, *Tug of War: The Battle for Italy 1943–45* (Pen & Sword, Barnsley, 2004)

Greenfield, Palmer, & Wiley, *US Army in World War II, The Organization of Ground Combat Troops.* (Center for Military History, US Army Washington, 1947)

Hapgood, David & Richardson, David, *Monte Cassino* (Da Capo Press, USA, 2002)

Hastings, Max, *Armageddon* (Macmillan, London ,2004)

Hingston, W.G., *The Tiger Triumphs. The Story of Three Great Divisions in Italy* (HMSO for the Government of India, 1946)

Holden Reid, Brian, 'Alexander' (In Keegan, John [Ed], *Churchill's Generals,* Weidenfeld & Nicolson, London, 1991)

Holland, James, *Italy's Sorrow: A Year of War 1944–45* (Harper Press, London, 2008)

Howard, Michael, *The Mediterranean Strategy in the Second World War* (Greenhill Books, 1993)

Jackson, General Sir Mike, *Soldier: the Autobiography* (Bantam, 2008)

Jackson, General Sir William, *The Mediterranean and Middle East Vol VI, Parts II & III (The Official History)* (HMSO, London, 1988)

Kazamias, Georgios, *Military Recruitment and Selection in a British Colony: The Cyprus Regiment 1939–1944* (In E. Close, M. Tsianikas and G. Couvalis [Eds.], *Greek Research in Australi. Proceedings of the Sixth Biennial International Conference of Greek Studies, Flinders University June 2005*, Flinders University Department of Languages – Modern Greek, Adelaide, 2007)

Keegan, John (Ed), *Churchill's Generals* (Abacus, 1999)

Kesselring, Field Marshal Albert, *Memoirs of Field Marshal Kesselring* (Greenhill, 2007)

Lee, Ulysses, *The Employment of Negro Troops. US Army in World War II* (Center for Military History, US Army Washington, 1965)

Leighton, R. M., *OVERLORD versus the Mediterranean at the Cairo-Tehran Conferences* (in *Command Decisions*, Center for Military History, US Army Washington, 1960)

Lewis, Norman, *Naples '44: An Intelligence Officer in the Italian Labyrinth* (Eland, 2002)

Linklater, Eric, *The Campaign in Italy* (HMSO, London, 1951)

Malony, Brigadier C. J. C., et al, *The Mediterranean and the Middle East Vol V (The Official History)* (HMSO, London, 1973)
, *The Mediterranean and Middle East Vol VI, Part I (The Official History)* HMSO, London, 1984)

Mansoor, Peter R, *The GI Offensive in Europe, The Triumph of American Infantry Divisions 1941–1945* (University Press of Kansas, Kansas, 1999)

Marshall, George C., *Marshall Papers*, (The George C. Marshall Foundation)

Matloff, Maurice & Snell, Edwin M., *Strategic Planning for Coalition Warfare 1941–1942* (Center for Military History, US Army Washington, 1980)

Matloff, Maurice, *Strategic Planning for Coalition Warfare 1943–1944* (Center for Military History, US Army Washington, 1959)

Mathews, Sidney T., *General Clark's Decision to Drive on Rome* (in *Command Decisions*, Center for Military History, US Army Washington, 1960)

Mavrogordata, Ralph S., *Hitler's decision on the defence of Italy* (in Command Decisions, Center for Military History, 1960)

BIBLIOGRAPHY

McCann, Frank D., *Brazil and World War II: The Forgotten Ally* (University of New Hampshire http://www.tau.ac.il/eial/VI_2/mccann.htm)

McNaughton, James, *Japanese Americans and the US Army, a Historical Reconsideration* (Army History Summer-Fall 2003, Washington)

Mohlamme, J. S., *Soldiers Without Reward: Africans in South Africa's Wars* (South African Military History Journal Vol 10 No 1, June 1995)

Montgomery, Field Marshal Bernard Law, *El Alamein to the River Sangro* (Hutchinson, London, 1952)

, *Memoirs of Field Marshal the Viscount Montgomery of Alamein* (Leo Cooper Ltd., London, 2005)

Neillands, Robin, *Eighth Army: from the Western Desert to the Alps, 1939–1945* (John Murray, 2004)

Office of the Chief of Military History, US Army, *World War II: The Defensive Phase* (Army Historical Series)

Orpen, Neil, *Victory in Italy* (Purnell, Cape Town, 1975)

Patton, George S., *War as I knew It* (Houghton Mifflin, 1995)

Peaty, John, *The Desertion Crisis in Italy, 1944* (RUSI Journal, June 2002)

Penteado, Lieutenant Colonel Carlos J. R. A., *The Brazilian Participation in World War II* (US Army Command & General Staff College Thesis. Fort Leavenworth, 2006)

Phillips, N.C., *Italy Vol 1: The Sangro to Cassino* (Historical Publications Branch, Wellington, 1956)

Plesch, Dan, *America, Hitler and the UN* (I.B. Tauris & Co. Ltd., London, 2011)

Rhodes-Wood, E. H., *A War History of the Royal Pioneer Corps 1939–1945* (Gale & Polden Ltd., Aldershot, 1960)

Ripley, Tim, *16 Air Assault Brigade* (Pen & Sword, Barnsley, 2008)

Saunders, H. St G., *The Green Beret* (Michael Joseph, London, 1949)

Saxon, Timothy D., *The German Side of the Hill: Nazi Conquest and Exploitation of Italy, 1943–45* (PhD Dissertation, University of Virginia, 1999)

Scheck, Raffael, *Hitler's African Victims: The German Army Massacres of Black French Soldiers in 1940* (Cambridge University Press, Cambridge, 2006)

Sheppard, G.A., *The Italian Campaign 1943–45* (Arthur Baker, London, 1968)

Schmitt, Deborah Ann, *The Bechuanaland Pioneers and Gunners* (Praeger, Westport, 2006)

Scudieri, Major James D., *The Indian Army in Africa and Asia 1940–42: Implications for the Planning and Execution of Two Nearly-Simultaneous Campaigns* (US Army Command & General Staff College Monograph. Fort Leavenworth, 1995)

Soherwordi, Syed, *'Punjabisation' in the British Indian Army 1857–1947 and the Advent of Military Rule in Pakistan* (Edinburgh Papers in South Asian Studies No 24, University of Edinburgh, 2010)

Stacey, Colonel C.P., *Military Cooperation within the Commonwealth 1939–1945* (Canadian Army Historical Section Report No 75, 1956)

Starr, Lieutenant Colonel Chester G., Jr, *Fifth Army History. Parts VI – XI, 1944–45* (Pizzi & Pizio, Milan, 1945)

Stoler, M.A., *George C Marshall: Soldier-Statesman of the American Century* (Simon & Schuster Macmillan, 1989)

Theunissen, Major A. B., *Major General W. H. Evered Poole, CB, CBE, DSO: 1902–1969, Personal Retrospects* (South African Military History Journal Vol 9 No 5, June 1994)

Truscott, Lucian K. Jr, *Command Missions* (E.P. Dutton, New York, 1954)
US ARMY, *3 Infantry Division Report*
  , *45 Infantry Division Report*
  , *82 Airborne Division Report*
Vigneras, Marcel, *Rearming the French* (US Army in World War II Special Studies, Center for Military History, Washington, 1989)
Von Senger und Etterlin, F.M., *Neither Fear nor Hope* (Greenhill, London, 1989)
Walker, Major General Fred, *General Walker's Story of the Rapido Crossing* (36th Infantry Division Association website)
Watson, Mark Skinner, *Chief of Staff: Prewar Plans and Operations* (Centre for Military History, US Army, Washington, 1991)
Wessels, Andre, *The First Two Years of War: The Development of the Union Defence Forces (UDF) September 1939 to September 1941* (South African Military History Journal Vol 11 No 5, June 2000)
Whitlock, F., *The Rock of Anzio: from Sicily to Dachau, a history of the US 45th Infantry Division* (Westview Press, Boulder, CO, 1998)
Verney, P., *Anzio 1944: An Unexpected Fury* (B.T. Batsford Ltd., London, 1978)

Index

INDEX

INDEX